SHAPING THEOLOGY

Challenges in Contemporary Theology

Series Editors: Gareth Jones and Lewis Ayres
Canterbury Christ Church University College, UK and Emory University, US

Challenges in Contemporary Theology is a series aimed at producing clear orientations in, and research on, areas of 'challenge' in contemporary theology. These carefully co-ordinated books engage traditional theological concerns with mainstreams in modern thought and culture that challenge those concerns. The 'challenges' implied are to be understood in two senses: those presented by society to contemporary theology, and those posed by theology to society.

Published

SHAPING THEOLOGY
Engagements in a Religious and Secular World

David F. Ford

Blackwell
Publishing

BLACKWELL PUBLISHING
350 Main Street, Malden, MA 02148-5020, USA
9600 Garsington Road, Oxford OX4 2DQ, UK
550 Swanston Street, Carlton, Victoria 3053, Australia

First published 2007 by Blackwell Publishing Ltd

1   2007

Library of Congress Cataloging-in-Publication Data

Ford, David, 1948–
    Shaping theology: engagements in a religious and secular world / David F. Ford.
        p.   cm.—(Challenges in contemporary theology)
    Includes bibliographical references and index.
    ISBN 978-1-4051-7721-4 (hardcover : alk. paper)—ISBN 978-1-4051-7720-7 (pbk. : alk. paper)
    1. Religion—Philosophy. 2. Theology. I. Title.

    BL51.F575   2007
    230.01—dc22

                            2007018808

A catalogue record for this title is available from the British Library.

Set in 10.5 on 12.5 pt Bembo
by SNP Best-set Typesetter Ltd., Hong Kong
Printed and bound in Singapore
by Utopia Press Pte Ltd

The publisher's policy is to use permanent paper from mills that operate a sustainable forestry policy, and which has been manufactured from pulp processed using acid-free and elementary chlorine-free practices. Furthermore, the publisher ensures that the text paper and cover board used have met acceptable environmental accreditation standards.

For further information on
Blackwell Publishing, visit our website at
www.blackwellpublishing.com

Shaping Theology

For Micheal, with an endless thank-you

So be reposed and praise, praise praise
The way it happened and the way it is.

("Question to Life")

For we must record love's mystery without claptrap.

("The Hospital")

And a bird gathering materials for the nest for the Word
Eloquently new and abandoned to its delirious beat.

("Canal Bank Walk")

There was a laugh freed
For ever and ever.

("Lough Derg")

In the final simplicity we don't care whether we appear foolish or not.

(*Self Portrait*)

A poet is a theologian.

(*Self Portrait*)

– Patrick Kavanagh

CONTENTS

PERMISSIONS

The following chapters are revised versions of essays previously published by the author and we are grateful to the publishers for permission to use the material:

1. 'Theology' in *The Routledge Companion to the Study of Religion*, ed. John R. Hinnells, Routledge, London and New York, 2005 (pp. 61–79).
2. *A Long Rumour of Wisdom. Redescribing Theology*, Cambridge University Press, Cambridge, 1992.
4. 'Reading Scripture with Intensity: Academic, Ecclesial, Interfaith, and Divine' in *The Princeton Seminary Bulletin*, Vol. XXVI.1 (new series), 2005 (pp. 22–35).
5. 'Developing Scriptural Reasoning Further: Reflections on Scripture, Reason and the Contemporary Islam-West Encounter' in Basit Bilal Koshul and Steven Kepnes (eds), *Scripture, Reason, and the Contemporary Islam-West Encounter*, 2007, Palgrave Macmillan. Reproduced with permission of Palgrave Macmillan.
6. *Knowledge, Meaning and the World's Great Challenges: Reinventing Cambridge University in the Twenty-first Century* in *Emmanuel College Magazine*, Vol. LXXXV, 2002–2003 (pp. 38–63); and in *Scottish Journal of Theology*, Vol. 57.2, 2004 (pp. 182–202); also published by Cambridge University Press, Cambridge, 2003.
7. 'Faith and Universities in a Religious and Secular World (1)' in *Svensk Teologisk Kvartalskrift*, Vol. 81.2, 2005 (pp. 83–91) and 'Faith and Universities in a Religious and Secular World (2)' in *Svensk Teologisk Kvartalskrift*, Vol. 81.3, 2005 (pp. 97–106).
8. '1 Corinthians and wisdom christology' in *Christian Wisdom: Desiring God and Learning in Love*, Cambridge University Press, Cambridge, 2007 (pp. 176–190).

9. 'Barth's Interpretation of the Bible' in *Karl Barth: Studies of His Theological Methods*, ed. S. W. Sykes, Oxford University Press, Oxford, 1980 (pp. 55–87). By permission of Oxford University Press.

10. 'The God of Blessing Who Loves in Wisdom' in *Denkwürdiges Geheimnis – Beiträge zur Gotteslehre*, ed. Ingolf U. Dalferth, Johannes Fischer, Hans-Peter Großhans, Festschrift für Eberhard Jüngel zum 70. Geburtstag, Mohr Siebeck, Tübingen, 2004 (pp. 113–126).

11. 'Tragedy and Atonement' in *Christ, Ethics and Tragedy. Essays in Honour of Donald MacKinnon*, ed. Kenneth Surin, Cambridge University Press, Cambridge, 1989 (pp. 117–130).

12. 'Apophasis and the Shoah: Where was Jesus Christ at Auschwitz?' in *Silence and the Word: Apophasis and Incarnation*, ed. Oliver Davies and Denys Turner, Cambridge University Press, Cambridge, 2002, (pp. 185–200).

Conclusion 'Epilogue: Twelve Theses for Christian Theology in the Twenty-first Century' in *The Modern Theologians – An Introduction to Christian Theology since 1918*, ed. David F. Ford with Rachel Muers, third edition, Blackwell, Oxford, 2005 (p. 761).

Every effort has been made to trace copyright holders. The author and publishers gratefully acknowledge the copyright holders for permission to reproduce copyright material, and apologize in advance for any inadvertent use of copyright material.

ACKNOWLEDGEMENTS

Many people have helped with the production of this book. First, I am very grateful to the editors of the 'Challenges in Contemporary Theology' series, Gareth Jones and Lewis Ayres, who initially suggested that I might contribute to this series. At Blackwell Publishing, I would like to acknowledge the support and assistance of Rebecca Harkin, Bridget Jennings and Karen Wilson. Finally, I would like to register my thanks to those involved with copy-editing and proof-reading the book: Jenny Roberts and Jason Fout.

There are innumerable debts of gratitude owed for the pieces collected in this book. Many are expressed in the acknowledgements accompanying my two monographs, *Self and Salvation: Being Transformed* and *Christian Wisdom: Desiring God and Learning in Love*; others are mentioned in the Introduction to this book. I will not repeat them, but specially mention two.

The first is to Paul Nimmo. Part of his job as Research Assistant in the Centre for Advanced Religious and Theological Studies in the Faculty of Divinity in Cambridge has been to help me with research and other areas of academic work. In doing so he has transformed my capacity to write and publish. In the case of this work, without him it would simply not have been brought together and prepared for press. I have especially come to be grateful for his direct and well-weighed judgements, not least about what should be published. His assistance has also enabled time for other things besides books on theology.

One of those things has been rereading the *oeuvre* of Micheal O'Siadhail in the course of co-editing and contributing to a volume of essays, *Musics of Belonging: The Poetry of Micheal O'Siadhail* (Carysfort Press). The present book is dedicated to Micheal, in continuing amazed gratitude for our friendship of over 40 years, and for the thoughtfulness and generosity of his love for me, for my mother and for so many others.

PROLOGUE

The last quarter of the twentieth century and the opening decade of the twenty-first has been a fascinating period in which to be a theologian. World events have made religion prominent in ways that were unimaginable earlier, and it seems likely that religious issues and conflicts will continue to attract public attention during the twenty-first century. The more private, personal aspects of religion and spirituality have also thrived among many people in the West, often with the help of vigorous marketing, and this commodification of religion has generally been as ambiguous as its role in world events. At the same time, higher education has been expanding rapidly, most of it in areas directly related to the economy or vocational subjects. Amidst immense changes, the main religious traditions have all been stretched, trying to discern (sometimes accompanied by divisive argument) what to welcome, what to reject, what to learn to live with and what to try to transform for the better.

Despite their expansion, however, universities have been among the slowest to respond to the renewed prominence of religion. They have had considerable intellectual investment in the sort of secular (or rather, to emphasize its ideological aspect, secularist) understanding that has refused to take religion seriously except to dismiss it as premodern or anti-modern – something for mature, intelligent, modern people to explain away and grow out of, not entertain as true or habitable. University-based theology has therefore been in a complex situation, trying to emerge from a history of academic defensiveness and to take advantage of a changing climate. Now many of the 'discourses of dismissal' are themselves being dismissed or at least thoroughly questioned, the 'masters of suspicion' are suspected, and the relativizers are relativized. This is a hopeful aspect of the postmodern, or, as I prefer to call it, late modern or 'chastened modern' context.

Yet it must also be recognized that, for a great many of the four to five billion people directly involved with the world's major religious traditions, participation is largely through the understandings, values, virtues, convictions and practices that shape ordinary life. Theology at its broadest might be taken as thinking about the questions that arise from precisely that ordinary living as well as from political conflict, commodified spirituality, core identities coping with large-scale change, or academic inquiry; and the questions are often hard to separate neatly from each other.

Given that conception of the scope of its task, this has been an extraordinarily stimulating period in which to talk, think, teach and write theology, let alone work it out in relation to particular lives and institutions. There has been a superabundance of resources from the premodern, modern and late modern periods. The theological voices of women and of a wide range of races, classes, continents, religions and other groups have been heard. Theologians have made daring intellectual and imaginative attempts to be brokers of the arts, the humanities and the human and natural sciences. The urgencies of religious conflict, economic injustice and environmental deterioration have evoked vigorous theological responses. My continuing education in all this has partly been due to more than 20 years spent editing *The Modern Theologians*.[1] The changes made from one edition to the next act as a record of broadening horizons, response to critical comments and developing judgements about the relative significance of theologians, movements and leading concerns.

Faced with that wealth of theologies, why contribute the few drops of one's own theology to the flood of publications? Trying to discern the core motives behind more than 30 years of writing theology runs many dangers, but if I were to risk identifying those that have emerged again and again (and that I hope have been more formative than less worthy ones), I would name three: a delight in conversation, a responsibility to give testimony, and a desire for wisdom.

Conversation

As I look at the chapters of this volume they remind me again and again of the conversations that contributed to them. There were the student–

---

[1]   David F. Ford with Rachel Muers (eds), *The Modern Theologians – An Introduction to Christian Theology since 1918*, 3rd edn (Blackwell, Oxford and Malden, MA, 2005); David F. Ford (ed.), *The Modern Theologians. An Introduction to Christian Theology in the Twentieth Century*, 2nd edn (Blackwell, Oxford and New York, 1997) and 1st edn (2 vols, Blackwell, Oxford and Cambridge, MA, 1989).

teacher conversations that lay behind the doctorate on Karl Barth: with my two supervisors, Stephen Sykes (who had previously been the Director of Studies who introduced me to theology, with lasting impact) and Donald MacKinnon (whose theological presence was perhaps the most intense I have known, often expressed more in monologue than dialogue); with Hans Frei, who originally inspired the thesis and accompanied it throughout; and with Eberhard Jüngel, in whose house I lived for a semester in Tübingen. There are chapters in this volume related to the work of Jüngel and MacKinnon (Chapters 10 and 11), reflecting and taking further those earlier engagements.

During the 15 years of my first academic post in the University of Birmingham there were collaborative conversations with co-authors who became close friends. My senior colleague Daniel Hardy and I set aside every Thursday morning to talk theology. As this continued year after year I remember frequently thinking: I have never experienced anything like this before. The sustained intensity, the unlimited range of topics (God and whatever God relates to) and the sheer generativity of ideas were overwhelming. We eventually settled on the theme of praising and knowing God as a key focus for theology and life. The book that emerged was an attempt to distil all that conversation, and felt like a thimble drawing from an ocean.[2]

Overlapping with that were five years of collaboration with Frances Young, a colleague in New Testament and Patristics, in the course of writing *Meaning and Truth in 2 Corinthians* together.[3] That was a different sort of exhilaration: the luxury of so many years spent on one short text. By the end, 2 Corinthians was still as fascinating as at first, and we felt we had hardly begun to fathom it. These years imprinted indelibly in me the need and the fruitfulness of intensive scripture study in which scholarship, hermeneutics and theology come together (see Chapter 8).

The 15 years in Birmingham were followed by 15 years in Cambridge, where the privilege of sustained conversation continued, both one-to-one and in larger groups.[4] During this time there was also the beginning of

---

[2]   David F. Ford and Daniel W. Hardy, *Jubilate. Theology in Praise* (Darton, Longman and Todd, London, 1984; US edition, *Praising and Knowing God*, Westminster Press, Philadelphia, 1985); revised and updated as *Living in Praise – Worshipping and Knowing God* (Darton, Longman and Todd, London, 2005).

[3]   Frances M. Young and David F. Ford, *Meaning and Truth in 2 Corinthians* (SPCK, London 1987; Eerdmans, Grand Rapids, MI, 1988).

[4]   For a summary of the most significant conversation partners see the acknowledgements in *Self and Salvation: Being Transformed* (Cambridge University Press, Cambridge, UK, 1999) and *Christian Wisdom: Desiring God and Learning in Love* (Cambridge University Press, Cambridge, UK, 2007).

Scriptural Reasoning, a forum in which Jewish, Muslim and Christian academics came together to study and discuss the Tanakh, Bible and Qur'an
(see Chapters 4 and 5). It owed its origins and further development to
conversation around texts in small groups. These included three successive
summer meetings for several days with Daniel Hardy and Peter Ochs at a
lake in Connecticut during which there was again that sense of amazement
at the generative possibilities of intensive conversation. The past decade of
Scriptural Reasoning has been the setting in which I have learnt most about
conflict in conversation, how it might be possible to maintain engagement
and even friendship in the midst of continuing, unresolved differences.

Through all these years, beginning even before studying theology, was
the most sustained conversation of all, with the poet Micheal O'Siadhail.
We met when I was studying classics in Trinity College Dublin, and it is
not easy to say what have been the effects on my theology of talking regu-
larly with him – mainly because they have been so pervasive and so
significant.[5]

Conversation has, therefore, been a vital social matrix for the chapters of
this volume, and it has ramified far beyond the core partners into seminars,
learned societies, consultations, church gatherings and disputes, inter-faith
dialogues and, above all, relationships with students. Those wider settings
are a reminder of the crucial role of institutional and other structures that
enable disciplined conversation and collegiality to flourish in the long term.
Shaping the field of theology and religious studies and the institutions
associated with it so as to enable conversational collegiality has been a
growing concern of mine since moving to Cambridge, as is evident in Parts
I and III of this volume.

The writings in both parts might be seen as an attempt to 'fix' aspects
of conversational exchanges in order to share them more widely, invite new
participants and stimulate fresh interplay. They might also enable new stages
in existing conversations, and new meanings beyond anything conceived by
the writer. The recognition of such connections between conversation and
writing is a reminder that books, articles and other carriers of information,
such as computers, do not strictly speaking contain knowledge or understanding. Rather, they are information storage facilities with immense
capacity, while knowledge and understanding reside in and among people,
the receivers and interpreters of information.[6] The vast quantities of infor-

---

[5]   See David F. Ford, 'Life, Work, and Reception', in *Musics of Belonging: The Poetry of Micheal
O'Siadhail*, ed. Marc Caball and David F. Ford (Carysfort Press, Dublin, 2007).
[6]   Cf. David F. Ford, *Knowledge, Meaning and the World's Great Challenges: Reinventing Cambridge
University in the Twenty-first Century* (Cambridge University Press, Cambridge, UK, 2003),
Chapter 6 below.

mation available mean that coping with it is beyond any individual and must be a social matter. Disciplined conversation over long periods among people who come to trust each other, and who internalize the disciplines of responsible conversation in their own thinking, is perhaps the main way both to come to terms with theological knowledge and understanding from the past and to become oriented as wisely as possible towards the future.

Testimony

Theological conversation has its primary setting before God and is done for God's sake. So it is not just a means to an end, an effective way to produce theological publications. The paradox is that, for it to work well in this way, there needs to be an irreducible dimension of delight in conversation and in God, no matter what its results. If that is given, there can be all sorts of results and overflows from it, but it is not merely instrumentalized as a way of achieving them. Good conversation before and about God, and about all reality in relation to God, tends to have an intrinsic thrust towards being shared more widely. The thrust is primarily towards God in praise, thanks, lament, and other forms of prayer; but it is also directed towards other people. This is the double dynamic of testimony: confession, acclamation and declaration to God, and witness to other people. If what has emerged in worship and conversation rings true, why keep it to ourselves? Theological writing is one form of this wider sharing with others, and is energized by delight in conversation – which, of course, often happens in mediated forms through the writings of others.

If one learns something that is worth sharing and rings true regarding God, God's purposes, reality in relation to God, and the traditions and discourses that deal with such matters, then one has testimony to give. This category shifts the emphasis from the dynamics of conversation as a key social energizer in doing theology to the subject matter of its first-order responsible speaking and writing. It is of course possible to do theology in a consistently second-order mode, analysing and commenting upon discourses in ways that bracket out one's own theological verdicts and commitments. That is not the main mode of this volume.

Many of the institutional and inter-faith positions taken in Parts I, II and III would be acceptable across a range of religious and secular commitments, while at the same time being coherent with Christian theological judgements. Yet settlements that try to do justice to the religious and the secular in their various forms are often tempted, or even pressured, to play down particularities and differences. Between faiths, it is vital that there be 'mutual space' within which each can testify. Scriptural Reasoning creates such a space by studying, conversing and arguing around the core scriptural testimonies of Judaism, Christianity and Islam. Settlements between the religious and the secular are sometimes distorted by attempts to impose or create 'neutral space' within which there can be no testifying, no direct discourse springing from distinctive religious understanding. Even stronger forms of secularism insist on anti-religious ground rules. Universities are good test cases for the relation between the religious and the secular. The suggestion in Chapter 7 is that secularist universities have failed to do justice to religions, with serious consequences for public understanding and for the religions themselves. The constructive proposal in response is that, at least in the West, the flourishing of universities themselves, and of wider society, would be best served by an 'inter-faith and secular' settlement. That might be described as secular in the minimal sense of enabling the coexistence and collaboration of those with very different commitments and ruling out the domination of any single religious tradition. But it allows for discourses that are nourished by distinctive testimonies.

Parts IV and V are more obviously concerned with matters to which Christians give witness as true, focused through the theological interpretation of scripture and questions related to God, salvation and Jesus Christ. The Conclusion looks ahead to twenty-first-century theology by suggesting 12 theses about its form and content.

Reflection on testimony (or witness or attestation) itself has been considered by me at some length elsewhere,[7] but here it is appropriate to note some of its features that suit it to be a key Christian theological category. Ricoeur lists several of these:

> Testimonies are real events whose depths no reflection can plumb. Testimony even divides itself, outside of reflection. There is first the testimony rendered by real acts of devotion up to death. Next, there is the testimony rendered to this testimony by witnesses to its witnesses . . . A dialogic structure of testimony is indicated here between testimony as act and testimony as narrative . . . Here to believe is to trust. With testimony, it seems to me, the problematic of truth coincides with that of veracity. It is in this sense that testimony is related to and dependent upon a hermeneutics: the believing confidence of a second-order testimony in the first, absolute testimony does not coincide with deductive knowledge or with empirical proof. It stems from the categories of understanding and interpretation.[8]

---

[7] Notably in *Self and Salvation: Being Transformed* – see index under each of the three terms for references.

[8] Paul Ricoeur, *Figuring the Sacred. Religion, Narrative and Imagination* (Fortress Press, Minneapolis, 1995), pp. 116–18; for a fuller discussion see *Self and Salvation: Being Transformed*, Chapter 4.

So testimony can be closely related to history and specifically to that of the Gospel narratives; it allows for both real reference and the cross-examination of that without reducing all truth to what is logically deducible or empirically verifiable; and positively it points to the irreducible elements of trust, understanding and interpretation.

At the heart of Christian faith is being embraced in love by the God of Jesus Christ in such a way that witness is an overflow of recognition, delight and gratitude. Thomas Mann's epic novel, *Joseph and His Brothers*, says of Jacob at the end of his life: 'Anyhow he simply loved to speak of her [his wife Rachel], even when there was no point at all – just as he loved to speak of God.'[9]

Could there be a better motive for writing theology?

Wisdom

The third motive, a desire for wisdom, can be dealt with most briefly because it figures repeatedly in the chapters of this volume. Wisdom has become for me the least inadequate term for what theology is seeking. It tries to embrace the imaginative, the intellectual, the passionate and the practical; it refers to the wisdom of God as well as to fallible human searching. Wisdom need not be competitive with the various other terms that describe theology, such as understanding, thought, knowledge, truth, reflective practice, dogma and doctrine. Yet it seems to me the most inclusive. While encouraging rigorous inquiry and thorough understanding it is also hospitable to the ethical and the aesthetic. Wisdom traditions are concerned with the long-term shaping of life in many dimensions, including the common good and the formation of the whole person.

In the introduction to her commentaries on Proverbs, Ecclesiastes and the Song of Songs a leading contemporary teacher of wisdom comments on the prominence of poetry and of women in that literature and concludes:

> But the portrayal of wisdom as a beautiful and alluring woman suggests something more. It suggests that wisdom is more than useful; it is desirable, in the strongest sense. Remembering that the sages' original audience was composed largely of young males, the student population of ancient Israel, we can see that the wisdom teachers are creating poems, some of them frankly

---

[9] Thomas Mann, *Joseph and His Brothers* (Penguin, London, 1978), p. 1181. For a theological interpretation see *Living in Praise: Worshipping and Knowing God*, pp. 187ff.

erotic (the Song of Songs), with the aim of cultivating healthy and life-giving desire. 'Wisdom is a tree of life to those who lay hold of her' (Proverbs 3:18). Great works of art stir because they awaken in us a longing for what is essential for our humanity. The poet-sages of ancient Israel enable us to see 'Lady Wisdom's' beauty, that we may love her, lay hold of her, live, and live well.[10]

What would the future be like if many of the next generation were gripped by that desire and were to pursue the wisdom of God passionately? The ramifications go way beyond the future of academic theologians and the institutions where they work, but at the least they share in the responsibility for arousing that desire and helping to fulfil it. The shaping of theology is inseparable from the education of desire in the ways of wisdom.

In a culture that is endlessly inventive in inflaming and manipulating desires, and gives massive rewards to those celebrities, entrepreneurs, politicians and others who succeed in this, how might Christian theologians with others be comparably creative in testifying that

> . . . wisdom is better than jewels,
> and all that you may desire cannot compare with her. (Proverbs 8:11)?

In universities where knowledge, know-how and information are often commodified or instrumentalized or divorced from rich understanding, ethical responsibilities and all-round educational formation, how might Christian theologians with others nurture a collegiality of wisdom-seeking conversation? In the bitter religious and other conflicts of the twenty-first century, can Christian theologians with others bring to bear the resources in their traditions that make for peace? Can they do such things in the debates and heart-searching of their own faith communities and in shaping life well before God in the midst of the complexities of ordinary living?

In sum, how, where, and by whom is to be found a prophetic wisdom immersed in the realities of life today yet oriented to God and God's future? If the present volume inflames a desire for such wisdom in even a few of its readers I will be satisfied.

[10]   Ellen F. Davis, *Proverbs, Ecclesiastes and the Song of Songs* (Westminster John Knox Press, Louisville, KY, 2000), p. 7.

Part I

THE WISDOM OF THEOLOGY

Chapter One

THEOLOGY

Definitions of Theology and Academic Theology

Theology at its broadest is thinking about questions raised by, about and between the religions. The name 'theology' is not used in all religious traditions and is rejected by some. It is a term with its own history, which will be sketched below. Yet there is no other non-controversial term for what this chapter is about, so it is used here in full recognition of the disputes and diverse associations surrounding it. Theology has many analogues or comparable terms such as 'religious thought', 'religious philosophy', various technical terms for the teaching and deliberative dimension of particular religions and even 'wisdom'. Indeed, wisdom (though itself a complex idea with different meanings and analogues in different traditions) is perhaps the most comprehensive and least controversial term for what theology is about. Wisdom may embrace describing, understanding, explaining, knowing and deciding, not only regarding matters of empirical fact but also regarding values, norms, beliefs and the shaping of lives, communities and institutions. The broad definition of theology given above could be refined by reference to wisdom. The questions raised by, about and between the religions include some that are not necessarily theological, and many of these are formative for the disciplines in the study of religion. One helpful (if still quite vague) further determination of the nature of theology by reference to wisdom is: at its broadest, theology is thinking and deliberating in relation to the religions with a view to wisdom.

This chapter is mainly about the narrower subject of academic theology as pursued in universities and other advanced teaching and research institutions, especially in settings variously called departments of religion, religious studies, theology and religious studies, theology or divinity. The primary focus is on this academic theology in its European history and its present situation in universities that are in continuity with that tradition and its

expansion beyond Europe. There have been numerous traditions of theology
(or its analogues) originating in other parts of the world and in various
religious traditions, some of which are increasingly significant within contemporary universities; but an appropriate way of portraying academic theology within one chapter is to concentrate on its characteristics in the
academic tradition that generated the field often called the study of religion
or religious studies.

In that tradition, as will be seen, theology is an inherently controversial
discipline because of its subject matter, because of its history, because of the
relations of other disciplines to religious issues and because of the nature of
modern universities and the societies that support them. Academic theology
is distinguished from theology in general mainly by its relation to the various
disciplines of the academy. So a preliminary definition of academic theology
(and analogues of theology) is that it *seeks wisdom in relation to questions, such
as those of meaning, truth, beauty and practice, which are raised by, about and between
the religions and are pursued through engagement with a range of academic
disciplines*.

The final preliminary definition to be considered is that of religion. This
too is a contested concept. For the purposes of this chapter it is sufficient
to identify religion in a low-key, non-technical way through a number of
generally accepted examples. Religion, it is assumed, includes such ways of
shaping human life in communities and their associated traditions as are
exemplified by Buddhism, Christianity, Hinduism, Islam and Judaism. This
is not an exclusive definition; it simply limits the scope of reference of this
chapter, while allowing that much of what it says could be applied to other
instances of religion and to traditions (such as cultures, philosophical schools,
or secular worldviews and ways of living) which might not be included in
a particular definition of religion. It is also a definition that does not entail
any particular position on such disputed matters as the essence, origin and
function of religion.

Before focusing on the discipline of academic theology it is important
first to say more about theology and its analogues in the broadest sense.

Theology Beyond the Academy

The religious communities mentioned in the definition above all place a
high priority on learning and teaching. An immense amount of time and
energy is spent on such activities as the study and interpretation of key texts,
and instruction in tradition, prayer and ethics. Much learning happens
through imitation, and the adoption of habits of thought, imagination,

feeling and activity, which are assimilated through participation in a community's life. Such learning and teaching have been important in helping those traditions survive and develop over many generations.

It is, however, never simply a matter of repeating the past. The texts and commentators raise questions that require consideration afresh by each generation; each period and situation raises new issues; there are conflicts, splits and challenges from inside and outside the tradition. Even when the verdict is that what is received from the past ought to be repeated and imitated as closely as possible in the present, that is a decision which cannot be arrived at without some deliberation. Thinking about appropriate ways to understand and act in the context of a particular tradition comes under my broad definition of theology. Such thought is pervasive and usually informal, and teaching usually aims at turning its basic features into implicit, taken-for-granted assumptions in the light of which questions are faced and behaviour shaped. Yet, because of the many factors which prompt internal and external questioning, explicit thought may also be provoked, and theological inquiry, in the sense described above, may be generated. What is the right interpretation of this text? How should children be educated in this tradition? What is the right response to legal or political injustice? Does God exist? If so, what sort of God? What about death, creation, salvation, gender issues? What, if any, is the purpose of life? How should those with very different traditions and conceptions be treated? Such questions may give rise to theological inquiry.

Yet it is not only those who identify with a particular community and its traditions who ask such questions. Religions provoke inquiry in many beyond their own members; and some of their own members may dissociate themselves from their community but may still (sometimes even more energetically) pursue such questions. In addition, there are public debates about every major area of life – medicine, politics, economics, war, justice and so on – which raise religious issues and require deliberation and decision. Such debates display various types of theological thinking, both implicit and explicit.

Therefore theology in the broad sense is practised not only within religious communities but also by many who are beyond such communities or in an ambivalent relationship with them; and it is also present between religious communities and in public debates, both within and between nations.

Finally, theological questions arise at all levels of education. They may be focused in religious or theological education, but, because of the considerations discussed above, they are also distributed through other subjects, and they are relevant to overall educational policy and practice.

Overall, it is important to remember that only a very small part of the theology going on in the world is taught and learnt in the university settings that are the main concern of this chapter.

Academic Theology: Early History in Europe

The Greek word *theologia* meant an account of the gods, and it was taken over by the early Christian church to refer to the biblical account of God's relationship to humanity. This close relationship to scripture was maintained through the Middle Ages in Western Europe, when theology in the narrower sense of a specific discipline studied in universities arose with the development of universities in the early thirteenth century. It is significant that these universities themselves had many characteristics in common with Islamic institutions from which Christian scholars learnt a great deal.

Before the foundation of universities, theology had been nurtured in the many monasteries around Europe and in associated rural schools. Theology was there inseparable from the duties of worship and prayer, pervaded by the life of the cloister. In the cities the cathedral schools, founded for training diocesan clergy, were important theological centres. In addition, theology in the cities became part of the guild-oriented activity of a new rising class of freemen, both students and teachers, who responded favourably to new forms of argument and teaching and to the rediscovery of forgotten writings of the past. Here theology in schools (hence the label 'scholastic') was becoming a specialty subject for professional, philosophically trained dialecticians. Anselm of Canterbury (1033–1109), based in a monastery, brought fresh systematic and argumentative rigour to theology, and described it as 'faith seeking understanding'. Peter Abelard (1079–1142) represented the new sort of teacher and dialectician. In Paris, the new religious movement embodied in the Augustinian canons of St Victor mediated between the claims of the monastery and the schoolroom. This was an age of discovery, compilation and integration, which culminated in producing what became (in addition to the Bible) the standard theological text for discussion in the university schoolrooms of Europe during the next four centuries. This was the *Sentences* of Peter Lombard (d. 1160), a collection of four books of the theological wisdom of scripture and of the early Fathers of the church.

After the formal establishment of the first universities in the first part of the thirteenth century, scholastic theology developed under a new influence, the mendicant religious orders of Franciscans and Dominicans. Both flourished in the new University of Paris. Thomas Aquinas (1225–74) among the

Dominicans and Bonaventure (1221–74) among the Franciscans developed distinctive ways of doing theology within the new universities. They drew on traditional monastic resources such as Augustine and Pseudo-Dionysius, and, especially in Thomas's case, on newly discovered texts of Aristotle as well. Their disputation-dominated educational environment produced several major theological syntheses, which remain classic texts. One persistently contentious issue remained the nature of theology. Whereas all agreed that it was a form of *sapientia* (wisdom) there was dispute about its status as a *scientia* (branch of rational knowledge relying on its own first principles).

In the later Middle Ages theology split into distinct 'ways' based on the religious orders. After 1450, as the Renaissance and other changes occurred in Europe, the dominance of Parisian theology was broken as many European universities established theology faculties. The largely Dominican faculty at Salamanca replaced Lombard's *Sentences* with Thomas Aquinas's *Summa Theologiae* as the basic text for classroom commentary. The Salamancan theologian Melchior Cano (1509–60) produced a systematic treatise combining various kinds of authoritative texts, scriptural, scholastic and Renaissance humanist, including historical and scientific, covering the main theological *loci* (places). This gave birth to systematic theology in the modern sense.

By this time, humanist scholarship, especially represented by Desiderius Erasmus (1466–1536), together with the initiation of the Protestant Reformation by a professor at the University of Wittenberg, Martin Luther (1483–1546), had begun a reaction against a scholastic theology that had become highly specialized and abstruse. The humanist and Protestant emphasis was on recovering the original sense of scripture and of early Christian writers. They produced scholarly editions of the texts based on the best possible manuscript evidence, and they interpreted the 'plain sense' of the texts with the intention of approximating as near as possible to what the authors meant. The result in Protestant universities was that the main task of theology became the interpretation of scripture studied in Hebrew and Greek.

Catholic theology continued to be scholastic in form, with Thomas Aquinas dominant, though often understood through the medium of later interpreters and summaries in manuals. Polemics between Catholics and Protestants increasingly shaped both sides, as they developed systematic statements of their positions and counterpositions. A further dimension was apologetics defending theological positions against an increasing number of critiques and challenges, some of which made a sharp distinction between 'revealed' and 'natural' religion and theology. During the eighteenth century, theology began to lose its role as the 'leading science' whose word carried authority for other faculties. The rise of sovereign states, whose practical demands were less theological than legal, gave pre-eminence to the law faculties. These in turn were superseded by the 'new sciences' that entered the curriculum, studying the 'book of nature'. Many of the ideas that had most effect on later discussion of theological issues were generated by those outside theology faculties, whether Protestant or Catholic.

During these centuries, theology also became increasingly differentiated into branches. By the twentieth century the main branches had become: systematic (or dogmatic or doctrinal or constructive) theology; historical theology; biblical theology; moral theology (or theological ethics); philosophical theology; practical (or pastoral) theology and mystical theology (or spirituality).

Academic Theology in the Modern University

A formative event in the shaping of the modern academic tradition of Christian theology in the nineteenth and twentieth centuries was the foundation of the University of Berlin in 1809, which became for many the archetypal modern university.[1] There was considerable debate about whether theology ought to be included in it. Some (such as the philosopher J. G. Fichte) argued that it had no place in a university committed to modern standards of rationality. The position which won was that of the theologian F. D. E. Schleiermacher, who affirmed the role of rationality in the university without allowing it either to dictate to theology or to be in competition with theology. He saw theology as a positive science or discipline (*Wissenschaft*), by which he meant that it was not included within any one theoretical discipline but that it related to several disciplines with a view to the practical task of educating those who would lead the Christian church. The usual pattern of theological faculties in the German university became that of the state overseeing and paying for a faculty which both owed allegiance to general standards of rationality (*Wissenschaft*) that presuppose academic freedom, and also was committed to training clergy for the state Protestant church. Two consequences of this make modern German theology a specially good focus through which to study the discipline in modernity.

First, it meant that theology was carried on in an environment where it was continually in engagement with and informed by other academic dis-

---

[1] Hans W. Frei, *Types of Christian Theology*, eds George Hunsinger and William C. Placher (Yale University Press, New Haven, CT and London, 1992), pp. 95ff.

ciplines in their most advanced forms. Christianity became the religion that was most thoroughly examined, explained, critiqued and argued about in the nineteenth-century European university.

Second, the attempt to hold together the requirements of academy and church built into theology the tendency towards a tension between 'reason' and 'faith'. This tension is one way of approaching the task of describing basic types of modern Christian theology.[2] These types are of wider relevance than to the German or the Christian context, and developing them will provide a helpful framework later in this chapter.

The German pattern might be described as confessional theology (in the sense of theology according to the belief and practice of one religious community or 'confession' of faith) funded by the state. This continues to be the norm in Germany and other countries which follow its pattern, and some universities contain both Roman Catholic and Protestant faculties of theology. In addition, some German universities teach religious studies or 'history of religions', and there is a fluid situation as regards the relations with theology.

Elsewhere, different patterns have emerged. Those in North America and England exemplify the main contrasting ways in which the discipline is present in universities today.

In North America the tendency has been to separate theology from religious studies. Theology has often been understood as a confessional discipline (whereas the description given above includes confessional theology but is not limited to it) and has been largely taught in institutions affiliated to a Christian church or group of churches. The main location of theology has therefore been the 'seminary' or 'divinity school', sometimes attached as a professional school to a non-state university. Because of the separation of church and state, theology has rarely been taught, except as intellectual history, at state-funded universities, but many church-affiliated universities have departments of theology. Departments of religious studies exist in many state and private universities. These embody various understandings of the discipline, ranging from a few which integrate theology with religious studies, to others which define religious studies over against theology (a position that has been represented controversially by Don Wiebe[3]). Judaism, numerically far smaller than Christianity, displays a comparable range of

---

[2] See Frei, *Types of Christian Theology*; David F. Ford with Rachel Muers (eds), *The Modern Theologians – An Introduction to Christian Theology since 1918*, 3rd edn (Blackwell, Oxford and Malden, MA, 2005).

[3] Donald Wiebe, *The Politics of Religious Studies: The Continuing Conflict with Theology in the Academy* (St Martins Press, New York, 1999).

relationships in the institutionalization of its theology or (to use a term which is preferred by many Jews) its religious thought (see pp. 19–21).

In Britain university theology has become largely state-funded, and has developed from being exclusively Christian and Anglican to embracing, first, other Christian traditions, and then, in the later twentieth century, other religions. Departments in British universities are called variously theology, religious studies, theology and religious studies, and divinity. Whatever the name, most now embrace both theology and religious studies.

Most universities in other parts of the world roughly correspond to the German (confessional theology), American (separation of theology and religious studies) or British (integration of theology with religious studies) models for the field, and both within countries and internationally there is a continuing debate about which is to be preferred. The next section will outline the main issues in the debate.

Theology in distinction from religious studies

Theology has advanced reasons why it should be separate from religious studies; religious studies has likewise had reasons for being separate from theology; and there have been advocates of integration who refuse to accept such separation. We will consider each set of reasons in turn, while recognizing that there are also those who interpret the reasons on one or both sides as rationalizations of religious, political or economic interests intent on maintaining or gaining power and influence.

Theology's reasons for favouring separation centre on three related considerations.

First, especially in the Abrahamic faiths (Judaism, Christianity and Islam) there is the role of God in knowing God, and of faith and commitment in doing theology. If theology includes knowing God (or analogues of God), and if knowing God depends on responding in faith and obedience (or on some other form of self-involving practice) to God's initiative, then surely those who are not believers cannot do theology?

Second, moving beyond the possible individualism of the first point, there is the relation of theology to a community and its tradition. If a particular theology is intrinsically connected to a particular community, then surely it can only be genuinely pursued in the context of that community? The logic of these points is to confine genuine theology to confessional faculties, seminaries, divinity schools or other institutions in affiliation with the community whose theology is being studied.

Third, there has been some theological suspicion of the very category of 'religion'. Whereas, for example, God in Jewish, Christian or Muslim belief can be understood as relating to and transcending all creation, religion has often been seen as one domain of human existence among others. The objection of theology to being paired with religious studies is that this constricts the scope of theology. The effect of the Enlightenment (not least through inventing the modern sense of the word 'religion') tended to be to privatize religion, so that it became a matter of private discretion with its proper sphere in human interiority. Where religion's public role was concerned, the tendency was to limit its power and to deny its contribution to public truth. Its competitors in the public sphere included not only nationalism, capitalism and communism, but also new understandings of the universe, humanity, history and society which were closely associated with various academic disciplines. When these disciplines focused on their limited concepts of religion, theology did not find that they could do justice to its questions of meaning, truth, beauty and practice.

Religious studies in distinction from theology

Religious studies, for its part, has been aware that its origins in European and American universities lay partly in a desire for academic freedom for the study of religion without being answerable to religious authorities. Institutional separation from theology had a political point.

Academically, the key issue concerned knowledge and the methods which lead to it. The study of religion developed as a loose alliance of disciplines whose main concerns were elsewhere. It has never had a generally agreed method or set of methods, despite many proposals. In one of the most comprehensive accounts of the field, Walter H. Capps finds its fragile coherence in an Enlightenment tradition stemming from Descartes and Kant in its conception of knowledge and method.[4] Religious studies has focused on questions such as the essence and origin of religion, the description and function of religion, the language of religion and the comparison of religions. But, in dealing with those questions through disciplines such as philosophy, psychology, sociology, phenomenology and anthropology, Capps suggests that the most fundamental feature of the field has been a broadly Kantian epistemology (if that can be taken as allowing for both empiricist and hermeneutical developments). The concern for academic

---

[4]   Walter H. Capps, *Religious Studies. The Making of a Discipline* (Fortress Press, Minneapolis, 1995).

autonomy in line with that tradition has often persuaded it to prefer separation from theology, except where theology (or its analogues) is willing to accept its terms. Capps is hospitable to theology which is willing to find a role contributing to his conception of religious studies, but he also recognizes the need to go beyond his own paradigm. The next section offers one conception of how that might be achieved.

The question about knowledge and methods is a mirror-image of the problems, mentioned above, which theology has with religious studies. Religious studies has usually wanted to bracket out, for example, any conception of God being involved in the knowing that goes on in the field; and its pursuit of questions of meaning, truth, beauty and practice has tended to be limited to the methods of its constituent disciplines. It prefers to use such methods in rigorous pursuit of what can be known and justified to dealing with larger or more synthetic issues without those methods or beyond them. Overall, therefore, a basic concern of religious studies has been that of the academic integrity of the field.

Theology integrated with religious studies

Those who advocate the integration of theology with religious studies rarely suggest that all theology and religious studies should be institutionally combined. They recognize that religious communities will want to have their own academic institutions in which confessional theology (or its analogues) would be the norm; and that many universities will want to specialize in their religious studies (e.g. by focusing on a few disciplines such as sociology, anthropology or phenomenology) so as to exclude theology as well as some other disciplines. There are many factors (historical, religious, political, economic, cultural) other than the overall conception of the field which help determine its shape in a particular institution. Their main point for integration is the academic case in principle for the inseparability of the two. One version of the case is as follows.

First, theology is not in competition with religious studies but needs it. If theology is to be rigorous in its pursuit of questions of meaning, truth, beauty and practice then it needs to draw on work in other disciplines. This will not just be a matter of using their results when they are congenial, but rather of entering into them from the inside and engaging both critically and constructively with their methods and results. Academic theology has done this much more thoroughly in some areas than in others. It has been most widely practised in relation to philosophy, textual scholarship and history. In each of these fields there are many practitioners who integrate their discipline with theology, and also many who do not. This gives rise to considerable debate about issues that are not likely to be conclusively resolved (a common situation in philosophy, textual interpretation and history). The argument is that for the health of the field it is desirable to have some settings where such debates can be carried on as fully as possible.

Second, theology is not just pursued by those who identify with a particular community, and it can be studied in many ways other than confessionally (see p. 6). Universities are obvious settings for those who wish to pursue theological questions in such ways. For the members of particular religious communities there can also be advantages in doing theology in dialogue with academics and students of other faith traditions and of none.

Third, religious studies need not be in competition with theology. Certain definitions of the field exclude certain definitions of theology (see above pp. 3–4), but other definitions of religious studies open it towards integration with theology. A key issue is how far questions intrinsic to the field may be pursued, and whether some answers to those questions are to be ruled out in advance. For example, is the question of truth concerning the reality of God as identified by a particular tradition allowed to be pursued and then answered in line with that tradition? If so, then the way is opened for critical and constructive theology within a religious studies milieu. If not, what reasons can be offered for cutting off inquiry and disallowing certain answers? Such cutting off and disallowing either appears arbitrary or it relies on criteria that are themselves widely contested and debated within the field. The irresolvability of the dispute over boundaries and criteria has been intensified by similar disputes, often bitter, in other disciplines with which religious studies and theology engage, such as literary studies, philosophy, history and the human sciences.

Fourth, the three main responsibilities of theology and religious studies can be argued to converge and so make integration appropriate for them in university settings. The first is their responsibility towards the academy and its disciplines. The requirement is excellence in the study and teaching of texts, history, laws, traditions, practices, institutions, ideas, the arts and so on, as these relate to religions in the past and the present. This involves standards set by peer groups, work within and collaboration between disciplines and a worldwide network of communication. The second is their responsibility towards religious communities. This includes the tasks of carrying out their academic responsibilities critically and constructively, educating members of religious communities as well as others, and providing forums where religious traditions can engage in study, dialogue and debate together. Universities have increasingly become centres of such interfaith engagement in which theological concerns with, for example, questions of truth and practice, go together with the use of a range of academic disciplines. The third is their responsibility to society and the realm of public life. Issues in politics, law, the media, education, medicine and family life often raise questions which require complex interdisciplinary, interreligious and international collaboration. These questions embrace theological as well as other matters.

Fifth, in the light of the above four points, the case for a fundamental dualism in the field is undermined. It is still appropriate to have institutions with particular emphases and commitments, but the overall intellectual and ethical 'ecology' of the field embraces theology and religious studies.

Types of Christian Theology

How can the field of academic theology be described so as to do justice to the range of theologies and their different ways of relating to other disciplines? One typology worked out in relation to Christian theology is that of Frei.[5] It takes account of the importance of institutional contexts both historically and today. Frei takes the University of Berlin as his historical point of departure (see above pp. 8–9), and his typology also relates to the American situation of theology and religious studies. He recognizes that there are very different types of theology, some of which are more at home in universities than others. His typology therefore grows out of the academic tradition with which this chapter is mainly concerned and it is limited to Christian theology; but it can also be developed in relation to other religious traditions. Its attempt to do descriptive justice to the current state of the field results in allowing both for the separation of theology and religious studies and for their integration.

There are five types on a continuum, of which the two extremes will be described first.

Type 1

This type gives complete priority to some contemporary philosophy, worldview, practical agenda or one or more academic disciplines. In its academic form it subjects Christian theology to 'general criteria of intelligibility,

---

[5]   *Op. cit.*

coherence, and truth that it must share with other academic disciplines'.[6] Immanuel Kant (1724–1804) is seen as the main historical exemplar of this in modernity. He applied his criteria of rationality and morality to theology and offered an understanding of religion 'within the bounds of reason alone'. In terms of the previous discussion, a Kantian Type 1 is in line with a conception of religious studies which insists on a particular set of epistemological criteria being met by any theology that is to be admitted to the academy. It therefore excludes other types of theology mentioned below. It also gives philosophy (of a particular type) priority as the main cognate discipline of theology.

Other versions of Type 1 use different external criteria to judge theology – for example, an ecological worldview, or a feminist ethic, or a political programme or an imaginative aesthetic.

Type 5

This type takes Christian theology as exclusively a matter of Christian self-description. It is the 'grammar of faith', its internal logic learnt like a new language through acquiring appropriate conceptual skills. It offers a scriptural understanding or a traditional theology or version of Christianity as something with its own integrity that is not to be judged by outside criteria. All reality is to be seen in Christian terms, and there is a radical rejection of other frameworks and worldviews. Examples include some types of fundamentalism (such as those seeing the Bible as inerrant and all-sufficient for theology) and also more sophisticated conceptions of a religion as a distinctive and embracing 'language game' or 'world of meaning'. In terms of the previous discussion, Type 5 is in line with a conception of theology which prefers separation from religious studies and other disciplines.

The two extremes of Types 1 and 5 can be seen to come together in their tendency to see everything in terms of some given framework (whether Christian or non-Christian) and to cut off the possibilities for dialogue across boundaries.

Types 2, 3 and 4

Between the two extremes come three types that in various ways incorporate dialogue.

[6] *Op. cit.*, p. 2.

Type 2 tries to correlate general meaning structures with what is specifically Christian. It interprets Christianity consistently in terms of some contemporary philosophy, idiom or concern, while trying to do justice to the distinctiveness of Christianity. One example is the German theologian Rudolf Bultmann (1884–1976), who reconceived the Christian Gospel in terms of existentialist philosophy. The overall integration is biased towards the general framework, and so this type is close to Type 1.

If Type 2 moves in the other direction towards a correlation which does not attempt a comprehensive integration, then it becomes Type 3. This non-systematic correlation is a thoroughly dialogical form of theology. Theological questions, methods and positions are continually being correlated with other questions, methods and positions. Theology can learn a great deal from other disciplines and positions without giving a single one overarching significance, and it is only from within the process of dialogue that judgements can be made. Schleiermacher is an example of this type, as is Paul Tillich (1886–1965), who correlated fundamental questions about life and history with the meaning offered by Christian symbols and ideas.

Type 4 gives priority to Christian self-description, letting that govern the applicability of general criteria of meaning, truth and practice in Christian theology, yet nevertheless engaging with a range of disciplines and with other worldviews and theological positions in *ad hoc* ways. In does not go to the extreme of Type 5, but still insists that no other framework should be able to dictate how to understand the main contents of Christian faith. It is 'faith seeking understanding', basically trusting the main lines of classic Christian testimony to God and the Gospel, but also open to a wide range of dialogues – not least because God is seen as involved with all reality. The Swiss theologian Karl Barth is of this type, resisting the assimilation of Christian faith to Western culture and ideologies, especially that of the Nazis. Type 4 sees Type 3 as inherently unstable: there can be no neutral standpoint from which to carry on dialogues, and therefore there has to be a basic commitment for or against Christian faith – which yet needs to be tested in encounter with other positions. A favoured cognate discipline of this type of theology as practised in Britain and North America is the more descriptive (rather than explanatory) types of social science.

Assessment of the types

Any complex theology is not likely to fit neatly into a single type, and the purpose here is not to set up neat pigeonholes enabling all theologians to be labelled. Many will display subtle blends and uncategorizable positions which resist easy description. Rather, the aim is to portray a range of types which spans the field and enables a judgement about theology in relation to other disciplines, including those embraced in religious studies. The judgement is that, while Type 5 is likely to be least at home in the university and Type 1 least at home in the Christian community, Types 2, 3 and 4 can, in different ways and with different points of tension, be at home in both. There are Christian communities that would exclude the first four types, and there are universities that would exclude the last four types, but these ways of drawing boundaries are controversial and many institutions are more inclusive. The practical conclusion is that an overview of the discipline of theology, as it has developed in universities carrying forward the European tradition, argues for a definition that can embrace all five types. This in turn supports the argument above in the previous section that it makes academic as well as theological sense to see the field as whole, embracing theology and religious studies. The different types of theology construe the field very variously, and particular institutions and traditions need to take fundamental decisions about which types they embrace – but that is the case in many other fields too.

Beyond Christian Theology

The above typology has been deliberately tradition-specific. The next question is whether something like those types does justice to the other religious traditions which are the examples being used in this chapter: Judaism, Islam, Hinduism and Buddhism. There was a blossoming of the study of these and other religious traditions in the universities of Europe and the US in the nineteenth century, though apart from the special case of Judaism the study was mostly outside theological faculties. A major factor in the rise of the field of religious studies was an attempt to do fuller academic justice to religions other than Christianity. From a standpoint at the beginning of the twenty-first century it is possible to see that attempt as having two main phases, the second still in progress and provoking much debate.

The first phase involved the establishment of religious studies over against theology (usually against confessional Christian theology). The main concern was for properly academic study through disciplines such as the philosophy, sociology, anthropology, psychology and phenomenology of religion.

The second phase has accompanied the multiplication of universities around the world and the growth of the study of theology and religious studies in them. The last half of the twentieth century has seen an unprecedented expansion in higher education and of the disciplines and subdisciplines that study religions. One crucial feature of this second phase has been that considerable numbers of academics and students in universities now study their own religion as well as the religions of others. This has led to debates similar to those which have surrounded Christian theology in the European tradition. How far is it appropriate to be a Jew and pursue critical and constructive Jewish thought in a university? If a Buddhist academic is discussing ethical issues, how far is it appropriate to develop Buddhist positions? Increasingly, the answer has been that it is appropriate; then the debate moves on to consider the criteria of appropriateness. But, once it is granted that members of traditions can contribute in such ways to academic discussions and utilize a range of disciplines in doing so, then what has been defined above as academic theology is being practised. The result is that the type of religious studies which defined itself against Christian confessional theology is now being challenged to 're-theologize'. Can it recognize the academic validity of inquiries, debates and dialogues which are theological (in the sense of seeking wisdom about questions of meaning, truth, beauty and practice relating to the religions and the issues they raise), which use various academic disciplines, and which relate to other traditions besides Christianity?

The impetus towards such theology has been strengthened by suspicion directed towards the ways in which religions have been studied by Western academics. For example, the accounts of Judaism by non-Jews (especially Christians) have been subjected to thorough critique (especially by Jews); Islam, Buddhism and Hinduism have struggled to resist the imposition of 'orientalist' identities projected by Western scholars; and Christians have often judged accounts of their faith to be distorted by post-Enlightenment academic presuppositions and criteria. In particular there has been a rejection of 'ideologies of neutrality' and associated positions such as the dichotomy between fact and value, or the separation of knowledge from ethics and faith. The key point has been: 'no one stands nowhere', and it is desirable that religious traditions (together with genders, races, classes and cultures) have their own academic voices that can speak from where they stand. Huge questions of epistemology, ethics, theology and the meaning of 'academic' are at stake here and are likely to remain in contention; but once they have been raised they are hard to suppress, and many institutions have created the settings for pursuing them. One such setting is the integrated field of theology and religious studies.

The typology suggested by Frei is an attempt to devise a conception of the field that fits such a setting. It is applicable to religions besides Christianity insofar as each is a tradition (or set of traditions) whose traditional identity can be rethought and developed in the present according to the five types. For example, there are those who assimilate Buddhist ideas and practices to a variety of non-Buddhist frameworks (Type 1); others are 'fundamentalist', or convinced of the self-sufficiency of a particular set of traditional Buddhist ideas and practices (Type 5); and others arrive at more dialogical identities which balance differently between those extremes (Types 2, 3 and 4).

Yet each of the sample religions with which this chapter is concerned has a distinctive history in relation to theology or its analogues. In line with this chapter's limited scope (focusing on theology in the university tradition begun in Western Europe in the Middle Ages, continued today in research universities that are successors to that tradition in and beyond Europe and America, and concerned especially with the relation between theology and religious studies) it is not possible to discuss the history of each tradition in detail. What are offered below are some considerations from the standpoint of each of the five traditions as they take part in theology and religious studies in contemporary universities. Most space is given to Judaism as the tradition which has, besides Christianity, been most intensively engaged with academic study and thought in the universities of Europe, North America and more recently Israel.

Judaism

The term 'theology' is often considered suspect among Jewish thinkers. This is partly because theology is sometimes seen as being about the inner life of God, which has not usually been a Jewish concern. Partly it has been a reaction of a minority against oppressive and dominant confessional theology: it has not been safe for Jews to condone public or university theological talk, since Christians (or others) could use it to seek domination or to proselytize. Partly, too, theology has been seen as abstractive, intellectualizing and even dogmatizing (in the bad sense) instead of practice-oriented discussion about community-specific behaviour. Perhaps the most acceptable term is Jewish religious thought.

The main institution for articulating Jewish religious thought has been the rabbinic academy, whose origins are in the 'yeshivah', a centre of learning and discussion going back to the Mishnaic period in Palestine, and continuing in the Talmudic academies of Palestine and Babylonia, and later in centres spread around the diaspora. The discourse of these centres combined study of biblical texts (with a view to expounding both its plain sense and also its relevance to traditional and current issues), ethical discussion, jurisprudence, literary interpretation, folk science and much else. The rabbinic academy is still the normative institution for the religious thought of most orthodox Jewish communities, and there are equivalents in other forms of Judaism – for example, rabbinical seminaries, Jewish colleges and other institutes.

There have been other non-university centres of Jewish religious thought besides the rabbinical academies. Beginning in the late Persian or Second Temple period, sages, and later rabbis and textual scholars, included devotees of the esoteric circles that generated Jewish mystical practice and literature or 'kabbalah'. These kabbalistic circles conducted 'theology' in the sense of studying the inner life of God, or at least those dimensions of God that are processual and descend into levels of human consciousness. Hasidism is a large, popular movement of lived kabbalah, and some contemporary Jewish academics are paying increasing attention to kabbalistic study.

One influential tradition in Jewish thought has been sustained by intellectuals, scientists and statesmen working in a succession of empires and civilizations – Persian, Greek, Roman, Islamic, Christian, modern European and American. They have been social and cultural brokers in statecraft, finance, medicine, the sciences and scholarship, and have produced much sophisticated and often influential thinking which mediates between Jewish and non-Jewish interests and understandings and which might be categorized under Types 2, 3 and 4 above. Examples include Moses Maimonides (1125–1204) in medieval Spain, the Jewish doctors, mystics, scientists, scholars and diplomats of Renaissance Italy, the Jewish intelligentsia in twentieth century New York, and communities of lively religious thought which flourish outside the universities in Israel.

Jews were long excluded from the Christian-dominated university tradition of Europe, but since their entry into these academic settings they have, considering their small numbers, been disproportionately influential in many disciplines. Some have approximated to Types 1 and 2 above, attempting to accommodate Jewish religious traditions to the categories of Western thought. This was developed in German universities in the nineteenth century, Moses Mendelssohn (1729–1786) being a major figure. Others studied Judaism according to the canons of *Wissenschaft* (see p. 8), with a strong historicist tendency. This tradition, known in German as *Wissenschaft des Judentums*, remains the strongest influence on Jewish academic religious study. At its heart is the study of Jewish texts by explaining how and in which contexts they were composed, and what their sentences meant to those who composed and received them. This study is 'theological' in the sense used in this chapter insofar as it sometimes argues that the religious meaning of the texts is exhausted by what can be elicited through its methods.

Out of this tradition of *Wissenschaft* have come more complex forms of interaction, brokerage or dialogue with various types of academic inquiry, perhaps best labelled 'humanistic Jewish studies'. The study of texts has been opened up by such approaches as hermeneutical theory, structuralism and deconstruction, and the range of human and natural sciences has been related to Jewish concerns. In terms of the types above, it has most affinities with Type 3, but relates happily to any of the first four.

Finally, a recent development has called itself 'postcritical' or 'postliberal', sometimes welcoming the label 'Jewish theology'. Influenced by literary studies, postmodernism, and twentieth-century Jewish philosophies originating in Germany, France and America, these thinkers try to integrate three elements: philosophical inquiry; academic studies of texts, society and history; and traditional forms of rabbinic text study and practice. Its main affinities are with Type 4 in its concern to maintain a community-specific identity while learning from a wide range of dialogues – including dialogues with other religious traditions.

Islam

Islamic theology shares some of the strategies and concerns of Christian and Jewish discourse about God, since all three traditions are rooted in ancient Semitic narratives of a just and merciful Creator, and have historically evolved under the influence of Greek thought. For some three centuries after the death of the Prophet Muhammad (632 CE) the theology of the new religion was stimulated by encounters with several eastern Christian traditions, a debt which was later to be repaid when Avicenna, Ghazali and Averroes exercised profound influence on theologians of the Latin West in the Middle Ages. In spite of these convergences, however, the term 'theology' has no one Arabic equivalent, and theology in the sense used in this chapter has been pursued across many of the traditional Islamic disciplines.

One such subject area is Islamic jurispurdence (*usul al-fiqh*), which incorporates discussions of moral liability, natural law, the status of non–Muslims and other topics which received exhaustive treatment of a theological nature.

Sufism, Islam's highly diversified mystical and esoteric expression, also included systematic expositions of doctrine and cosmology in which mystical and exoteric teachings were juxtaposed, frequently in order to justify speculative or mystical insights to literalists.

A further discipline of great historic moment was Islamic philosophy (*falsafa* or *hikma*), which inherited late Greek philosophical syntheses and developed them into multiple religious systems. Many of these were regarded as too unscriptural and were therefore frequently confined to the status of private belief systems among elite circles.

Interacting with all these disciplines was *kalam*, conventionally translated as 'Islamic theology'. This is primarily a scriptural enterprise, applying forms of reasoning of Greek origin to the frequently enigmatic data of revelation. Ghazali (d. 1111) and Shahrastani (d. 1153) incorporated aspects of the *falsafa* tradition to shape *kalam* into a highly complex and rigorous Islamic world-view. Their tradition, known as Ash'arism, is still taught as Islam's orthodoxy in most Muslim countries. Orthodox status is also accorded to Maturidism, a theology which prevails among Muslims in the Indian subcontinent, Turkey, Uzbekistan and the Balkans. The debates between these schools are due mostly to the greater weight attached to rationality by Maturidism over against the comparatively more scriptural Ash'arism.

There have been various institutional settings for these types of theology, perhaps the most distinguished being Al-Azhar University in Cairo. In the twentieth century there have been many new universities. Those in Saudi Arabia, for example, have rejected the forms of reasoning from scripture found in both Ash'arism and Maturidism in favour of a strict literalism. These 'fundamentalists' (*Salafis*) are in a polemical relationship with traditional institutions such as Al-Azhar, and it may be that this engagement has become a more significant and widespread activity than the engagement with the discourses of modernity. In terms of the types used in this chapter, the main debates are between a Type 4, which inhabits and interprets the Qur'an with the aid of traditional Greek-influenced rationality, and a Type 5, which finds the Qur'an self-sufficient.

So far there has been comparatively little Muslim theology analogous to Types 1, 2 or 3. This is partly because of the widespread acceptance of the divinely inspired status of the Qur'anic text, and a rejection of the relevance of text-critical methodologies. There are some modern Muslim theologians open to post-Kantian approaches to metaphysics, found in more secular institutions such as Dar al-Ulum, a faculty of Cairo University, or the Islamic Research Academy of Pakistan. Perhaps partly because the Qur'an contains comparatively little cosmological or other material that might clash with modern science, the defining controversies in modern Islam concern the extent of the relevance of medieval Islamic law to modern communities. So it is in matters of behaviour rather than belief that the greatest range of types is found.

It is in universities in the European tradition that some of the potentially most far-reaching developments are now taking place. Due to the establishment of large Muslim communities in Europe and North America, making it now the second largest religion in the West, Muslim scholars and theologians are increasingly present in faculties of theology and religious studies. The study of Islam has shifted there away from 'oriental studies', and new forms of dialogue and interpretation are being developed.

Hinduism and Buddhism

Hinduism and Buddhism both have long and complex intellectual traditions of thought in many genres and many types of institutions. As with the other religious traditions, the university plays only a small role in contributing to Hindu and Buddhist religious or theological thought in the sense of a pursuit of wisdom. 'Hinduism' and 'Buddhism' themselves are terms which became popular due to Western interpreters in the nineteenth century but which mask the deeply plural phenomena that more developed understanding of these traditions now suggests. Nineteenth-century university studies often approached these from the angle of philology, with more systematic studies of the religious dimensions frequently shaped by colonial concerns. The earlier conceptualizations of Hinduism concentrated on the Sanskritic (Brahmanical or elitist) forms as representative, with continuing repercussions.

India in the twentieth century has been one of the most important countries for dialogue between religious traditions, including Hinduism, Buddhism, Christianity and Islam. This dialogue has been deeply affected by Hindu and Buddhist approaches that insisted not only on theoretical and doctrinal discussion and disputation, in which argument (*tarka*) based on textual exegesis (*mimamsa*) plays a prominent part (and where the argumentation has been vigorously intra- and inter-religious in both traditions), but also on experience or realization of the goal *(anubhava/saksat-kara, dhyana,* ultimately *moksa/nirvana)*, in what is an integrated grasp of truth-in-life.

This in turn encouraged suspicion of Western academic study applied to religion, especially the stress on the 'objectivity' of truth and knowledge and the tendency to separate understanding from practice. In Indian universities, the secular constitution led to religious traditions being studied mainly in departments of philosophy in ways similar to the more 'neutralist' approaches to religious studies in the West, and this reinforced the alienation of universities from the more wisdom-oriented inquiries of those concerned with the contemporary development of religious traditions and dialogue between them. In other countries of the East, however, there are other patterns – in Thailand, for example, where Buddhism is for all practical purposes the state religion, the study of Buddhism is privileged in the universities.

The numbers of Hindus and Buddhists living in diaspora in the West, together with large numbers of Westerners who now practice versions of these faiths, have begun to transform the situation of Hinduism and Buddhism in Western universities, where the late twentieth century saw a blossoming of posts related to them. The pattern has been repeated of a move from 'oriental studies' to 'religious studies' to a pluralist situation where oriental studies and religious studies continue, but there are also Hindus, Buddhists and others engaged in deliberating about questions of meaning, truth, beauty and practice with a view to wisdom for the contemporary situation.

Christianity

So far, Christian theology has been dealt with mainly in its history as a discipline, its relation to religious studies and its types. The contemporary situation of Christian theology is described using the five types in *The Modern Theologians*.[7]

Of the traditions described above, the closest parallel is with Judaism, and there are analogies in Christian theology for most of the strands in Jewish theology. There is rapid growth at present in studies and constructive contributions to 'theology and . . .' topics, the accompanying fields including notably philosophy, ethics, politics (leading to 'theologies of liberation'), the natural and human sciences, culture and the arts, gender (leading to feminist and womanist theologies), race, education, other religions and postmodernity. The German and other European and North American academic traditions continue strongly, but the most obvious new development in the twentieth century has been that of theological traditions in other countries and cultures. African, Asian, Latin American and Antipodean theologies have all emerged (often displaying acute tensions between the types described above), and many of these are networked in transregional movements.

At the same time, major church traditions have undergone theological transformations, most noticeably the Roman Catholic Church through the Second Vatican Council. At present the Orthodox Church in formerly Communist countries is having to come to intellectual (and other) terms with exposure to massive global and local pressures; and the Pentecostal movement (reckoned to number over 300 million) is beginning to develop

---

[7]   *The Modern Theologians, op. cit*, pp. 2–3.

its own academic theology. Between the churches there have developed ecumenical theologies and theologies advocating or undergirding common action for justice, peace and ecological issues. As with other religious traditions, the spread of education has meant that far more members of churches are able to engage with theology, and there are local and international networks with university-educated laypeople addressing theological issues in relation to the Bible, tradition, and contemporary understanding and living.

The Future of Theology

Viewed globally, the vitality of theology in the twentieth century was unprecedented: the numbers of institutions, students, teachers, researchers, forms of theology and publications expanded vastly. It is unlikely that this vitality will diminish. Questions of meaning, truth, beauty and practice relating to the religions will continue to be relevant (and controversial), and the continuing rate of change in most areas of life will require that responses to those questions be constantly reimagined, rethought and reapplied. Higher education is likely to continue to expand, and there is no sign that the increase in numbers in members of the major religions is slowing. The convergence of such factors point to a healthy future, at least in quantitative terms.

Theology in universities is likely to continue according to a variety of patterns, such as the three mainly discussed in this chapter. Quantitatively, the main setting for theology or religious thought will continue to be institutions committed to particular religious traditions. There will also continue to be university settings in which religious studies is pursued without theology. My speculation is that the nature of the field, including its responsibilities towards academic disciplines, religious communities and public discourse, will also lead to an increase in places where theology and religious studies are integrated. The history of the field in recent centuries has not seen new forms superseding old ones (religious studies did not eliminate theology in universities) but the addition of new forms and the diversifying of old ones. Beyond the integration of theology and religious studies, further diversification is imaginable as theology engages more fully with different religions and disciplines and attempts to serve the search for wisdom through each.

Within the university it is perhaps the theological commitment to wisdom that is most important and also most controversial. Seeking wisdom through pursuing fundamental questions in the context of dialogue between radical commitments is never likely to sit easily within universities. Yet in a world where the religions, for better and for worse, shape the lives of billions of people, there is a strong case for universities encouraging theological questioning and dialogue as part of their intellectual life.[8]

---

[8]   I am indebted to four other scholars who are joint authors of parts of this chapter: John Montag, SJ on the early history of theology in Europe, Timothy Winter on Islam, Julius Lipner on Hinduism and Buddhism (all from the University of Cambridge); and Peter Ochs on Judaism (University of Virginia).

Chapter Two

A LONG RUMOUR OF WISDOM: REDESCRIBING THEOLOGY

One of my predecessors as Regius professor of Divinity at the University of Cambridge was the great Reformation theologian, Martin Bucer, the quincentenary of whose birth we celebrated in 1991. He was trained as a Dominican, steeped in Thomas Aquinas; he was then deeply influenced by Erasmus and also by Luther and Zwingli; and he in turn influenced leading Reformation theologians, notably Calvin. He had a genius for friendship and also for peacemaking across deep divisions. On his extensive travels through Europe he communicated and tested his theology in debate with all-comers, academics and non-academics, Catholics and Protestants. He focused above all on the city of Strasbourg, its politics and economics as well as its church life. When he was forced to leave there he came to Cambridge to be Regius Professor of Divinity in 1550 and wrote one of his most important works, *De Regno Christi*,[1] on the reshaping of English society. Sadly, he could not withstand the Cambridge climate and he died the next year in 1551. It was a turbulent life, thoroughly involved in the formative events of his time with all their twists and turns. Professor Gordon Rupp called him, in a neat, anachronistic metaphor, 'the greatest ecclesiastical spin bowler of the age'.[2] He is also a good example of passionate dedication to the search for a wisdom which engages with the best available scholarship and with the deepest issues of religion and society.

---

[1] *Melanchthon and Bucer*, vol. XIX in The Library of Christian Classics, ed. by Wilhelm Pauck (SCM Press, London, 1969).
[2] Gordon Rupp, *Protestant Catholicity* (Epworth Press, London, 1960) p. 24.

Three Responsibilities

Over four hundred years later we find ourselves in a Europe undergoing comparable transformations. The question I want to ask is: what is theology in this situation? My short answer is that theology is the seeking after a wisdom which has at least this much in common with Bucer's theology, in that it has three main responsibilities: to the academy, to religious communities and to the wider society. I will treat each in turn, with most attention paid to the academic responsibilities. But it is worth bearing in mind the source of my title in the last stanza of Micheal O'Siadhail's poem 'Motet':

> O my white-burdened Europe, across
> so many maps greed zigzags. One voice
> and the nightmare of a dominant chord:
> defences, self-mirroring, echoings, myriad
> overtones of shame. Never again one voice.
> Out of malaise, out of need our vision cries.
>
> Turmoil of change, our slow renaissance.
> *All things share one breath.* We listen:
> clash and resolve, webs and layers of voices.
> And which voice dominates or is it chaos?
> My doubting earthling, tiny among the planets
> does a lover of one voice hear more or less?
>
> Infinities of space and time. Melody fragments;
> a music of compassion, noise of enchantment.
> Among the inner parts something open,
> something wild, a long rumour of wisdom
> keeps winding into each tune: *cantus firmus*,
> fierce vigil of contingency, love's congruence.[3]

'Something wild' – that quite provocatively goes somewhat beyond the notion of responsibility that I will be exploring. The connotations of responsibility are perhaps too sober, too cool and even moralistic (in the bad sense) to allow for the inebriations that have been part of the full-blooded pursuit of wisdom, whether in Plato, Augustine, Dante, Luther, Mother Julian, Gandhi, Einstein or Donald MacKinnon. There are desperate wrestlings with reality at its darkest points, leaps, strange intuitions, doubts that can, and sometimes do, subvert the whole enterprise, perseverance

---

[3]   *The Chosen Garden* (Dedalus, Dublin, 1990) p. 82.

through years of aridity, frustration or bewilderment, experiences that put the self in the passive voice – one is gripped, addressed, judged, forgiven, illuminated, called, consoled, loved – and there are intoxicating joys. This wild and dangerous side to theology should qualify any domestication of it into a set of responsibilities to the passing forms of university, religious community or society. Yet those responsibilities remain essential. We will return to the poem later. Now I want to take a sober look at the responsibilities, beginning with a general description of the type of theology that is done in the setting of English universities.

Public Theology

First, we need to keep university theology in perspective. If theology at its broadest may be defined as a thinking relation to religions and to the questions of truth and life that they raise, then it is obvious that most theology is not academic. It goes on as part of ordinary life among those, estimated at between three and four billion, who make up the membership of the world's main religions,[4] and also among those of the remaining two billion or so who are provoked to thinking by encounter with the religions and the questions they raise. And even within academic theology, most is not done in universities.

Next, we need to recognize the distinctive institutional setting for theology and religious studies that we have in English universities. Its crucial feature emerges most clearly from a comparison with the situation in Germany and the United States. Put simply, in Germany university theology is publicly funded and largely confessional along lines laid down by the Reformation – there is usually a Catholic and Protestant faculty in the same university and the churches have control over most senior appointments. In the United States, with its strict separation of church and state, public funds may only go to religious studies, and other theological pursuits are variously funded, usually through churches, charitable donations and fees. In England, as the confessional constraints in university theology in the older universities were slowly removed and as newer universities started departments afresh, there developed, often with conscious rejection of both the German and American models, a publicly funded realm where the polarity between theology and religious studies need not dominate. This is a precious achievement to which the greatest danger is, perhaps, a failure to recognize its strengths and a tendency to fall back into fruitless polarities. I want to describe it so as to elucidate its wisdom and its potential.

[4]   See D. Barratt, *Encyclopedia of World Christianity* (Oxford University Press, Oxford, 1982).

In the Faculty of Divinity of the University of Cambridge the clearest sign of moving beyond any dichotomy between theology and religious studies came in 1969 when it was decided to change the BA course from the Theological Tripos to the Theology and Religious Studies Tripos. This move was late in comparison to many other English universities; it was an attempt to do fuller justice to other religions besides Christianity. When a theology or divinity faculty (I sometimes find the ancient term 'divinity' attractive in face of the manifold misunderstandings and misrepresentations of 'theology', but on the whole I prefer to use 'theology') which is not confessional extends its studies to cover more religions, that is a change in scope rather than basic academic character. What I mean is that there is no aspect of a religious studies faculty that should not also be found in a good theology faculty: the same disciplines apply to each religion. What then is specifically theological beyond these shared aspects? It is dangerous to generalize because there is no widely agreed distinction between theology and religious studies. But what theology tends to include, whereas religious studies need not necessarily do so, are such elements as the encouragement to discuss and take positions on the truth claims of a religion, and the freedom to contribute constructively as well as critically to the lively contemporary debates within, between and beyond religious communities as well as about them. This allows for and even encourages a theological truth and wisdom which I will explore further towards the end of this chapter.

What term might be applied to the discourse that goes on in the Faculty of Divinity in Cambridge and in other faculties and departments like it around the country? The least inadequate that I can find is 'public theology'. It is engaged with the worldwide public presence of the religions. There is no single agreed definition of religion. In many ways I find the term 'religion' unsatisfactory, but I use it in a fairly low-key way to refer to the sort of entities that Hinduism, Buddhism, Christianity, Judaism, Islam and so on are. More important than agreement on definitions is the need to recognize the multidimensional nature of religions. My colleague Professor Nicholas Lash has recently described the main dimensions under variations on headings from Schleiermacher (feeling, knowing and doing); from Newman (devotion and passion, fellowship and organization, and thought, philosophy and theology); and from von Hügel (the mystical, the institutional and the intellectual).[5] What does public theology do? It encounters specific religions in all these aspects and it tries to adopt the methods of study appropriate to them. This encounter may be 'in faith', with personal involvement in a

---

[5]   Nicholas Lash, *Easter in Ordinary. Reflections on Human Experience and the Knowledge of God* (SCM Press, London 1988) p. 140.

particular tradition, or it may not. It seems to me to make no more sense to try to define and legislate for the appropriate subjective condition in which to come to the academic study of theology than it does to do so in the case of poetry, economic theory or music – though that is not to say that there are not important differentiations in capacity. Surprising things happen in the theological encounter, both to those within the religion studied and to those outside it. And one thing that commonly happens is that the crude spatial picture of 'inside' and 'outside' is replaced by a more sophisticated notion of boundaries and relationships.

Clearly, a thoroughgoing encounter will have to draw on many disciplines, and here we enter the public world of international academic life. It is hard to think of a discipline that is not related to the questions raised by the study of religions. This underlines the obvious fact that theology is not one field in the way in which, for example, geology is. It does not have a subject matter that can be neatly circumscribed, because it is the nature of religions to pervade the whole of life, individual and corporate, and to offer a comprehensive horizon embracing all reality. In this respect it is more like philosophy (at least in some of philosophy's self-understandings) than any other discipline and for theology one of the most important relationships is with philosophy. (Happily, this relationship at present shows some signs of entering a more interesting and mutually respectful phase in England and elsewhere.) One danger for theology, as for philosophy, is that it may be fragmented into all the fields where it may be relevant. So why not have religious history in the history faculty, philosophy of religion or philosophical theology in philosophy, Hebrew in oriental studies, New Testament in classics, sociology of religion in sociology and so on? That happens already in some cases, though usually in the University of Cambridge with joint affiliation to two faculties. And in some universities there is no theology or religious studies as a separate unit. There is a fundamental issue here, on which I will simply give my summary judgement: that a specific religion is not adequately studied if it is fragmented into specialist aspects without coordination. Its aspects are coinherent in ways that quite often make nonsense of attempts to deal with it in fragments. Justice is not done to the complexity and dynamics of its distinctive existence over time. Above all, its multidimensional wisdom is missed.

Responsibilities to the Academy

So public academic theology has as its subject matter the religions in their various dimensions, encountered and responded to through various disciplines, with the questions of truth and life pursued wherever they lead, but needing some integration if the pursuit is to be adequate. How can its responsibilities within the university be summarized?

First, it needs to be as good as possible at the study of languages, texts, history and traditions, laws, practices, institutions, politics, economics, social life, intellectual life, psychology, science, art, music, architecture, and so on, in so far as these are relevant to the religions. These all appear in religions as mediations of meaning and life. In all of these studies, specialists in theology have wider peer groups with whom to be in communication over content, criteria and the whole state of particular fields. I take it for granted that most of the academic study and research in theology and religious studies comes under this broad heading and that a faculty which fails in this is not academically credible. It is also obvious that it is intrinsic to such studies that they constantly expand, bringing a perpetual longing for more colleagues!

Secondly, through all that, questions about truth as well as about norms and practice need to be asked, and both critical and constructive contributions encouraged. Here it is especially important to be able to handle religions as wholes, to engage with their particularity rather than with religion in general. One of the implications of this is the need to relate specialties to each other where questions which transcend any one of them are at stake. Theology is in a good position to try to achieve models of good practice in relations between disciplines. It is also a field where profound disagreements cannot be avoided, not least about the nature of the field, and so it can help to contribute to the university an ethos of dialogue without suppression of fundamental disputes.

Thirdly, there is the responsibility to give a good education to undergraduates and graduates. There are few subjects that allow enagement with such a wide range of areas and skills and with such intensity. A student can specialize in some of the fields already mentioned as well as take part in the overarching questions of philosophy, hermeneutics and systematic theology. There are many themes and issues of considerable existential importance to the student and of wide relevance to society. The result is that theology can at its best offer an education well suited to our complex world. It can be imaginative and richly rational and can offer as much as any other the sheer joy of understanding and even wisdom. It is also significant that the centuries-long limiting of university theological education in England to those preparing for official church ministry has long since ended. Education of clergy of course continues to be important but this is not the vocation of the large majority of our graduates. They range over the whole gamut of careers, and these lay theologians are, I believe, in their own statistically small way, an important presence in our society.

The Task of Universities

So much for the main responsibilities of theology in the university. But universities themselves are not unproblematic settings. In the face of enormous changes they often seem curiously unable to state a convincing public case for themselves. When challenged to justify themselves their rhetoric has often run hollow. Not only that, but there seems to have been a constriction of the very space to debate vital issues transcending specialties, such as the relation of knowledge to power, rational justification and the nature of truth. The creation of institutional space for this sort of fundamental dialogue and dispute to happen is, I believe, one of the primary justifications for the university in a pluralist society. Theology needs to be part of this; and the universities, unless they are to limit the debates quite arbitrarily, need to do academic justice to the religions that billions are members of and to the questions that they raise.

The most embracing way to characterize this is as a search for wisdom. I will say more about theology as wisdom later. For now I use wisdom in the sense that the philosopher Mary Midgley (a wise representative of the 'common sense in plain language' tradition of British philosophy) does in her sharp and, I think, convincing analyses of academic life at present.[6] Wisdom here is about taking the risk of facing the large questions, about refusing to separate specialization from human wholeness, being alert to the powerful hidden and sometimes open agendas of those shaping our 'knowledge industry', and about meeting the demands of people outside the universities for serious discussions of wide topics. One task of the university is to help society transcend itself in various ways, above all in its knowing, its perspectives on itself and the world, and its quality of judgement. That is both a risky task and one which it is ultimately fatal for the university to ignore. There is a great thirst for meaning and wisdom. There is also, of course, widespread disillusion with many of the 'packages' of meaning that have been passed on (in the religions and in other ways), and there is much despair that there are meanings to be found. But in this situation it is extraordinarily important both that the profundities of meaning from the past be studied, criticized, retrieved and made available for the present, and that there be meditation and discussion about their implications and about new possibilities. The academic study of theology has a role to play here.

---

[6] *Wisdom, Information, Wonder, What is Knowledge For?* (Routledge, London and New York 1989).

Responsibilities to Religious Communities

I turn next to the responsibilities of academic theology to the churches and other religious communities. With the exception of some posts in Oxford and one in Durham the departments and faculties of theology in English universities are not committed to any denomination or religion. In Cambridge this has not, of course, always been the case, but there has been a steady, sometimes painful development towards the present situation in which one's religious allegiance is no longer a criterion for admission as a student or appointment as any University Teaching Officer. The requirement that the Regius Chair of Divinity be occupied by an ordained Anglican priest was repealed in 1977 and I am in fact the first non-clergyman to hold it in 452 years (though I notice the university regulations still require me on occasion to wear a cassock). It seems to me an undoubted advantage that admissions, appointments and curricula are no longer determined according to one church. But what does that mean for particular faith commitments in the study of theology?

I would suggest that these do and should play a full part in the discipline. Everyone has commitments and the properly academic approach is, when they are relevant to any topic, to try to identify them and discuss them. Yet this is of course a very sensitive area. On the one hand there is the view that faith is a disqualification in the academic study of religions, leading inevitably to bias and inappropriate advocacy. Those are serious dangers and have often occurred, but they are by no means limited to theology. They are just as relevant to economists commenting on the economy, lawyers with deep convictions about justice and punishment, historians, architects, literary critics and so on. The answer to improper advocacy or manipulation of a discipline to serve one's own belief or ideology is not to ban all advocacy but to have it take place in a setting where rigorous argument and consideration of alternatives are normal.

On the other hand, in the communities of faith there are also fears and prejudices. These too can appeal to much evidence. The dominant modern academic discourses have on the whole given some cause to religions to be defensive – they have variously patronized them, explained them away, historicized them, marginalized them, ignored them, privatized them, trivialized them, refuted them, neutralized them, and in general suspected them. Often theology has been felt as giving the unkindest cuts of all. Yet it is sad to the point of tragedy when this leads, as so often, into a suspicion of intellectual life as such, as if faith might be unintellectual or anti-intellectual. The main religions present in England, Judaism, Christianity, Hinduism and Islam, all have distinguished intellectual heritages. They are also at present involved in complex and rapid transformations. For them not to think about these matters is not an option. The question is about the quality of thought and whether whatever contribution the academy can make is offered and welcomed.

What are the theological needs of the main religious communities? I would suggest that they are for a high quality of enagement with what comes from the past, for discernment and judgement about the present and future significance of their traditions, and for the provision of 'ordered learning'.[7] This shows how much an overlap there is with what I have taken the tasks of university theology to be – studying the elaborate particularity of religions, exploring questions of truth and practice and offering a good education. The overlap means that there should be (and in fact, of course, there are) close links between church and university. Indeed, historically the differentiation of the two came late and the nature of the differentiation is the pivotal issue. For example, how does theology in the Faculty of Divinity at Cambridge differ from that in the ecumenical Cambridge Federation of Theological Colleges? It differs not necessarily in content, standards or even in personnel, but primarily, I suggest, in the priority the theological colleges must give to the welfare of the particular faith communities they represent and to preparing their students for one type of vocation. As institutions, the faculty and the colleges have primary responsibilities towards different, though overlapping communities, the universities and the churches. But if either loses its sense of responsibility towards the other then both are impoverished. This is not necessarily an easy relationship, least of all for those who wear both hats, but the sustaining of its complexities (and sometimes ambiguities) is essential to the health of public theology. And here again there are instructive analogies in other faculties such as law, medicine and architecture.

Such institutional relationships need not be limited to Christianity. In Birmingham, for example, two centres for the study of Islam and of Judaism in the Selly Oak Colleges are integrated with the university and do a great deal of undergraduate and graduate teaching under its auspices. Once the deep misconceptions and prejudices on both sides have been faced then the way is open for initiatives such as these. The University of Birmingham is a good example of a self-consciously secular foundation which has recognized in its policy over the years the significance of what I have called public theology within the academy, including the responsibilities this carries in a multifaith society.

---

[7] Cf. Edward Farley, *The Fragility of Knowledge: Theological Education in the Church and the University* (Fortress Press, Philadelphia, 1988) chap. 5.

I would make one final point on this relation of universities and religious communities, with the Christian churches of England in mind. I see the most important item on their theological agenda at present being the education of their general membership for living in truth and wisdom. As traditional habits and supports for faith weaken in the society generally, as faith becomes less a part of the atmosphere, so the need for thorough learning of the faith increases. A religion is at least as many-layered and complex as a language and culture, and if people are to be more than tourists in relation to their traditions then there needs to be ordered learning of them and of their contemporary significance. Theological education has largely been limited to clergy and they have, usually with the collusion of the laity, kept it mostly to themselves. 'Mind-stretching' is not a term most Christians would apply to their learning of the faith. This is now being seriously addressed in some churches. There is a quiet revolution happening in many places through study courses, lay training, small groups and new forms of congregational learning (it is quiet because the media almost never report such things). But there is also a serious worry: the content can easily bypass the deepest questions posed through academic theology and other disciplines. Some of those questions go to the heart of both Christianity and of late modernity. The failure to make appropriate connections here is especially dangerous in a society with modern communications and widespread education in other areas, but for those called to love God with all their minds it is also a radical failure in integrity.

Responsibilities to Society

The third responsibility of academic theology is to our society as a whole. This will of course be achieved largely by fulfilling the other two responsibilities. But besides those there is, from society's standpoint, a wider reason for having public theology. It is desirable for a society to have as high a quality of public discourse as possible in relation to the religions and the questions of truth and life that they raise. If religions are not studied in universities then they do not go away; what happens is that the level of public debate on religious matters and on the wide range of issues to which religion is relevant is to that extent impoverished. A dimension of our social and moral ecology is distorted. The Chief Rabbi, Jonathan Sacks, in his Reith lectures, 'The Persistence of Faith',[8] has made an eloquent plea for the public importance of religion in terms of that metaphor of a moral

[8]   *The Persistence of Faith* (Weidenfeld and Nicolson, London 1991).

ecology. I would extend his conception by including academic theology as one niche. It draws its social significance not only from the intrinsic importance of the questions it pursues or the quality of the education it can give but also from the sheer historical and contemporary impact of the billions of religious adherents. Like it or not, the religions not only persist but often flourish. Many of the major international developments in the modern and late modern Period have been closely connected with religions. Even the standard objection to religious participation in the public sphere, that it means bigotry, fanaticism, wars, intolerance and insoluble debates, looks less persuasive when one notes the performance of religion's replacements in the marketplace: nationalism, capitalism, communism, fascism and other ideologies have an unrivalled record in human killing and misery. One need not even think that religions are on the whole beneficial in order to see the wisdom of promoting high-quality discourse within them, between them and about them. This is not a recipe for harmonious public life – rather it guarantees the airing of deep differences – but at least the sponsoring of spheres of respectful study and communication is a step in that direction.

Of its three responsibilities theology is probably least adequate to this one. If one looks at formative discourses in our society in recent decades there is relatively little high-quality theological contribution. On the whole, it is hard to think of theological treatments of the legal system, the economy, education, science, technology, medicine and the formation of our culture that have entered the mainstream of debate. This is not only the fault of theology – there is considerable resistance to seeing religion as living, thoughtful and publicly significant – but theology has often allowed itself to be marginalized or confined within restricted areas of philology, history, sociology or philosophy. That would have been unthinkable to Bucer or to his great predecessor against whom he reacted, Thomas Aquinas. To imitate them is not necessarily to say what they said but to do what they did in such diverse ways: they engaged with their contemporary world and rigorously related it, critically and constructively, to what they found in Christianity and in several intellectual traditions. The organization of academic theology on the whole severely limits this in ordinary theological education. We have the irony of students studying the law and economics of ancient Israel but having no place to engage with contemporary parallels.

What this amounts to is a one-sided orientation to the past which is to the detriment of present public significance. But we need to be very wary of any sense of competition between engagement with the past and the present. It is not just theological wisdom that insists on the inseparability of the two. Nor do we want to suggest that rigorous specialties are to give way to dilettantist involvements in current affairs. Disengagement from the past and failure to cultivate scholarly and philosophical skills would be betrayal of the whole enterprise of theology and religious studies. What is needed are ways to focus collaboratively across disciplines on aspects of the shaping of contemporary life. The aim is to offer analyses and assessments of issues and new developments, and, in Edward Farley's phrase, 'vividly imagined and severely criticized' possible courses of action.[9] There are many ways of attempting this. On my arrival in Cambridge I discovered that the Faculty of Divinity had for some time been germinating a new dimension, provisionally called a Centre for Advanced Religious and Theological Studies. I find this immensely attractive as a way of reproportioning the faculty so as to fulfil in a deliberate and well-resourced manner that third responsibility, while enriching its commitment to the other two. The centre is envisaged as sponsoring projects and programmes to do with the current relevance of theology in the ways just described, cooperating with specialists within the faculty and beyond it, and working through networks reaching to continental Europe, America and elsewhere.

Now let me sound a different note about this responsibility to society. I have emphasized the powerful, formative public discourses and developments. But vast numbers of people find themselves apparently written out of those scripts. They are not spoken to or spoken for and they have little possibility of speaking for themselves. They are marginalized, unable to take a worthwhile part, perhaps overwhelmed by the complexity, rapid change and vast scale of what they are part of, perhaps members of those diverse (and constantly changing) groups who find themselves severely disadvantaged in our late modern world. In relation to these, the public profile of theology is higher. Recent decades have seen a transformation in the theological scene as a growing number of theologies of liberation (largely within Christianity but also in Judaism and Islam) insist that genuine theology must be rooted in resistance to oppression – of the poor, of some racial groups, of lower classes, of women, of homosexuals, of minority cultures, of animals and of nature. These highly controversial theologies have changed the consciousness and the agenda of the theological world even where they have been largely rejected. Each theologian has to face a multiple confrontation with their claims. They have provoked many theological crises, not only among those they identify as oppressors but also among those they champion. They probe, sometimes crudely, sometimes with nuanced perception, the ways we have been shaped in the dimensions of our identity – gender, class, race, nation, wealth, status and so on – and they challenge us to change our perceptions, commitments and practice.

[9]   Edward Farley, *Fragility of Knowledge*, chap. 7.

These prophetic voices are not to be domesticated. I am not now going to attempt the task of following through their many implications, but I would make just two points about their role in the university, each of which would need further discussion if time allowed.

First, I think there is wisdom in the sort of phrase that is preferred by my colleague Dr Janet Martin Soskice, 'women and religion'. It draws attention to new voices until now largely absent from theology. The field has been changed irreversibly by these and the other previously unheard voices around the world. But the phrase also avoids any suggestion that there is a common 'line' or even that issues of gender are the main determinant of what all women contribute to religion and theology. It may be in some cases, but it is an open question. There are also 'men and religion', 'Jews and religion', 'Christians and religion', 'atheists and religion' and so on, with complex overlaps and interrelations between them. What I think needs to be avoided is the threat of a new sort of confessionalism in which not religious orthodoxy but political correctness is the criterion. This threat of quasi-confessionalism is one to which the wisdom learnt from handling the more usual confessionalism should be applicable – perhaps we have learnt a little about how to cope with religious divisions without either losing integrity or engaging in violence. It raises again the difficult issues of proper and improper advocacy, the other side of which is the nature of the university as a place where fundamental disagreements can cohabit in dispute and dialogue.

Secondly, I would argue that these theologies are by no means alien to my description of a public theology with three responsibilities. They all tend to major on the transformation of society, but those which have developed most also have strong connections with both universities and religious communities, often in challenging forms. The very use of the term 'responsibility' embodies one of their main contentions: that there is no divorcing the ethical from the academic. The question is whether it is a better or worse ethic and how far it serves a wisdom that is in tune with what that last stanza of 'Motet' calls 'a music of compassion'.

Wisdom

But what about that wisdom which has cropped up as a seeming cure-all from time to time? I choose it as a term that has deep resonances in the Hebraic, the Hellenic and many other traditions. It is characteristically particular yet reaches for universality. It is long-term and social, an achievement of generations. It is involved in the good shaping and reshaping of character, of patterns of life, of institutions and of discourses. It is about insight into the many-faceted complexity of reality combined with right practice within it. It refuses to be content with knowledge that does not raise further questions about its relations with other knowledge and with the whole ecology of reality. Wisdom grows through habits of attentiveness, listening and respect that allow for otherness to the point of mystery. It is expressed in many genres, perhaps most typically in the epigrammatic wisdom saying. Yet it is more appropriately associated with people than with texts, and with their engagement in the complexities of living. Its presence is most urgent and apparent at the raw edge of life, responding to the new in ways that are impossible to catch adequately in sayings, principles or theories.

Yet the wisdom that has been written down in the past has extraordinary potential for transforming the present and the future. I think of two formative encounters in my own life. Years before deciding to study theology I accidentally picked up Dietrich Bonhoeffer's *Ethics* and was gripped by that rich intensity of rigorous thought, faith and practicality.[10] It gave content for the first time to the word theology, and I remain grateful that that was the source of my first impression. Years later, while studying classics, I remember being taken over for a whole evening, lengthening into night, by this passage from Plato's Seventh Letter:

> If the hearer has the divine spark which makes the love of wisdom congenial to him and fits him for its pursuit, the way described to him [Plato has just described its rigours] appears so wonderful that he must follow it with all his might if life is to be worth living . . . Only after long partnership in a common life devoted to this very thing does truth flash upon the soul, like a flame kindled by a leaping spark, and once it is born there it nourishes itself thereafter.[11]

How easy it is to do years of academic study without much glimpse of anything like that!

And so on down the years – the pivotal points of theological pilgrimage have been times of encounter with wisdom in many forms – teachers, colleagues, students, friends, critics, novels, philosophies and so on. Not the least important has been poetry, of which you have heard that example by Micheal O'Siadhail. The first stanza of 'Motet' suggests the present situation of Western civilization in the shadows of past imperialisms and other forms of dominance and exploitation.

[10]   *Ethics* (Collins, London, 1964).
[11]   Plato, *Phaedrus and the Seventh and Eighth Letters* (Penguin, London, 1973), pp. 135 f.

O my white-burdened Europe, across
so many maps greed zigzags. One voice
and the nightmare of a dominant chord:
defences, self-mirroring, echoings, myriad
overtones of shame. Never again one voice.
Out of malaise, out of need our vision cries.

That reflects something of the postmodern diagnosis of a hopelessly fragmented culture, compromised by the corruptions of power, and it echoes
the postmodern determination: 'Never again one voice.' But then in the
second stanza there is another note, a hope for renaissance. I am reminded
of the suggestion of the philosopher Stephen Toulmin that after the Enlightenment's preference for grand overviews, systematic integrations and projects that homogenize people, places and knowledge, we have the possibility
of recovering in a new way some of the attractive wisdom of the Renaissance about diversity without fragmentation, many voices with a *cantus
firmus*.[12]

But can we be so positive? 'And which voice dominates or is it chaos?'
There we have two radical doubts about the very possibility of wisdom of
the sort I have been talking about. 'Which voice dominates?' – is it ultimately about power relations that are a function of violence? Is the imposition of meaning by force the only form of unity or harmony? Is there no
true peace, *shalom,* to be hoped for?

'Or is it chaos?' – this perhaps goes even deeper, the suspicion that there
is no meaning, despair about the point of the quest for wisdom. I see widespread despair of this sort around in our universities. It is often well disguised
– as Kierkegaard, in his unnervingly penetrating account of modern despair,
The Sickness unto Death,[13] said, despair is frequently embodied in hectic
activity and busyness. The bracketing out of large, apparently insoluble questions is often wise for specific purposes, but as a habit it has terrible effects
on the academy. In the face of a pervasive despair about energetic academic
pursuit of those big questions, is it surprising that many theologians take
refuge in respectable specialties and many philosophers find ways to con-
strict their scope of operations drastically in comparison with other periods?
The rumour of wisdom can be ignored or even actively denied.

Then there is the final question put by that stanza: 'does a lover of one
voice hear more or less?' In a pluralist situation, that is the pivotal one for

[12] Toulmin, *Cosmopolis: The Hidden Agenda of Modernity* (Free Press, New York, 1990).
[13] Søren Kierkegaard, *The Sickness unto Death: A Christian Psychological Exposition for Upbuild-
ing and Awakening*, ed. and transl. by Howard V. Hong and Edna H. Hong (Princeton University
Press, Princeton, NJ, 1980).

academic theology, and my vision of theology and religious studies turns
on the answer. There do have to be the generalizations, attempted overviews
and embracing concepts. The first part of this chapter has used such concepts
as responsibility and wisdom in order to sketch how the heterogeneous
practitioners in this field might be part of a common enterprise. But you
may have sensed a certain abstraction, the inability of that level of talk to
come to grips with many of the most urgent and interesting issues. The
main reason is that one does not have to press far before one comes upon
the deep particularity of concepts such as responsibility or wisdom. In theology this leads to conceptions that are both particular and transcendent,
such as responsibility before God and the wisdom of God. How can these
have academic justice done to them? Of course one can bring many disciplines to bear on them, say what they have meant to others and so on. But
what about actually listening and speaking in responsibility before God?
What about receiving the wisdom of God? Unless one is quite arbitrarily
to limit the human quest for truth and wisdom one must allow for this. No
one here can escape his or her own particularity: Hindu, Jew, Christian,
Muslim, agnostic, atheist or some other.

What might that involve for the lover of the voice of the Christian God?
It means, first, being in the tradition of wisdom communicated by the Old
Testament. Here wisdom is above all identified with God – as the opening
of Ecclesiasticus says:

> All wisdom is from the Lord:
> she dwells with him for ever. (Eccles. 1:1)

so that intrinsic to the formation of a wise mind is habitual relationship
with God in love, praise, prayer, and a wide range of responsibilities, but
above all the responsibility for passionate, whole-hearted and disciplined
pursuit of wisdom wherever it is to be found. This wisdom is as much
political and economic as it is personal and religious. It is also strongly self-
critical and revisionist – as in the Book of Job's devastating critique of key
elements in its own wisdom tradition. This theocentric and self-critical
understanding is further specified in Christian thought. To see Jesus Christ
crucified as 'the wisdom of God' (1 Cor. 1:24) is to find oneself wrestling,
in continuity with Job, with a range of radical questions about death, suffering, evil, sin, bodiliness, weakness and foolishness – but above all about
Jesus Christ. Further: to affirm this God as trinitarian is to be part of one
of the most extraordinary adventures of wisdom. It is partly about discerning
a dynamic order of love and truth that is infinitely abundant, generous and
welcoming. It stretches the mind in all directions – God, the cosmos, history,

religion, society and self. It draws one into confrontations, unexpected alli-
ances, mysteries and commitments. The mind is disciplined and challenged
by trying to conceive radical otherness, by qualification of all positive statements and by the need never to forget the *via negativa*. And it is a particularly
fascinating adventure at present as we find that in the twentieth and early
twenty-first centuries (in some contrast with the nineteenth) this deep
grammar of Christian faith is helping to generate new trinitarian speech
and theology among Catholics, Protestants, Orthodox, Pentecostals, libera-
tionists, feminists, Asians, Africans and others. Might Geoffrey Wainwright
even be right in his (to some) astonishing verdict that for our period the
doctrine of the Trinity is especially the one by which the Christian church
stands or falls?

Does the lover of the voice of this God hear more or less? There are no
inevitabilities here but the crucial possibility is that the voice bearing this
rumour of wisdom might be so heard and loved that the result is fresh and
fruitful wisdom for today.

I have a great hope, for others and for myself, for wisdom with something
of that quality, engaging critically and creatively with the religions and their
questions of truth and life. I have this, of course, in my particularity. I am a
lover of one voice. I trust that this will help in hearing more, not less.

It is worth meditating theologically on that hope. In classical Christian
theology there are two principal temptations which threaten a life of hope.[14]
The first is presumption, thinking you have already what you hope for and
relaxing the arduous tension of living in hope. One version of this is the
dominant voice asserting mastery. There are many other forms of academic
presumption, greatly encouraged by the pressures to publish. The second
temptation is to despair, believing that there is no fulfillment possible. This,
as I have mentioned, is the more serious academic threat. But there are also
two virtues which are especially supportive of hope. There is magnanimity,
which both Aristotle and Aquinas call 'the jewel of all the virtues'. It is about
aspiring to great things, stretching the spirit always towards greater possibilities. The vision of public academic theology that I have sketched risks doing
this. It would be much simpler to limit it to just one of the responsibilities
or perhaps two of them – and there are many who advocate that. Sustaining
the complexities of all three and also seeing wisdom as the goal will always
seem too much. But here the other supporting virtue comes in: humility.
This is about recognizing limits and proportions. It balances any claims to
docta sapientia, learned wisdom, with severe reminders of *docta ignorantia*,
knowing what we do not know. If one plays further with the fanciful

---

[14]   For a clear account see Josef Pieper, *On Hope* (Ignatius Press, San Francisco, 1986).

etymology that traces it to the Latin word for ground, *humus*, then one might say that in my vision it is about the disciplined, long-term and eco- logically sound cultivation of each specialty field in theology and religious studies. Excellence here is the *conditio sine qua non* of a good faculty. The study of all that wealth of particulars and the patient discerning of their character and interconnections is the staple, humble task of most of us most of the time. The challenge, in the hopeful pursuit of wisdom, is to keep together magnanimity without presumption and humility without despair.

Now to return to the final stanza of the poem, indeed to its last line. 'Love's congruence' is the ultimate hope. But it is preceded by that 'fierce vigil of contingency'. In our universities, religious communities and societies we are faced with extraordinarily diverse threats, risks, possibilities and challenges. In the midst of rapid change, rumours are often decisive for how people act and otherwise respond. And of course one person's rumour can be another's reliable testimony. Public theology is engaged in a vigil that con- cerns long traditions of testimony and their present participation in the contingencies of our world. I hope that all of us, in our own particular ways, will join with magnanimity and humility in this vigil and that we who are theologians and scholars of religion will do something for our part to sub- stantiate some particular rumours of wisdom as testimony to be trusted.

Note

I am immensely grateful to friends and colleagues who helped in conceiving and discussing this chapter, especially Mr Micheal O'Siadhail, Revd Professor Daniel W. Hardy, Revd Professor Frances H. Young, Professor Christopher Brooke, Dr Janet Martin Soskice and Dr Alan Ford.

Part II

WISDOM AMONG
THE RELIGIONS

Chapter Three

FAITH AND CHANGE:
A CHRISTIAN
UNDERSTANDING

In a BBC broadcast in 2001, the Chief Rabbi Dr Jonathan Sachs said that the events of September 11 were the greatest challenge to the religions of the world since the wars of religion in Europe during the sixteenth and seventeenth centuries. In this chapter I will start from there in order to draw from history some positive lessons about civil society and about the possibility of peace with integrity between religious traditions that have been in deadly conflict, as well as some negative lessons about secularism and about religious responses to modernity. I will suggest that there is a need to do better justice to the character of our society as 'religious and secular' and to the nature of healthy religious responses to modernity. Next, I will propose 10 theses about Christian faith and change. I will conclude with six items for a future agenda between Christians and Muslims that might enable them to work out together better ways of drawing on the resources in their traditions for peacemaking amidst current changes.

Learning from History: A Key to the Relationship of Faith to Change

The period of the sixteenth and seventeenth centuries is a good place for a Christian and a European to start in considering 'Faith and Change'. Its religious wars played a crucial part in a transformation of Europe that involved changes which still shape our world: the development of nation states; secularization (with separation of religious from political and other institutions, and religion having less identifiable cultural influence); colonizing and imperialisms that affected most of the rest of the world; the global spread of Christianity; political, scientific, technological and industrial revolutions; constitutional democracy; and mass education. None of the world faiths has been insulated from these developments, and all have in fact changed as a result of them; but Christianity has had a uniquely direct involvement with them.

A key question in the aftermath of September 11 is therefore: what lessons can be learnt from that history? The imperative of learning from history is deeply embedded in Christian scriptures. It is indeed a vital key to the relationship between faith and change. A great deal of the Old Testament is historical narrative from which lessons are continually being drawn; the prophets are concerned with discerning the meaning of the events of their time in relation to God's purposes; the wisdom literature is distilled from centuries of trying to understand personal, social and economic life with a view to human flourishing (and what prevents it); and the praising and lamenting of the Psalms are often closely related to the ups and downs of Israel's history. The New Testament pivots around the historical events of Jesus Christ's life, death and resurrection, in the light of which past, present and future are understood. Life now is lived oriented towards the Kingdom of God, as portrayed in the parables of Jesus, and faithful anticipation of that requires alert responsiveness to new events, tasks, possibilities and people.

Each period of Christian history has provoked attempts to understand its meaning in the purposes of God. Perhaps the most influential in the West has been Augustine's *City of God*, written during the collapse of the Roman Empire. The greatest trauma after that was the rise of Islam, and a good deal in medieval European and Byzantine Christianity can be understood as responding to Islam – militarily, intellectually, religiously.

Then in the fifteenth century came the Reformation and the split in Western Christianity. This was a time of vibrant Christian renewal, as well as devastating warfare which discredited Christianity in the eyes of many. The danger to which the Chief Rabbi points is that a similar discrediting, this time applying to all the conflicting religions, may be happening on a global scale now – already religion is a leading factor in many major conflicts.

But what if September 11 were to act as a shock sufficient to mobilize Muslims, Christians and others to try to avoid loss of life on the scale of the seventeenth century's Thirty Years War, and instead to find a wisdom that could contribute to a more peaceful and flourishing world in which the resources of the religions for peace are drawn upon more fully than ever before? From both Christian and Muslim standpoints, it is better to trust that this rather than religious war is in accord with the will of a God of peace, and that the seeking of the required wisdom will be blessed by God.

But what might be the lessons of the European wars of religion?

Two positive lessons from European wars of religion

There are two major positive lessons.

The need for civil society. One constructive and partly successful response to deadly religious conflict was to develop the institutions, laws and customs of civil society. This was in many countries as much the project of Christians who were appalled at the bloodshed in the name of their faith as it was of those who were disillusioned with Christianity as well as with war. There was collaboration among those who wanted peace through constitutional settlements, civil institutions, and distributions of power and privilege that limited the possibility of religious differences leading to inter-national or civil war.[1] There was also resistance, refusal to cooperate, and even violence from those who wanted the settlement to be on their terms alone. But overall the advocates of civil society succeeded, and for all the debates about the quality of its civility there is a broad consensus that civil society itself has been a major contributor to the common good.

It is no accident that one of the most insistent demands since September 11 has been for what one might call a more civil global society.[2] The Chief Rabbi's challenge might be developed as follows: can Christianity, Islam, and the often non-religious or anti-religious protagonists of contemporary capi-talism,[3] find the resources to weave a fabric of meaning that might shape

[1] For an account of some of the leading eighteenth-century approaches to history and the lessons that were learnt by historians, philosophers, jurists and others in the period after the wars of religion see J. G. A. Pocock, *Barbarism and Religion*, vols 1 and 2 (Cambridge University Press, Cambridge, UK, 1999). On the efforts in international law in a later period to create a more civilized world see Martti Koskenniemi, *The Gentle Civilizer of Nations: The Rise and Fall of International Law* (Cambridge University Press, Cambridge, UK, 2001). Koskenniemi is especially concerned to learn from international law's successes and failures, and suggests that its 'fall' and widespread replacement by 'instrumentalism' has left the world poorly equipped to move towards a better global civil order. Yet his sharply perceptive history and analysis, which includes discussion of ethics, morality, norms, conscience, universality, inter-dependence, human rights, rationality, tradition, and natural law, is extraordinarily inattentive to religion. Islam, Christianity, even 'religion' do not appear in the index. Perhaps it is too much to hope that such inattention will become less common among Western academics after September 11.

[2] For a study of civil society by an international team of contributors who cover historical and contemporary aspects of it in the West and in the Southern hemisphere see Sudipta Kaviraj and Sunil Khilnani (eds), *Civil Society: History and Possibilities* (Cambridge University Press, Cambridge, UK, 2001).

[3] It is important also to take into account at least three other areas: Judaism, China and India. These, together with Christianity and Islam, have in common the engagement with capitalism and the presence of long and still lively wisdom traditions.

the values, principles, agreements, laws, institutions and exchanges needed for global civil society?

The need for ecumenism. Another lesson is that it is possible for religious traditions which have engaged in deadly conflict to change with integrity and, without resolving all their differences, to live in peace, with their main emphasis on conversation and cooperation. That is in fact the story of the European churches. Its climax came in the twentieth-century ecumenical movement.[4]

Much of the inspiration for this came from beyond Europe, but within Europe a crucial factor was the experience of total war and mass killings justified by ideologies. There are many interpretations of that movement's significance, and there have been many other factors in the transformation of Europe's religious situation.

Yet it is likely that any efforts to increase understanding and make peace between religions today would have to include elements whose worth has been shown where the ecumenical movement has been effective: every level – local, regional, national and international – is involved; there are bilateral and multilateral dialogues and agreements; a good deal of thorough study, discussion and publication has been essential; where the process has gone well, both leadership and extensive institutional support (including financial) have been important; and there is realism about the timescale required – divisions that developed and were reinforced over centuries need time to be understood and negotiated, and attempts to take short cuts can be more disastrous than not engaging at all.[5]

Two negative lessons

The partial successes of civil societies and of the ecumenical movement offer resources that can lead in the direction of the wisdom needed in the

---

[4]   For a perceptive summary of the ecumenical movement's history and significance (together with a short bibliography) see Geoffrey Wainwright's article in *The Oxford Companion to Christian Thought,* ed. Adrian Hastings, Alistair Mason and Hugh Pyper (Oxford University Press, Oxford, 2000), pp. 189ff.
[5]   A new major feature of world Christianity which has so far had little to do with ecumenism is the Pentecostal-Charismatic movement – it is estimated at about 300 million people and growing rapidly. Its main impact has not been in Europe, so is outside the scope of this section. It is a form of lively, popular religion that has often flourished in modern urban settings, and has learnt to practise and spread Christianity amidst rapid change. For a broad sociological account of Pentecostalism see David Martin, *Pentecostalism: The World Their Parish* (Blackwell, Oxford, 2002).

present situation, but the negative lessons of the European experience also need to be learnt. These are primarily two.

The failure of secularism in a religious and secular world. First, the civility of the European settlements was extremely partial and prone to violence. Religious warfare was succeeded by imperial conquest and rivalry; French, Russian and other revolutions; and a twentieth century in which secular ideologies of communism, fascism and capitalism flourished and fought, resulting in hundreds of millions of casualties. The lesson of this is that secularism has failed even more terribly than religion.

The symbolism of September 11 was profound: it focused on the global economics of the World Trade Center and the global military power of the Pentagon (and may also have been aimed at the global political power of the White House). The main response has been in terms of military muscle and an alliance based on America's political, economic and military power. The lesson of European history and its global influence is that, whatever its short-term justification, this is unlikely by itself to lead to the peace of global civil society.

Those secular forces centred on money and arms only have access to the resources of soul, wisdom, compassion, and hope when they are set in a larger, richer fabric of meaning and purpose. One modern version of such a fabric is secular humanism with a vision of a civil, humane and just world. Desirable though that might be, it is often unaware of its dependence upon older, religiously influenced institutions, understandings and patterns of life, and has hardly yet displayed the depth, resilience and life-shaping capacity needed to form communities that can heal the divisions of our world.[6]

We have to face the religious and secular reality of our world. This reality is seen in two ways. First, the main secular ideologies have either failed or shown their serious inadequacy, and even in crude statistical terms the vast majority of the world's population are likely to identify with one or other of the world's faiths for the foreseeable future. Second, the secular myth of a neutral framework, with rational criteria against which to measure quality, costs and benefits (over against more partial, biased, traditional frameworks and criteria associated with religions) rightly appears less plausible than previously. Nobody has a neutral overview from nowhere, and the superiority complex of modernity in relation to religion (for all its justification in

---

[6] Koskenniemi, in *The Gentle Civilizer of Nations, op. cit.*, is a good example of this. He recognizes the weaknesses of all the secular attempts to meet the problems of international affairs and ends on a rather despairing note, while also ignoring the significance of the world's religions.

the terrible record of religion, but now balanced by a comparable secular record) can be seen as one strategy of one worldview in a bid for universality and power.

The alternative is a global civil society in which participants (including those with no religious commitment) find resources for peacemaking and serving the common good within their own traditions and through conversation and deliberation with others, and learn how to understand each other and collaborate without anyone being able to assume the role of neutral referee enforcing agreed rules. For that, intensive engagement between the participants is vital, seeking a wisdom that does justice to history and to each other as well as to their own convictions.

Inadequate religious responses. The second negative European lesson is about the failure or at least serious inadequacy of many Christian responses to the massive transformations of which the religious wars were part.

The least adequate responses are at the extremes of a continuum. One extreme allows the transformations and accompanying modern understandings to assimilate Christianity. This is adaptation in which nothing distinctively Christian is allowed a formative role. It is clearly inadequate from a Christian standpoint, since it evacuates Christianity of any continuing relevant content. Yet even a Christianity that is in principle against such assimilation can easily slide into it. The danger is increased by the circumstance that modern Western culture has been in closer symbiosis with Christianity than with any other faith. It may be that important lessons about alertness to assimilation and wise ways of avoiding it can be learnt by Christians from Muslims living in the West.

The other extreme attempts to prevent the transformations having any effect, preserving unchanged an earlier form of Christian faith and practice, and refusing any dialogue with modern understandings.

One form of this is attempted withdrawal from the modern world. The Christian critique of this questions its conception of God and Jesus Christ, its failure to affirm the goodness of creation (including many aspects of modernity), its avoidance of responsibility towards society, and its despair of possibilities of transformation for the better.

Another form tries to fight the modern world, dominate it, and reshape it according to its own religious vision. The Christian critique of this again relates to the conception of God and Jesus Christ, the goodness of creation, and a discerning response to modernity. In addition, there are questions about what form of communicating and spreading the gospel are in harmony with the content of the gospel and the example of Jesus Christ, and about the lessons to be learnt from the bloody history of such totalitarian religious ambitions.

Faced with extremes of assimilation to modernity or radical rejection of it, is there an alternative that has Christian integrity?

I see most types of Christianity today coming somewhere between the extremes on that continuum.[7] They try to understand Christian faith in continuity with its origins and combine it with critical and constructive engagement with modern life and understanding. Faith and change are not alternatives: the key issue is to discern how they relate to each other. There is here a wisdom that needs to be worked out afresh in each period and situation.

This is especially urgent after September 11, because most discussions have lacked a crucial category for describing reality. This is the category of a religion that is neither absorbed by modernity nor simply rejects it, but is engaged in simultaneously affirming it, judging it and transforming it. If Muslims and Christians were to agree that this embodies the best wisdom of both of our traditions, that could be a momentous step forward. It could be the basis for intensive discussion about what is to be affirmed, and why, how, where, when, and by whom it is to be affirmed; about right judgement before God of modernity, our religious traditions, and our current situation; and about desirable transformations that follow from those affirmations and judgements and that draw on the resources of our traditions.

Christian Faith and Change: 10 Theses

What is the Christian understanding of faith and change that underlies the position being advocated: to refuse both assimilation to and rejection of modern changes, and instead to attempt to find a wisdom that appropriately affirms, judges and transforms them? I will put forward briefly for discussion 10 theses on Christian faith and change,[8] any one of which could do with a chapter to itself.

---

[7] For a fuller discussion of this with reference to the types of Christian theology in the last two centuries see David F. Ford with Rachel Muers (eds), *The Modern Theologians – An Introduction to Christian Theology since 1918*, 3rd edn (Blackwell, Oxford, and Malden MA, 2005), especially the Introduction, in which a fuller account of a typology relevant to the present argument is given. Looking at the history of Christianity from the New Testament and the early Church and on through its later developments, I see there too the mainstream emphasis avoiding the two extremes described above.

[8] I hope that, if Muslim participants agree on the wisdom of affirmation, judgement and transformation, they might offer an Islamic understanding of them, or analogous concepts.

1   Christian faith is above all in God who is intimately involved in ongoing history for the good of the whole of creation. Creation and human history are to be paid close and appreciative attention (feeding into praise and thanks to God) as being given by God and oriented to God's glory and full life with other people before God.

2   Change can be for the better, in line with the good purposes of God, or for the worse. Human participation in history requires continual discernment, learning, and taking of responsibility in the interests of change for the better. The most serious danger is idolatry, in which what is not God is absolutized, and relations with God, other people and creation are distorted. Discerning and resisting the tendencies to idolatry, and educating desire to be non-idolatrous, are basic services to our societies.[9]

3   In Jesus Christ God has come together with the world so as to affirm radically its created goodness, to judge its sin and evil, and to transform it into the Kingdom of God. Jesus Christ was involved with change for the better and for the worse. The threefold realism of affirmation (seen especially in his ministry of healing, feeding, teaching, etc.), judgement (especially in his death), and transformation (especially in his resurrection) embodied in the crucified and risen Jesus Christ is at the heart of Christian involvement with change in history.[10]

4   The Holy Spirit 'poured out on all flesh' is the continuing eventfulness of God in history, opening it up to God's purposes and enabling ongoing affirmation, judgement and transformation.

5   Christians are called to be affirmed, judged and transformed by God through Jesus Christ for the sake of the affirmation, judgement and transformation of the world. This calling centres on their participation in the worshipping community of the church.

6   With regard to the massive changes associated with modernity, there is a demanding task of wise discernment, accompanied by efforts,

[9]   For a perceptive historical, philosophical and theological treatment of this in the context of relations between religious traditions, see Nicholas Lash, *The Beginning and the End of 'Religion'* (Cambridge University Press, Cambridge, UK, 1996) especially Part One 'A Meeting-Place for Truth' and within that pp. 19ff. on 'Education from Idolatry, and the Purification of Desire'.

[10] For a clear statement of this see Dietrich Bonhoeffer, *Ethics* (Collins, London, 1964), especially Chapters 4 and 5.

in collaboration with others, to heal both the religious traditions and modernity. Essential to Christian discernment is continuing conversation around scripture, drawing on the resources of tradition, the worldwide Christian community and the worldwide academic community. The indwelling of scripture through worship, prayer, study, the arts, academic disciplines, discussion, debate, and living in the world in faith is at the heart of lively Christian wisdom in response to change.

7   In relations with Muslims, whose own scriptures are likewise vital to discernment with regard to faith and change, any worthwhile mutual understanding will have to include sharing in the processes of scriptural interpretation (and the responses to historical developments involved in that) in both traditions. There should also be participation in this by Jews, as the eldest siblings of the Abrahamic faiths. Such intensive, long-term conversation around seminal texts while seeking wisdom for the contemporary world is a model of how to ensure that participants in a pluralist situation (including others besides Jews, Christians and Muslims) engage with each other at a level that allows for the discovery of shared wisdom.

8   Institutions, organizations and other structured focuses of life in society are vital arenas for facing the challenges of modernity (together with many serious challenges that have little to do with modernity). In line with my analysis of the importance of civil society in our religious and secular world, these must become places where religious resources for peace and flourishing are available. What is the potential for this in national and local government, the health service, business, the judicial system and prisons, education, the media, entertainment, and so on?

9   Part of the task of collaborative discernment and healing is to do with modern knowledge, its applications, and its institutions. Universities in particular are places where Christians, Muslims, those of other faiths, and those identified with no faith, come together in learning, teaching, scholarship and research with responsibilities in relation to students, knowledge, understanding and applications that are vital to the shaping of our world. At present many universities in the West (and elsewhere too) are strongholds of secularism. If they are to contribute constructively to understanding and peace in a religious and secular world they need to become religious-and-secular universities, where there can be sustained engagement with

questions of truth and practice raised by, between and about the world's religions.[11]

10 Human history and achievements, together with society and its institutions, should not be seen as ultimates – they are penultimate. God and God's Kingdom alone are ultimate, and the beginning of wisdom is to recognize this. Realizing the right relation of the ultimate to the penultimate is at the heart of wise living. A wrong emphasis on the penultimate can lead to compromising Christian faith, to assimilation, and to idolatry. An emphasis on the ultimate out of right relationship to the penultimate leads to fanaticism, religious warfare, and other forms of idolatry. Jesus Christ is neither compromiser nor fanatic, but lives affirming, judging and transforming the penultimate sphere while also orienting it towards ultimate transformation.[12] His followers are called to live in that dynamic, their basic act being to recognize the ultimacy of God through worship and through prayer for the Kingdom of God. One important penultimate goal in the present situation is a non-idolatrous, religious and secular civil society.

Items for a Future Agenda Between Christians and Muslims

The events of September 11 have already produced considerable changes. In the light of the above understanding, what sort of agenda between Christians and Muslims might now help to generate further changes for the better?

1 *The ultimacy of God.* In what ways can the horizon of a God of peace, wisdom and compassion be shared by Christians and Muslims? Can

[11] The same holds for schools. The UK government's recent recognition of the desirability of more faith-based schools is an important landmark in affirming that Britain is a religious and secular society. In historical perspective this might later appear as a sign of official recognition (and by a political party that has had a militantly anti-religious secularist strand) that the assumption of a linear 'progress' from religious past to non-religious future is not only wrong but damaging and dangerous. The task now is to make sure that the way these schools are conceived embody the lessons of history. One predictable reaction to September 11 was to condemn the whole idea because religions breed division and conflict. That 'either-religious-or-secular' line needs to be countered by a 'religious-and-secular' approach in which both religious communities and other parties show they have learnt from the best and worst in history.
[12] For a fuller account of the relation of ultimate and penultimate see Bonhoeffer, *Ethics, op. cit.*, Chapter 4.

we identify what in the relations of Christians and Muslims, and in their relations with others, most fully glorifies God? How can we help each other to be faithful to God in the current testing of our capacity for wisdom, peacemaking and compassion? What practices of prayer for each other should each adopt? How do we handle the fact that Muslims and Christians identify God very differently?

2   *Affirmation, judgement and transformation.* Can Muslims and Christians collaborate in trying to find a wisdom of affirmation, judgement and transformation in relation both to each others' traditions and practices and to the developments of modernity? In dealing with modernity, is it right to avoid both extremes of assimilation and outright rejection? If so, how can this best be done by each community and by both in collaboration?

3   *A non-idolatrous religious and secular civil society.* Is this the right interim goal, given the lessons of history and the present world situation? If so, how can it best be developed by Christians, Muslims and others, both nationally and internationally?

4   *Forms of collegiality for seeking and sharing wisdom.* If the above items are to be taken seriously, appropriate groups, settings, structures and procedures are needed to enable Christians and Muslims to study, discuss, deliberate, and decide together. One concern which might be built into all wisdom-seeking is to explore the possibility of agreeing on common and truthful *descriptions* of each community and its history and present situation. Christians and Muslims each have well-developed internal forms of collegiality, but almost no joint collegiality. This is the greatest single practical lack in the present situation between the two. What forms might joint collegiality take? Who might initiate them? How might they be resourced? What might Christians and Muslims need to learn from each other,[13] and what might both of them learn from other traditions?[14] What are the most stubborn issues, and how can they be faced? Is such collegiality fatally

---

[13] If I ask about areas in which Christians in Britain might have lessons to learn from Muslims, they would include: insistence on faith needing to relate to the whole of life; the shaping of life with the help of disciplines such as regular prayer times; alertness to over-assimilation, compromises and idolatries; importance of family life; wisdom about dealing with racism; honouring education and those who teach; global solidarity with fellow-worshippers; and generous almsgiving.

[14] It is fascinating to trace how much each already owes to Jews and to Greeks. It may be that the present unprecedented availability of (and often engagement with) other traditions such as Hinduism, Buddhism, Confucianism, the modern natural and human sciences, and the arts of many cultures is an opportunity for enrichments, developments and joint learning among Christians and Muslims that would dwarf their debt to Judaism and Hellenism.

undermined by the missionary nature of each faith, or are there ways to have both collegiality and missionary integrity?

5   *Signs of Muslim–Christian service of the common good.* How might Muslims and Christians collaborate in serving the common good in every area of life? Instead of living up to the image of religion as causing division and conflict, how can they together serve peace, justice, the flourishing of civil society, and the seeking and sharing of wisdom for the common good? The aim should be to create signs of peacemaking in each sphere – politics, business, law, education, the media, and so on. What are the priorities here?

6   *Movements, networks, institutions, groups, friendships: the issue of scale.* The problems and possibilities between Christians and Muslims are so profound and extensive that it is unlikely that anything less than a movement (cf. the ecumenical movement discussed above), or even more than one movement,[15] would be able to have the desired impact. It is also possible to imagine networks, institutions and groups, with the face-to-face level being crucial if the essential element of trust is to be built up. But it is probably wise that there should be no master-plan. Perhaps the main lesson of the ecumenical movement is that it began in friendships. The most challenging question is: are Muslims and Christians open to the friendships that God is inviting them into today?

[15]   It is instructive that the ecumenical movement among Christians began as distinct movements (especially the missionary movement, Faith and Order, and Life and Work) whose coalition into the World Council of Churches has only ever been a very partial success.

Chapter Four

READING SCRIPTURE WITH INTENSITY: ACADEMIC, ECCLESIAL, INTERFAITH, AND DIVINE

When given the chance to reflect on 'Faith in the Third Millennium: Reading Scriptures Together,' my thoughts converged on four kinds of intensity: academic, ecclesial, interfaith and divine.

An Academic Intensity: Scholarship, Hermeneutics, and Theology

The first, an academic intensity, is connected especially with a five-year period during my time as a lecturer at Birmingham University. At the suggestion of my friend and colleague, Frances Young, she and I co-authored a book called *Meaning and Truth in 2 Corinthians*. It brought five years of intermittent but intensive conversation, study, translating, and writing together with a Master's course and a discussion group of colleagues also focused on this short, dense letter. What were the lessons from all this for reading together – besides the happy and by no means unimportant confirmation that study and friendship can so richly enhance each other?

The first was *how crucial and generative the activity of translating is*. We had both been trained in Greek and Latin classics, which meant that both of us were dissatisfied with all the available translations; but I do not think either of us had tried collaborative translation before. Franz Rosenzweig said that you know a text for the first time in translation. (And there is a sense in which our most important relationships, whether between friends, disciplines, traditions, religions, or generations, are exercises in translation.) Wrestling together with Paul's knotty, concentrated Greek not only led into all dimensions of philological scholarship; it also threw up one historical, literary, hermeneutical, and theological issue after another. I remember the feeling of sheer inadequacy when faced with chapters 8 and 9 about the collection for the poor in Jerusalem. Nils Dahl said these chapters are 'impossible to translate'.[1] Paul is using one key term of his Gospel after another in order to speak simultaneously about actual finances and the 'economy of God'.[2] The metaphorical and the literal are complexly inter-connected, and this embodies linguistically 'the coinherence of the financial and divine economies: in 2 Corinthians the mutuality of spiralling giving and thanksgiving culminates in the ultimate value, the glory of God (8:19; 9:13)'.[3] 'Thanks be to God for his inexpressible gift' (9:13). Again and again the labor of translating difficult passages led us on into questions for which scholarship – whether philological, historical, sociological, or literary – was not sufficient, but neither was hermeneutics alone nor theology alone.

This was the second lesson, *the necessary coinherence of approaches to a text such as this*, which generally means that interpretation must be collaborative, a conversation between readers steeped in differing disciplines and their habits of inquiry. This in turn calls for practices of long-term collegiality that are rare enough in the academy. Appropriate academic intensity requires forms of sociality that pose a little-recognized challenge to our institutional creativity. How can we create settings and encourage relationships that enable the best practice of such disciplined reading together?

---

[1]   N. A. Dahl, *Studies in Paul* (Augsburg, Minneapolis, 1977), p. 31.

[2]   'The collection itself is called *charis* (grace, gift of grace, favor, benevolence, gracious work, 8:6, 7, 19; cf. 8:1, 9; 9:14; 1 Cor. 16:3), *koinonia* (partnership, sharing, fellowship, 8:4; 9:13; cf. Rom. 15:26), *diakonia* (ministration, service, relief work, 8:4; 9:12, 13; cf. 8:19, 20 [the verb *diakonein*], and Rom. 15:21), *eulogia* (open-handedness, blessing, liberality, willing gift, 9:5; cf. 9:6), *leitourgia* (service, voluntary public service, priestly religious service, 9:12; cf. Rom. 15:27), *haplotes* (single-minded commitment, simplicity, generosity, 8:2; 9:11, 13), *hadrotes* (large sum of money, plenitude, liberal gift, 8:20), *perisseuma* (overflow, abundance, 8:14), *endeixis tes agapes humon* (proof of your love, demonstration of your love, 8:24), *sporos* (seed-corn, seed, resources, 9:10; cf. 9:6) and *ta genemata tes dikaiosunes humon* (the offshoots, harvest or yield of your righteousness, 9:10; cf. Hosea 10:12). Even this limited focus shows the collection linked into key terms in Paul's Gospel and 2 Corinthians. The ordinary word for collection, *logeia* (1 Cor. 16:1, 2), is not used at all here. The chapters are certainly about money and basic attitudes to possessions and prosperity, but these are inseparable from the character and glory of God, the practice of faith and love in the church and the dynamic reality of grace. The metaphorical application of economic terms to the gospel is given a new development as key gospel concepts, including economic ones, are in turn directed at reconceiving financial attitudes and relationships.' (Frances Young and David Ford, *Meaning and Truth in 2 Corinthians* (SPCK, London, 1987; Westminster, Philadelphia, 1988), pp. 176f.)

[3]   Ibid., p. 180.

A third lesson has taken longer to draw. It came clear last year when thinking about another co-authored book, called *Thinking Biblically: Exegetical and Hermeneutical Studies* by Andre LaCocque, an Old Testament scholar, and Paul Ricoeur, among many other things a hermeneutical philosopher. (I think Paul Ricoeur, with Karl Barth, is among the very greatest Christian minds of the twentieth century – two thinkers of the Reformed Protestant tradition who are also deeply complementary to each other, and converge, one through philosophy and the other through theology, on the utter centrality of biblical interpretation.) LaCocque and Ricoeur draw together the more retrospective, archaeological approach of LaCocque with the more prospective approach of Ricoeur, who engages with the text's reception through the centuries and with its meaning for today. Thinking about the traditions and disciplines of interpretation which they bring to bear on texts from Genesis, Exodus, the Psalms, the Song of Songs, and other books, it is as if they are attempting to recapitulate the most fruitful exegetical and hermeneutical practices of the Western academy since the foundation of universities alongside the monastic schools of Medieval Europe. There is, especially in Ricoeur's rich and daring exposition of the Song of Songs, something of the monastic *lectio divina*, a meditative, contemplative reading allowing for many senses, and oriented above all towards the worship of God. That monastic tradition often resisted the scholastic, argumentative discourse of the new universities and their concern with Aristotle and other philosophers, but Ricoeur shows how to learn from the scholastics too as he discusses the *Ego sum qui sum*, 'I am who I am', of Exodus 3:14. As the Middle Ages turned into the Renaissance and early modernity, scholasticism was in its turn challenged by the humanists. The Christian humanists' return to sources, their emphasis on Greek and Hebrew, and their appreciation of poetry, rhetoric, and history are all reflected in the studies of LaCocque and Ricoeur. And in later modernity we might discern the strands most obviously represented by the two authors: the strongly *wissenschaftlich* German philological and historical critical tradition, and that of philosophical and theological hermeneutics.

The lesson I draw from this is that *we read scripture together not only with those in the various disciplines of the academy but also with our predecessors in the communion of saints*; and these include monastic saints, scholastic saints, humanist saints, hermeneutical saints and (even!) saints who are historical critics. It would be surprising if each of the regimes of reading that have at various times dominated the academy did not have something to teach us (even when practised by those we might not identify as within the communion of saints at all), and this encourages us to welcome representatives of all of them (the religious and the secular, and those who are complexly both) into the circle of those with whom we read and discuss scripture.

An Ecclesial Intensity: Wisdom Interpretation for the Church in the World

I now turn from the academic intensity of scholarship, hermeneutics and theology to a second, which I am naming *an ecclesial intensity*, one centred in the church in the world. This has many aspects – local, regional, political, ecumenical, and more – but for now I will confine myself to one formative involvement of my own over another five-year period.

The 1998 Lambeth Conference for the 800 bishops of the Anglican Communion took Second Corinthians as its theme text, studied together by the whole conference in small groups every day in the context of morning prayer. I was part of a group that organized the opening and closing plenary sessions with a focus on the Bible through drama, video, discussion, and addresses. This later led into my participation, as leader of the Bible studies and theological adviser, in four annual meetings, between 2000 and 2003, of the Archbishops and Presiding Bishops of the Anglican Communion, called Primates' Meetings.

As is well known, during all this time the Communion was engaged in vigorous argument, especially over issues relating to homosexuality; and these in turn were inseparable from deep differences over the interpretation of scripture. This has been one of the most public and long-running disputes in our time over how to read scripture together. I need not remind you that this is not just an Anglican problem: the issues here resonate around the world in many Christian churches and in other religious and non-religious communities. So although I am selecting the tradition that I know best, there are analogous tensions in other churches and traditions.

Within the Anglican Communion, the culmination of the most recent phase was the publication of the Windsor Report by the Lambeth Commission on Communion set up by the Archbishop of Canterbury.[4]

---

[4] Its discussion of scripture is under the heading of 'The Bonds of Communion'. What it says about the authority and interpretation of scripture in the Church is as good as any brief statement I have read. Its finely balanced affirmation of authority says:

> 'If the notion of scriptural authority is itself to be rooted in scripture, and to be consonant with the central truths confessed by Christians from the earliest days, it must be seen that the purpose of scripture is not simply to supply true information, nor just to prescribe in matters of belief and conduct, nor merely to act as a court of appeal, but to be part of the dynamic life of the Spirit through which God the Father is making the victory which was won by Jesus' death and resurrection operative within the world and in and through human beings.' *The Lambeth Commission on Communion: The Windsor Report* (Anglican Communion Office, London, 2004), p. 39.

What is to be learned regarding reading scripture together from this Anglican experience between Lambeth 1998 and 2005? One encouraging result is that it shows it can be done fruitfully; the discouraging thing is how easily this achievement can, at least in the short term, be undermined, ignored, or undone, especially through the activities of well-financed and well-organized interest groups skilled in dealing with the media. The 1998 Lambeth Conference sub-group that spent over two weeks considering human sexuality was made up of over 50 bishops, ranging from Bishop Jack Spong to conservative Nigerians. They began extremely polarized but ended by agreeing on a common statement that was no empty compromise.[5] Yet this sub-group report was brushed aside by the highly politicized plenary session that discussed sexuality. In successive Primates' Meetings something similar happened. In each one that I attended, a common life interweaving worship, the study of scripture, serious listening to each other in a spirit of mutual accountability, the sharing of issues from each province, and engaging with a wide range of demanding questions, from canon law and theological education to HIV/AIDS and world poverty, led to unanimous joint statements. Yet surrounding each meeting, and sometimes penetrating the meeting places, were the dedicated lobbyists pressing hard for quick, decisive, and inevitably divisive solutions according to their own clear criteria. And in between meetings the political pressures were sustained, encouraged by

---

This recognition of an authority that is part of the dynamic of the Spirit involved with all the contingencies and complexities of history and community life, and open to fresh interpretations, leads it to recognize the current situation as, against the odds, an opportunity for the Bible even to become a means of unity:

> If our present difficulties lead us to read and learn together from scripture in new ways, they will not have been without profit. . . . In fact, our shared reading of scripture across boundaries of culture, region and tradition ought to be the central feature of our common life, guiding us together into an appropriately rich and diverse unity by leading us forward from entrenched positions into fresh appreciation of the riches of the gospel as articulated in the scriptures. (Ibid., p. 42).

[5] The ingredients, as observed by a member of the plenary group that I was part of, Dr Tim Jenkins, a social anthropologist, included shared worship, small group Bible study, thorough preparation by resource people, a commitment to respectful conversation, a really able secretariat of three bishops (who produced a draft proposal each day, circulated it, registered and coped with criticisms and disagreements, and redrafted it overnight), all enabling a process of coming to a common mind. This process was one in which no one was expected to give up a convinced position (especially on the way scripture was to be understood) and so bishops had to allow a certain discretion and integrity to each other, while at the same time they took into account and took responsibility for the effects of their own position on other participants and dioceses, offering to each other an imaginative understanding and compassion.

some of the Primates, often exerted through the mass media, but also through creating single-issue solidarity across continents.

But it is worth trying to name the sort of scriptural interpretation that went on in that sub-group at Lambeth, in the Primates' Meetings at their best, and probably (though here I do not speak as an eyewitness) in the Commission that produced the Windsor Report. How might we describe this interpretation?

It is *centered in worship*, the primary locus for reading scripture together. It grows out of *intensive, respectful conversation* in community, conversation around both scripture and the issues of church and world. It is alert to the *varied modes of interpretation* in the tradition and in the contemporary church and academy and it appreciates the abundance of meaning in Scripture. It is *imaginative and compassionate* in understanding and assessing the interpretations of others. It recognizes the *immersion in messy history* both of the biblical characters and authors and of the whole intricate and conflictual tradition of interpretation, including ourselves.[6] It *resists the temptation to reach for the security and satisfaction of clear, decisive answers* to questions in dispute among faithful Christians, and the consequent temptation always to speak emphatically in the indicative and imperative moods, when it might be more appropriate to use the interrogative mood, or the exploratory subjunctive mood of 'may be' and 'might be', or the optative mood, the 'if only' of desire to see face to face in the future while acknowledging that now we see through a glass darkly. It is willing, on the one hand, to enter into *dispute for the sake of God's truth and love*, allowing that challenge, disagreement and admonition can be life-giving in any good family life, but, on the other hand, it is also willing to *live patiently with deep problems*, if necessary for many years, rather than break up a family bound together by the blood of Christ. Finally, it trusts that, if the two great commandments are about love, and

---

[6] Part of sensitivity to history is exploring why a particular issue regarding scripture has become so 'hot' at a particular time. What are the conditions for it becoming the focus of attention? In whose interest is it that this be at the centre of attention? Should this centrality be affirmed or challenged? If its importance is granted, is it so important as to be church-dividing? One example worth reflecting upon is that of predestination to salvation and damnation. This has been deeply divisive, especially among Protestants, and has split churches, local communities, and families. There is a great deal of scripture relevant to it and no single interpretation has been generally agreed. Why at some periods has it been 'hot' enough to divide the church whereas at others, without being resolved, it has not been central? Are there lessons to be learned from the ways in which this issue has at times been taken off the boil and enabled not to be church-dividing even while also not having been given a clear, decisive answer?

God is love, then *no interpretation is to be trusted that goes against love* – that is Augustine's great *regula caritatis*, the rule of love. *If love is the rule, then the 'how' of reading scripture together is as important as the 'what'.* To come to conclusions in a separate group about what the Bible means and then to try to impose these on others by polemical websites, worldly political strategies, and a good deal of caricature, selective quotation, and anger, is deeply unchristian. But to follow an ethic of holy communication in love, to apply to our reading together the maxims, for example, of the letter to the Ephesians (that great epistle of unity, much of whose ethical teaching concerns the use of language):

> Let no evil talk come out of your mouths, but only what is useful for building up, as there is need, so that your words may give grace to those who hear. And do not grieve the Holy Spirit of God, with whom you were marked with a seal for the day of redemption. Put away from you all bitterness and wrath and anger and wrangling and slander, together with all malice, and be kind to one another, tenderhearted, forgiving one another as God in Christ has forgiven you. Therefore be imitators of God, as beloved children, and live in love, as Christ loved us and gave himself up for us, a fragrant offering and sacrifice to God (Eph. 4:29–5:2).

That is, to be committed to long-term patience with each other, often to give up chances of political advantage, and therefore to be politically vulnerable.

I suggest that one possible name for all this is: *a wisdom interpretation of scripture.* Wisdom in a full biblical sense somehow catches the blend of understanding, sensitivity to historical circumstances and to persons, concern for human flourishing, and passion for God and God's purposes that are in line with the wisdom and love through which all things were made. And it allows for the arts as well as the sciences, for depths beneath depths, for complexity that resists any overview, even for paradoxes, unresolved difficulties, unclarity, and the mystery of God. Just think of Job!

And thinking of Job immediately sets this wisdom in the context of the most terrible anguish, the cries of those who suffer, who seek against all the odds to make sense of things. Wisdom in the Bible is closely related to cries: the cries of wisdom herself, the cries for wisdom, for justice, for forgiveness, for peace, for prosperity, for healing, for life, for God; and the cries of God. I remember the effect at the Primates' Meeting in Kanuga in 2001 of the Rev. Gideon Byamugisha, someone with HIV/AIDS who gripped the whole gathering with his account of the AIDS pandemic, its implications, and what might be done about it. Really hearing this cry put the church's internal difficulties into another perspective and directed attention to scripture in a different way. As we interpret scripture in order to work out our salvation in fear and trembling before God (Phil. 2:12), that we hope is the beginning of wisdom, *are we within earshot of the cries of our world that go up to God?*

Above all, are we within earshot of the cries of Jesus Christ from the cross, and of Paul's proclamation of 'Christ crucified . . . the wisdom of God' (1 Cor. 1:23–4)? In my judgement, the most significant event of the meetings during those five years centred on the cross. It happened in Porto, Portugal in 2000, in the course of a Bible study on the Letter to the Ephesians. A discussion of 'the Father from whom every family in heaven and on earth takes its name' (Eph. 3:14) led into a discussion between two African archbishops about authority in families. This connected with the discussion of Ephesians 2 about being brought together by the blood of Christ, 'For he is our peace; in his flesh he has made both groups into one and has broken down the dividing wall, that is, the hostility between us' (Eph. 2:14). The core realization was that if it is virtually unthinkable to turn away and break off from our natural families, how much more unthinkable and scandalous should it be to turn away from those with whom the blood of Christ unites us? The measure of suffering to which we are called for the sake of our unity is nothing less than that seen in the crucifixion of Jesus Christ. This led into a statement in the meeting's communiqué that seems to me to give a prophetic wisdom for Christians in our new millennium: 'As in any family, the assurance of love allows boldness of speech. We are conscious that we all stand together at the foot of the cross of Jesus Christ, so we know that to turn away from each other is to turn away from the cross'. And that statement is quoted in the final sentence of the recent Windsor Report.

One final lesson from those five years was a growing realization that, if time were to be given to the Anglican Communion to continue together, one area above all would need to be addressed: theological education. It had become clear that theological education was actually deteriorating in many regions, and that many clergy, let alone laity, were not being formed in ways of prayer, worship, scriptural understanding, and engagement with the world in the best traditions available. The pivotal issue was the interpretation of scripture. In the aftermath of one standard Book of Common Prayer it was apparent that the common language of the Communion has to be shaped afresh by the Bible, but that it has not anything like a common mind about the ways in which the Bible should be studied, interpreted, taught, and lived. This is a core challenge to be met if there is to be a healthy Anglican Communion; *I have become increasingly convinced that here in the reading of scripture together there is also a core challenge for Christianity as a whole.*

An Interfaith Intensity: Jews, Christians, and Muslims Reading our Scriptures Together

Now to the third intensity, which is closely related to the academic and the ecclesial. Of recent publications that manage to describe and embody wisdom in interpretation I think the best and most accessible is the publication of the Scripture Project sponsored by the Center of Theological Inquiry in Princeton, edited by Ellen Davis and Richard Hays, and called *The Art of Reading Scripture.*[7] They summarize their joint conclusions in nine theses on the interpretation of scripture: distillations of their wisdom which are as good guidelines as any yet offered for reading scripture together in the twenty-first century.[8] The eighth of the nine theses reads: 'Christians need to read the Bible in dialogue with diverse others outside the church'.[9]

The third intensity is the engagement of a community of Jews, Christians, and Muslims in what is called Scriptural Reasoning. Its origins are in a Jewish group called Textual Reasoning that began to meet at the American

---

[7] Eerdmans, Grand Rapids, MI, 2003.

[8] The nine theses are as follows:

1. Scripture truthfully tells the story of God's action of creating, judging, and saving the world.
2. Scripture is rightly understood in light of the church's rule of faith as a coherent dramatic narrative.
3. Faithful interpretation of scripture requires an engagement with the entire narrative: the New Testament cannot be rightly understood apart from the Old, nor can the Old be rightly understood apart from the New.
4. Texts of scripture do not have a single meaning limited to the intent of the original author. In accord with Jewish and Christian traditions, we affirm that scripture has multiple complex senses given by God, the author of the whole drama.
5. The four canonical Gospels narrate the truth about Jesus.
6. Faithful interpretation of scripture invites and presupposes participation in the community brought into being by God's redemptive action – the Church.
7. The saints of the church provide guidance in how to interpret and perform scripture.
8. Christians need to read the Bible in dialogue with diverse others outside the church.
9. We live in the tension between the 'already' and the 'not yet' of the Kingdom of God; consequently, scripture calls the church to ongoing discernment, to continually fresh rereadings of the text in the light of the Holy Spirit's ongoing work in the world. (Ibid., pp. 1–5).

[9] Ibid., p. 4.

Academy of Religion (AAR) in the early 1990s, with Professor Peter Ochs as one of its founding members. They are Jewish text scholars (of scripture and Talmud), philosophers, and theologians who found that there was little deep engagement between their different discourses centred on texts and reasoning, and so they started to study together. Some Christians, myself among them, used to sit in on their argumentative, learned, and extraordinarily lively sessions. Soon we joined together to form a second group of Jews and Christians, Scriptural Reasoning, studying the Tanakh and the Bible; and a few years later were joined by Muslims with the Qur'an. Scriptural Reasoning is now, like Textual Reasoning, a unit with a life of its own in the programme of the annual meeting of the AAR, there are groups in various parts of the world, an international Scriptural Reasoning Theory Group that has been meeting twice a year at AAR and in Cambridge, a grassroots body called the Children of Abraham Institute (CHAI), the online *Journal of Scriptural Reasoning*, a research group focusing on medieval scriptural interpretation in Judaism, Islam, and Christianity that is convened at the Center of Theological Inquiry, a postgraduate programme in the University of Virginia, and much else.

The core identities of Judaism, Christianity, and Islam have always been inseparable from their scriptures and accompanying traditions of study, interpretation, argument, doctrine, ethics, and worship; and this is unlikely to change in the third millennium. *It makes deep sense for these rich and widely influential reading traditions to engage as thoroughly as possible with each other.* They are already complexly related in content, and also with regard to issues of transmission, translation, normativity, methods of interpretation, contemporary relevance, and so on. Both historically and in many parts of the world today, communities that look to these scriptures have lived and are living together, often with considerable tensions. But whereas both the academic and the ecclesial intensities of scripture reading are served by many forms of collegiality, the interfaith intensity has almost a complete lack of collegiality. Where in our world do Muslims, Jews, and Christians gather to read our scriptures together in mutual hospitality and attentiveness? *I believe that a crucial challenge for faith in the third millennium is to create new forms of collegiality gathered around our scriptures and their accompanying traditions of interpretation and application.*

The practice of Scriptural Reasoning is to spend some time in plenary discussion but most time in small groups studying passages of the three scriptures that in some way relate to each other. We have focused on texts concerning revelation, law, economics, teaching and learning, prayer, love, and much else. In February 2005, a group in Cambridge was joined by Rowan Williams, the Archbishop of Canterbury, for a two-hour session on

Joseph and Potiphar's wife in the Qur'an and Tanakh, and, from the New Testament, the woman who anointed Jesus's feet. Hebrew, Arabic, and Greek flew around the room; the Hadith, the Talmud, and patristic and medieval interpretations were drawn in, and all sorts of contemporary issues raised. In the phrase coined by Dr. Aref Nayed, each of us brings to the table our 'internal library'. When all these libraries are resourcing the reading of three texts at the same time, the result can be a dazzling intensity that combines the premodern, modern and postmodern that can produce startling surprises, that defies overview, systematizing or adequate reproduction in print, but yet – for those of us with academic vocations – has an intrinsic impulsion towards a theorizing, a doing of philosophy and theology, and a writing that can never do anything like full justice to what is going on but still tries to approximate to it as well as possible.

What happens at best in such sessions is close engagement with each other's texts in a spirit simultaneously of academic study, of being true to one's own convictions and community, and of truth-seeking and peace-seeking conversation wherever that might lead. It does not usually lead to consensus – the differences between us often emerge more sharply, and at these points there is often a deepening awareness of the meaning of one's own faith. It does often lead to friendship. *The mutual hospitality of each being both host and guest in relation to the others is at the heart of this collegiality.* Each tradition needs to offer its best food, drink, and cuisine.

For me that means preparing and offering those academic and ecclesial intensities in coinherence. In particular, that involves striving to embody and communicate something of what I have tried to describe through my account of the best practices of interpretation in the Anglican Communion in recent years. All of the strands in that wisdom interpretation cry out to be worked through appropriately in Abrahamic, interfaith reading of scripture: the intensive, respectful conversation in community, focused on both scripture and the issues of church and world; the abundance of meaning in scripture and the consequently varied modes of interpretation in the academy, in the tradition and in the contemporary church, synagogue, and mosque; the value of imagination and compassion in understanding and assessing each others' interpretations; recognition of immersion in messy history; the need to resist the temptation to reach for the security and satisfaction of clear, decisive answers to questions in dispute among Jews, Christians, and Muslims, and to value mutual questioning and exploration; the willingness, on the one hand, to enter into dispute for the sake of God's truth and love, and, on the other hand, to recognize the strength of our bonds in the family of Abraham and the call to live patiently with our deep differences; and throughout to conduct our reading according to an ethics, and even politics, of justice, love, and forgiveness.

Yet, as in the Anglican Communion, so in each of the Abrahamic faiths: such practices of wise reading are extremely vulnerable. The politics of scriptural interpretations can be crude, manipulative, and literally violent. I do not think that Scriptural Reasoning, or any other peace-loving practice among Jews, Christians, and Muslims, can flourish without building up of forms of dedicated collegiality and collaboration that are prepared to meet strong opposition within each community and in the secular world. Our world needs such signs of hope, and it needs the resources for peacemaking that each of these traditions can offer. And among these resources is one that is incomparable.

God, The Ultimate Intensity

This is the fourth intensity: God. In recapitulating the lessons learned from recent Anglican experience I omitted the first: reading needs to be centred in worship as its primary location. This points to the most obvious (yet extremely easy to ignore) truth about Muslim, Christian, and Jewish scriptures: that they are above all concerned with God. Within each tradition, doing justice to this is a never-ending challenge. Between them it is even more difficult and sensitive. For most members of each tradition, including myself, worship together by Muslims, Christians, and Jews is not appropriate. But if, as people who pray, we enter into joint scripture study together, perhaps this is as near as we can or should come to sharing in the intensity of worship that is at the heart of synagogue, church, and mosque. Around the Scriptural Reasoning table are people who acknowledge that *this reading is done before the living God*, however differently we might identify God.[10] Reading in the presence of the God of Abraham, the God of peace who

---

[10]   This is not to imply that Scriptural Reasoning must be confined to practising Jews, Christians, and Muslims. Within universities, for example, it can be appropriate to have scholarly readers of scriptures who are not necessarily members of one of the three traditions: they might be members of other religious traditions or not identify with any. This creates a different dynamic than when all are Jews, Christians, and Muslims, but one that is especially relevant to the complexities of our religious and secular world. My view is that within universities there should ideally be both types of groups; but in practice, given the complexity of the religious identity of many people today in both religious and secular contexts, together with the related complex interplay of religious and secular dimensions in communities labelled either 'religious' or 'secular', actual groups are likely to have very different make-ups and often be extremely hard to categorize. Such complexifying of boundaries is intrinsic to any worthwhile, transformative interfaith practice in a religious and secular world.

wills to bless all peoples through Abraham: that is the ultimate source of encouragement and hope for such reaching together.

And there is a consequent lesson for our reading, one which I believe goes to the heart of each of our traditions, and which, if we learn it well and follow through its endless implications, will guide us into the richest scriptural wisdom of all. The lesson is that each of us, both within our own traditions and when we come together, should *read our scriptures for God's sake*. We are to read for the sake of God and God's purposes. This is the ultimate orientation of reading among Jews, Christians, and Muslims. Of course our reading can have worthy penultimate motivations and aims, but the ultimate desire is to hallow the name of God; to bless, praise, and thank God; to acknowledge that God is great, good, compassionate, forgiving, holy, and has whatever other perfections are expressed in worship; to relate to God all that we are and think and hope and do; and to read and live in ways that please God.

Epilogue: On Friendship

Finally, a word on one of God's purposes, friendship. I remember a distinguished graduate of Princeton Theological Seminary, Dr. Preman Niles, saying to me that in his view the success of the first decades of the Christian ecumenical movement was to a considerable extent due to friendships that were formed across Protestant and Catholic boundaries and were strong enough to endure severe pressures. Much more than friendship is, of course, required if a major movement is to flourish long term; but, without friendships at the heart of it, it is unlikely that its fruitfulness will have the right quality and depth. Might it be that relations between faiths have in our century something of the same urgency and sense of *kairos* that the Christian ecumenical movement had in the mid-twentieth century, and that they will both flourish in this millennium only if they are engaged in simultaneously? And might it be that in such exchanges and extensions of friendship among readers of Tanakh, Bible, and Qur'an that the clearest signs of hope for faith in the third millennium are to be found and, hopefully, multiplied?

Chapter Five

DEVELOPING SCRIPTURAL REASONING FURTHER: REFLECTIONS ON SCRIPTURE, REASON AND THE CONTEMPORARY ISLAM–WEST ENCOUNTER

What is needed in current encounters between Islam and the West? That is a question that inevitably has many answers according to participants, situations, issues and spheres of life. Scriptural Reasoning, in which Jews, Christians and Muslims study and discuss their scriptures together, is one response.[1] I see it as a wisdom-seeking practice that has so far proved adaptable to varied participants, situations, issues and spheres of life, and just because of this is facing challenges about its future shape. At its heart is conversation around the scriptures, but that cannot be performed in print. The next best thing in a written format is to have a dialogue between those who have studied together. In what follows the main aim is not to recount the story and elements of Scriptural Reasoning (which are well covered elsewhere, especially by a recent issue of the journal *Modern Theology*),[2] but to ask how it might be developed further so as to play its role in the engagement

---

[1] See chapter 4, pp. 67–70.
[2] *Modern Theology*, vol. 22, no. 3, July 2006, also published as *The Promise of Scriptural Reasoning*, ed. David F. Ford and Chad C. Pecknold (Blackwell, Oxford, 2006).

between the Abrahamic faiths in a Western context and also between the faiths and secular understandings and forces.

Interactive Particularity

That last sentence deliberately rephrases the 'Islam–West encounter' in terms of Islam as a religion that is located (among other places) in the West, where it relates in particular ways both to other religions and to the secular. Scriptural Reasoning has its roots in just this situation in the US and Britain, though it is now being practised also in non-Western countries and one question about its further development concerns its transferability elsewhere. Moreover, its main institutional setting so far has been that quintessentially European institution, the university. Again, it is now being practised in other settings too, and its adaptability to diverse institutions and communities (schools, civil service, citizens' groups, business, media, the arts, interfaith families, and professions such as healthcare or law) raises further issues about its future.

The reason why its further development in different places and settings raises so many questions is that it has to be reinvented, or at least improvised upon, in each one. It is a form of 'interactive particularity'.[3] Just as in the study of scriptures the participants' particular concerns, backgrounds, traditions, formations, and ways of reading make a crucial contribution to conversations around specific texts, and often require complex discussion and negotiation in order to be understood and allowed to interact, so formative factors may change with each shift in setting and type of participant. Scriptural Reasoning has so far been worked through in a very limited number of settings, and the number of potential forms is immense. This should be no surprise, since Judaism, Christianity and Islam have each for many centuries generated, and continue to generate, a variety of ways of reading, inhabiting and applying their scriptures, and when the three come together the possibilities are further multiplied.

The problem then becomes how to cope with the variety, intensified by the deep differences between the three. There can be no formula for this. Each tradition within itself has ways of coping with diverse and conflicting interpretations (often, of course, unsuccessfully, if success is measured in terms of agreement), and part of Scriptural Reasoning is exploring how far

[3]   A term I owe to Daniel W. Hardy. Dr Ben Quash, Academic Coordinator of the Cambridge Inter-Faith Programme, has employed it in papers on the academic design of that programme.

these work in this new interaction. The results of the exploration come in many forms, ranging from readings of specific texts to general statements of rules,[4] or of maxims,[5] but the general statements are best seen as distillations of the particular readings, the outcome of an apprenticeship in one form of interactive particularity.

The practical conclusion for the present chapter is that, for me as a Christian interpreter of scripture, the aim of developing Scriptural Reasoning further in the service of contributing to the contemporary Islam–West encounter requires an attempt to do three things. First, there should be further interpretation of Christian scriptural texts. Second, there should be careful listening and response to Jewish and Muslim interpretations of their scriptures. Third, there should be an attempt to distil wisdom for the Islam–West encounter (as understood above). My way of trying to fulfil those requirements will be to comment in turn on essays by Steven Kepnes and Basit Koshul, doing further scriptural interpretation where appropriate, and concluding with suggestions for the further development of Scriptural Reasoning.

Hagar, God and Modernity

The heart of Kepnes' paper is its interpretation of the story of Hagar and Ishmael in Genesis 16: 7–14 and other texts. They are seen as

> a warrant for Jews and Christians to take Islam seriously, not only as the third monotheism, but as a tradition that is rooted in Genesis and whose origin and destiny is intertwined with Israel . . . Jews and Christians have a warrant in their scriptures to engage with the Muslims not as strange Others but as long lost members of the great family whose destiny is to be a light of truth and healing to all the nations of the world.[6]

The actual interpretation, while supporting that lesson, cannot be reduced to it. Kepnes accumulates significant details about Hagar: God speaking to a woman – a slave-girl – for the first time in Torah; the resonances elsewhere

---

[4]   Cf. Steven Kepnes, 'A Handbook for Scriptural Reasoning', in *Modern Theology*, vol. 22, no. 3, July 2006, pp. 367–83.

[5]   Cf. David F. Ford, 'An Inter-Faith Wisdom: Scriptural Reasoning between Jews, Christians and Muslims' in *Modern Theology*, vol. 22, no. 3, July 2006, pp. 345–66, especially pp. 348–51.

[6]   Steven Kepnes, 'Islam as Our Other, Islam as Ourselves', in *Scripture, Reason, and the Contemporary Islam–West Encounter*, ed. Basit Bilal Koshul and Steven Kepnes (Palgrave Macmillan, Basingstoke, UK, 2007, p. 109).

in scripture of the encounter at a well, the journey to Egypt, the blessing of descendants, going out into a wilderness (in the stories of Eve, Abraham, Isaac, Rebecca, Joseph, Moses); the form of the question God asks her (one that 'seeks out a person's integrity and ability to respond and take responsibility'); the command to return and submit to Sarah understood as a test; the meaning of her name ('the stranger') in the context of Torah commanding love of the stranger as of yourself (Leviticus 19: 33); and her being the only person in scripture to name God, 'You are El-roi.' There is an interweaving of Hagar with other key figures, so that the otherness of Hagar, as a figure of the otherness of Islam, becomes inextricable from Israel's identity – biological, historical, ethical and theological. The climax, in line with the interpretation of Tikvah Frymer-Kensky, is:

> Hagar the stranger, Hagar the servant, Hagar wife of Abraham and mother of Ishmael *is* Israel! She presages, she prefigures, Israel's suffering in Egypt. And in her deep connection to God, and in the fact that God sees and listens to her suffering and rewards her with a multitude of offspring, Hagar also prefigures Israel's ultimate redemption![7]

Kepnes does something similar with Ishmael as the one whose name means 'God hears', whose destiny as one who 'shall live at odds with all his kin' can be translated as 'he shall dwell alongside all his kinsmen', and who later in Genesis 25: 9 appears as a dutiful son to Abraham and brother to Isaac at Abraham's burial.

What is happening here? Kepnes is using a combination of plain sense and figural interpretation to complexify the lessons to be drawn from Israel's foundational narratives. Any Jew who takes Torah seriously as revelation is offered a way to regard Muslims as 'family', as ambivalently related to Israel, but yet as having a significant positive role in history under God. A text that has frequently been used to justify stereotypes of Islam and hostility between Islam and Israel is opened up to fresh meaning. Kepnes also engages with the New Testament (to which I will return below) and with the Qur'an, complementing his reinterpretation of Genesis with suggestions as to where Christians and Muslims might find the resources for similar sorts of interpretation in their scriptures. In other words, his rich exploration of Genesis acts as an invitation, model and challenge to others in relation to their canonical texts.

I want to take up that challenge now as a Christian reader. The first move is to examine Kepnes' interpretation of the Genesis stories. It seems to me

---

[7]   Ibid, p. 111.

exemplary, and there is nothing in it with which to disagree. Yet it is not just a matter of not disagreeing; this is masterly and inspired reading, both plain sense and figural. The main potential for further interpretation is in the figural. Kepnes suggests that vestiges of the Hagar pattern can be seen in Jesus beginning his ministry with baptism followed by his journey into the wilderness. He explains further: 'Hagar is a counterpart of Abraham in prophetic sight, she is a positive counterpart to Eve, and her wandering, suffering, and blessing are counterparts to Israel's slavery and redemption and she even sets a pattern that is followed by Moses and Christ!'[8] The typology of Jesus and Hagar might have been taken further in terms of Jesus being tested, his relationship with God, his obedience, his identification of himself with slaves, his parallels with Adam, Joseph and Moses, his rejection and suffering, and his identification with Israel. It also might have been turned around, figurally identifying Jesus with God in the Hagar story. The most fruitful possibility here is the story of Jesus meeting the Samaritan woman at Jacob's well in John 4. Here too a fundamental, divisive difference is at stake, between Jews and Samaritans; the naming of Jesus (as prophet, Messiah, saviour) is central; the woman is drawn into the ministry of Jesus by becoming a witness to him; and 'worship in spirit and truth' transcends the differences between the Samaritans worshipping God on the mountain sacred to them or the Jews worshipping in Jerusalem.

Taking up the theme of Hagar's ambivalence in Hebrew scriptures, Kepnes follows through this 'treatment of the other as both different and the same, foe and friend' in the New Testament, where 'we see an equally ambivalent portrait of the most clear and obvious other to the Christian, the Jew'. He notes the hermeneutical challenge of the Old Testament for Christians:

> Holding on to the Jewish scriptures as Christian scripture, simply put, is not easy. Certainly, from the standpoint of narrative and logical coherence it does not really work. To pull it off, Christianity must develop a complex, self-contradictory hermeneutic which says at once that Jewish scripture is revealed and wrong. Its way of Torah, its way of the law, is both necessary and superseded. Its promise to the children of Abraham both nullified and fulfilled.[9]

The thrust of Kepnes' argument here is both contentious and generous,[10] in effect saying that, in the light (or chiaroscuro) of the ambivalence intrinsic

---

[8] Ibid, p. 114.

[9] Ibid, pp. 114–15.

[10] For example, I would propose 'revealed and limited' rather than 'revealed and wrong', and 'necessary and fulfilled' rather than 'necessary and superseded', both preferred phrases being understood in the light of an 'already/not yet' eschatology which embraces Jews, Christians and others.

to Jewish scriptures, the Christian ambivalence about both Jews and their scriptures makes a certain sort of sense. Christians are being very Jewish! Above all this need not entail a dichotomous, mutually exclusive relationship. Yet such a statement, generalizing from a specific interpretation of Hagar, must also be exposed to other texts, including difficult ones. As it happens there is in fact an explicit New Testament interpretation of the story of Hagar, and it is difficult. Paul writes to the Galatians:

> Tell me, you who desire to be subject to the law, will you not listen to the law? For it is written that Abraham had two sons, one by a slave woman and the other by a free woman. One, the child of the slave, was born according to the flesh; the other, the child of the free woman, was born through the promise. Now this is an allegory: these women are two covenants. One woman, in fact, is Hagar, from Mount Sinai, bearing children for slavery. Now Hagar is Mount Sinai in Arabia and corresponds to the present Jerusalem, for she is in slavery with her children. But the other woman corresponds to the Jerusalem above; she is free, and she is our mother. For it is written, 'Rejoice, you childless one, you who bear no children, burst into song and shout, you who endure no birth pangs; for the children of the desolate woman are more numerous than the children of the one who is married.' Now you, my friends, are children of the promise, like Isaac. But just as at that time the child who was born according to the flesh persecuted the child who was born according to the Spirit, so it is now also. But what does the scripture say? 'Drive out the slave and her child; for the child of the slave will not share the inheritance with the child of the free woman.' So then, friends, we are children, not of the slave but of the free woman.
>
> For freedom Christ has set us free. Stand firm, therefore, and do not submit again to a yoke of slavery.
>
> Listen! I, Paul, am telling you that if you let yourselves be circumcised, Christ will be of no benefit to you. Once again I testify to every man who lets himself be circumcised that he is obliged to obey the entire law. You who want to be justified by the law have cut yourselves off from Christ; you have fallen away from grace. For through the Spirit, by faith, we eagerly wait for the hope of righteousness. For in Christ Jesus neither circumcision nor uncircumcision counts for anything; the only thing that counts is faith working through love.
>
> You were running well; who prevented you from obeying the truth? Such persuasion does not come from the one who calls you. A little yeast leavens the whole batch of dough. I am confident about you in the Lord that you will not think otherwise. But whoever it is that is confusing you will pay the penalty. But my friends, why am I still being persecuted if I am still preaching circumcision? In that case the offense of the cross has been removed. I wish those who unsettle you would castrate themselves!

For you were called to freedom, brothers and sisters; only do not use your freedom as an opportunity for self-indulgence, but through love become slaves to one another. For the whole law is summed up in a single commandment, 'You shall love your neighbor as yourself'. If, however, you bite and devour one another, take care that you are not consumed by one another.

Live by the Spirit, I say, and do not gratify the desires of the flesh. For what the flesh desires is opposed to the Spirit, and what the Spirit desires is opposed to the flesh; for these are opposed to each other, to prevent you from doing what you want. But if you are led by the Spirit, you are not subject to the law. Now the works of the flesh are obvious: fornication, impurity, licentiousness, idolatry, sorcery, enmities, strife, jealousy, anger, quarrels, dissensions, factions, envy, drunkenness, carousing, and things like these. I am warning you, as I warned you before: those who do such things will not inherit the kingdom of God.

By contrast, the fruit of the Spirit is love, joy, peace, patience, kindness, generosity, faithfulness, gentleness, and self-control. There is no law against such things. (NRSV, Galatians 4: 21–5: 23)

That is an urgent, passionate appeal to the Galatians not to listen to those who were making circumcision a condition for non-Jews to be admitted to the church. It exaggerates for the sake of the argument and seems about as dichotomous as possible: two contrasted covenants; two contrasted mothers and sons; slave versus free; flesh versus Spirit or promise; the present Jerusalem versus the Jerusalem above; and the resolution by expulsion: 'Drive out the slave and her child!' This pattern has been tragically instantiated in Christian relations with Jews century after century.

Yet even this text has resources for a more complex reading that opens towards conclusions analogous to those Kepnes arrives at through Genesis. Partly this relies on seeing that this is a conflict within the Christian family about the conditions for admission. Paul is not objecting to Jews being circumcised but to them imposing circumcision on Gentiles who become Christians. In other words, in a largely Jewish church it is a protest against the majority imposing homogeneity according to their law. Paul is arguing for the maintenance of difference within unity, grounded in belonging to Christ. He had earlier concluded:

As many of you as were baptized into Christ have clothed yourselves with Christ. There is no longer Jew or Greek, there is no longer slave or free, there is no longer male and female; for all of you are one in Christ Jesus. And if you belong to Christ, then you are Abraham's offspring, heirs according to the promise. (Galatians 3: 27–9)

One might see through the history of Christianity a slow awakening to just how radical that is: the first century faced the Jew/Gentile issue, but it has never gone away; the eighteenth and nineteenth centuries faced the slave/free issue, but it too is still with us in many forms; and the twentieth century faced the male/female issue and that continues as a current concern. So if one wants to imagine a contemporary parallel to Paul as a Jew arguing on behalf of Gentile Christians, it might be found in those men who argue for women's ordination or other forms of equality or empowerment for women, but without ignoring sexual differentiation.

Beyond the immediate argument (which one might say was appropriately either/or: being half-circumcised was not an option – though, as Paul exclaims in exasperation, castration might be), there is a great deal in the passage that encourages peaceful relations across differences, above all living in the Spirit with the fruits of love, joy, peace, patience, kindness, generosity, faithfulness, gentleness and self-control (5: 22–3). Throughout the argument Paul is reaching for things that go deeper than the division. The righteousness of faith working through love refers to something he regards as more fundamental than circumcision/uncircumcision, and might be seen as a classic instance of 'abduction' that moves beyond a contrast to a new level. Similarly, he appeals to Abraham as father of Jewish faith prior to the law of Moses, to the fruits of the Spirit as in accordance with and transcending the law, to creation,[11] and above all to being 'in Christ' – all his readers being fellow-Christians. His allegorical midrash on the story of Hagar is polemically employed in the argument about circumcision and is not his last word on law and gospel or on Jesus as Messiah for Jews and Gentiles. Later in Romans 9–11 he wrestles explicitly with the problem of his fellow Jews who reject his gospel and comes to the extraordinary, non-dichotomous conclusion that 'God has imprisoned all [Jews and Gentiles] in disobedience so that he may be merciful to all.' He follows this with a passionate cry of amazement at the mystery of God, who is supremely the one who goes deeper than divisions and can embrace the apparently irreconcilable: 'O the depth of the riches and wisdom and knowledge of God! How unsearchable are his judgements and how inscrutable his ways!' (Romans 11: 32–3). One might follow the Pauline tradition further into the letter to the Ephesians, with its rich theology of unity and differentia-

---

[11]   Cf. 'For neither circumcision nor uncircumcision is anything; but a new creation is everything!' (Gal: 6: 15).

tion between Jews and Gentiles (2: 11–3: 6), all taken up into prayer to the God of love (3: 14–21).[12]

The power of Kepnes' argument from Genesis seems to me to lie in what he says about God in relation to Hagar and Ishmael, supported by his inspired exploration of the multifaceted narrative. That can be used as a complementary strategy in exploring the contemporary implications of Paul's interpretation of Hagar. My first strategy has been to see it as a midrash, focused on a specific intra-Christian quarrel (yet complicated by the fact that Judaism and Christianity did not yet have distinct identities), which can have devastating effects if generalized to later contexts, whether Jewish–Christian or (perhaps more of a danger in the current situation) Christian–Muslim. When it is read in that way it remains ambivalent (in its drive to expulsion, for example), but its resources for peacemaking 'in the Spirit' can also be recognized. What Paul says in the rest of Galatians and in later letters (especially to the Romans) allows for an approach to identity and otherness analogous to that proposed by Kepnes. So there is scope for Kepnes' interpretation of Hagar to be used to complement my interpretation of Galatians. As is widely recognized, there can be more than one midrash on a particular text in different circumstances, and it is often not appropriate to use a simple logic of contradiction in order to choose between them. A more general lesson in this regard has been repeatedly learnt in intra-Christian ecumenical discussions, where the investigation of deep differences has been greatly helped by understanding the contexts of positions that have come to be reified in opposition to each other, usually with supporting scriptural references.

I am less convinced by Kepnes' suggestion that there is a straightforward contrast between his reasoning from scripture and characteristically modern reasoning that follows a 'logic of dichotomies'. I want to affirm what he says positively – that, for example, 'scripture offers us concepts of connectedness: creation, revelation, covenant, redemption' and 'figures of mediation', but to question the implied dichotomy between scripture and modernity.

Kepnes says:

[A] closer look reveals, in almost every page of the Torah, the New Testament, and the Qur'an, elements and figures that lie outside of neat dichotomies and divisions. Scripture is filled with lacunae, gaps, inconsistencies, and mysterious

---

[12]   For my own application of Ephesians to the question of Jesus as Messiah and relations between Jews and Christians see David F. Ford, 'A Messiah for the Third Millennium' in *Modern Theology*, vol. 16, no. 1, January 2000, pp. 75–90; also in *Theology and Eschatology at the Turn of the Millennium*, ed. James Buckley and L. Gregory Jones (Blackwell, Oxford, 2001), pp. 73–88.

sayings, images, and parables that defy simple logic. Scripture, again in the
words of Ochs, is 'vague', its meaning unclear and hidden.[13]

Yet that list of scriptural features could equally well be said of a multitude
of modern novels, poems, songs, dramas, operas, science fiction and films,
with analogous things to be said about painting, sculpture, dance, cartoons,
music and architecture. Among historians, philosophers and theologians
there has also been considerable resistance to what Kepnes describes as
normative dichotomous logic. He is in danger of over-generalizing and so
ignoring the considerable resources in modernity that can resonate strongly
with his interpretation of scripture.

There have, of course, been philosophies such as Kepnes describes, and
they have had, and continue to have, great influence. But modernity has by
no means been monolithic and it too has resources to aid in Kepnes' project
(and mine) of fresh engagement with scriptures. Such resources are not only
found in the arts and discourses listed above but also in certain forms of
polity and social dynamic. The importance of all this for the future of
Scriptural Reasoning is that it needs to be nourished by and learn from
such arts and discourses and to shape its own collegiality and politics in line
with wisdom that has modern as well as premodern dimensions. This in
turn has consequences for the Islam–West encounter, which has great need
of such wisdom. I now turn to Basit Koshul's attempt to work out such a
wisdom in Islamic terms.

The Qur'an and the Bible, Islam and the West

In Scriptural Reasoning the relationship between Qur'an, Tanakh and Bible
is not generally thematized explicitly but is worked out piecemeal through
interpreting the three in conversation with each other. It is recognized that
they are not only different in themselves but also play very different roles
in each of the three traditions (and within various strands in each tradition),
but the most fruitful way of handling this is not to attempt to sum up and
agree on positions; rather it is repeatedly to bring the texts and their traditions of interpretation into dialogue with each other. One difference is that
the only text that speaks about itself is the Qur'an. The nearest parallel
within Jewish scriptures is probably the editing of and reflection upon Torah,
and within Christianity the engagement by the New Testament writers both
with the Jewish scriptures and with Jesus Christ as God's Word. Koshul's

---

[13]   Kepnes, 'Islam as Our Other, Islam as Ourselves', p. 116.

proposal, that the way the Qur'an engages with Jewish and Christian scriptures is a model for the relationship of Islam to Western modernity, therefore potentially opens up some of the deepest issues between the three at the same time as inviting the other two to think through their responses to modernity.

Koshul claims that the Qur'an 'does the impossible' in its simultaneous critical and affirmative attitude to the Bible, and after quoting many passages in illustration he concludes as follows:

> In short, the manner in which the Qur'anic Self relates to the biblical Other can be summarized in the following terms:
>
> 1. Critical engagement that sees the Self distancing itself from the Other,
> 2. Constructive engagement that sees the Other as affirming the Self,
> 3. An invitation by the Self to the Other to come to a common understanding so that both can work together toward a common goal.[14]

This is taken by him as a warrant for Scriptural Reasoning since it encourages Muslims to study with Jews and Christians and opens up a large space for interpreting together. Further, it seems likely that Muslims themselves are always going to have considerable discretion as regards the proportioning of 1, 2 and 3. There is likely to be discussion about just how each of the Qur'anic passages is to be applied to particular biblical texts, and if, as Koshul insists, there are Qur'anic and traditional warrants for Muslims (including the Prophet himself) to learn from Jews and Christians, then the way is opened to develop ongoing collegiality centred on the different scriptures.

What might a Christian response to that be? Because the Bible, as Christians understand it, does not have anything to say specifically about the Qur'an there can be no question of comparing texts on the same topic. But it is appropriate to see whether the threefold pattern Koshul discerns has parallels in the Bible. In the Old Testament it might be seen in the fundamental affirmation of all reality through God's creation and blessing (Koshul's 2); in God's radical judgement on sin and his alienation from those who disobey him or do evil (Koshul's 1); and in God's commitment to ending the alienation, healing the relationships between God, human beings and creation, and living with people in a covenant relationship (Koshul's 3).

---

[14]   B. B. Koshul, 'The Qur'anic Self, the Biblical Other and the Contemporary Islam–West Encounter', in *Scripture, Reason, and the Contemporary Islam–West Encounter*, ed. Basit Bilal Koshul and Steven Kepnes (Palgrave Macmillan, Basingstoke, UK, 2007, p. 18).

Two comments might be made on those parallels. First, they ground Koshul's points in God's activity. This is a God who affirms, judges and transforms through drawing into a covenant and community. That is implicit in Koshul's points – God is involved in them all. As with Kepnes' interpretation of the story of Hagar, and mine of Paul's wrestling with the problem of the gospel and his fellow-Jews, the engagement with scripture's complexities, ambivalences and impossibilities points to the radical need for deeper engagement with God. It is of course possible to throw up one's hands and despair of making any sense, but for Jews, Christians and Muslims one practical implication of finding difficulties in their scriptures is that they must wrestle further and, through this agony of searching and argument, attend more intensively to God.[15]

Second, I have changed Koshul's order, putting the affirmation first. I do not know whether Koshul would set any store by his order. It would appear to me that the Qur'an could support my order as well as his, and there are some advantages in putting affirmation first, especially in an inter-faith setting where there has been a long history of giving priority to the critical engagement and self-distancing. More radically, by centring all three on God I have put the affirmation of God as God at the root of them all.

In Koshul's own key terms there is a noteworthy development later in his paper. As he seeks out what is to be affirmed and negated in the Enlightenment he reaches the daring conclusion that 'the only unredeemable aspect of the Enlightenment is that its stance toward non-Enlightenment paradigms is one of critique-condemn-replace'.[16] Any such priority of critique is denied. His alternative is:

> A more sane approach 'albeit a more courageous, complex and nuanced one' and one that is built on scripturally (Qur'anically) reasoned grounds is redeem-reform-embrace . . . [a] life-affirming approach that will lead to enhanced understanding on the part of a troubled and alienated Self as a result of its critical but empathetic encounter with the alien Other.[17]

This seems to embrace any critique within affirmation, reform and redemption – all of which, in Qur'anic terms, are rooted in God.

---

[15]   Job is a model of such wrestling in Jewish and Christian scriptures. For my interpretation of the book of Job see *Christian Wisdom: Desiring God and Learning in Love* (Cambridge University Press, Cambridge, UK, 2007), Chapters 3–4.
[16]   Koshul, 'The Qur'anic Self', p. 32.
[17]   Ibid. p. 33. The quote within the extract is from Abdal Hakim Murad, 'Faith in the Future: Islam After the Enlightenment', in *Islamic Studies*, vol. 42, no. 2, Summer 2003, pp. 245–58.

The New Testament confirms the pattern and order I have suggested. The incarnation of Jesus can be seen as the most fundamental affirmation of humanity and of all creation by God, even while deeply alienated.

In the beginning was the Word, and the Word was with God, and the Word was God. He was in the beginning with God. All things came into being through him, and without him not one thing came into being. What has come into being in him was life, and the life was the light of all people. The light shines in the darkness, and the darkness did not overcome it. (NRSV, John 1: 1–5)

The ministry of Jesus is fundamentally affirmative and transformative, giving the good news of the Kingdom of God, forgiving, healing, feeding and teaching, while also including vigorous judgement. The death of Jesus can be seen as the most radical judgement of all, exposing the truth of a world that turns away from God. The resurrection of Jesus opens the way to transformed life with God and each other in the Spirit in covenantal community. In this it is the living Jesus Christ who is the affirmer, judge and transformer.

What does all this mean for the Islam–West encounter? Koshul sees the Qur'an opening up a third way distinct from fundamentalist rejection of the West and acculturated liberal assimilation to it. In place of such one-sided responses he proposes a differentiated response in line with the Qur'an's engagement with the Bible, culminating in the pattern of redeem-reform-embrace discussed above. He judges modernity by how it deals with philosophical and religious conceptions and practices relating to wisdom, illumination and the Divine, and, using more specifically Islamic categories, with faith, peace/surrender and grace/plenitude. These are rich criteria, and at times he seems to be heading for dichotomous confrontation,[18] but he is drawn back by his own categories to give a richer account. This involves a dual insider/outsider perspective of affirmation and dissent. Central to the affirmation is his correlation of the modern ideals of individualism, universalism and materialism with the dignity of the human being, equality before the law and the value of the material/profane world. He even claims that Islam is in a better position to affirm these than other religious traditions, despite frequent failures to realize them in Islamic countries.[19]

---

[18]   E.g. 'Enlightenment philosophy categorically rejects all philosophical and religious notions of wisdom, illumination and the Divine' (ibid. p. 20).
[19]   His diagnosis of why for many centuries Islam has often failed to realize Qur'anic principles in its political life calls for a hermeneutic of self-critique as well as self-affirmation, especially with regard to Qur'anic interpretation.

The climax is an exploration of the relationship of a Qur'anic concept of 'thinking' or 'reasoning' ('aql) with Enlightenment 'reason'. Here he breaks free of any stereotype of the thought of the modern West and acknowledges the importance of the mature understanding of reason seen in thinkers such as Wittgenstein, Heidegger, Adorno and Levinas, who have related critically to the narrower Enlightenment notion of reason and offer 'novel possibilities of bringing the Enlightenment tradition into conversation with the Scriptural traditions'.[20] It might even be possible to find 'mutual grounds' between the two. His conditional conclusion is: 'If there is a strong claim that is being made it is that engaging with the Enlightenment tradition on these mutual grounds would be as Qur'anically authentic as the Qur'an's use of the Bible in its engagement with Judaism and Christianity, should these mutual grounds be found'.[21]

Mutual ground is distinct not only from ground 'owned' by one party but also from neutral ground. Mutual ground is owned by none of the participants but is a place of mutual hospitality, with each able to be host and guest at the same time. Neutral ground tends to exclude what is most distinctive in favour of a lowest common denominator of values and discourse that can be shared. There is nothing wrong with such commonality, but where there are serious differences and yet no opportunity for participants to engage out of their deepest convictions the possibility of peaceful and constructive collegiality is very limited. Mutual ground does not have to require prior agreement on fundamentals: the point is to have a space where differing fundamentals can be discussed. In Koshul's terms, it is where there can be critical, affirmative and collaborative engagement. This is why scriptures are so well suited to being the focus. Each can act as host to their own scriptures, welcoming them to their own most sacred 'ground', while also being guests of the others. In this interactive particularity the matters most important to the identity of each can be explored – and these will often be in tension or in conflict with each other.

Yet what about those parts of the Enlightenment tradition as Koshul describes them in their alienation from 'wisdom, illumination and the Divine'? How might 'mutual ground' be found between them and the Abrahamic scriptural traditions? This is a crucial issue for the Islam–West encounter. I would propose it as the second part of a threefold strategy, which I find implicit in Koshul's paper.

[20]   'The Qur'anic Self,' p. 31.
[21]   Ibid., p. 31.

1   Corresponding to the first part of Koshul's paper on Bible and
     Qur'an, the three Abrahamic faiths need to engage in Scriptural
     Reasoning on mutual ground, in the course of which they can
     explore how their core identities are to be articulated and developed
     today and can learn from each other through affirmation, criticism
     and collaboration.

2   Corresponding to the second part of Koshul's paper, there is need
     for similar 'mutual ground' engagements with the more secular ele-
     ments of modern thought and culture, in which there should likewise
     be scope for affirmation, criticism and collaboration. In fact, an
     enormous amount of this has gone on in recent centuries, especially
     in universities where the religions have been represented.[22] There is
     of course always the danger that Koshul notes of the religious being
     assimilated to the secular. Yet my reading of twentieth-century Chris-
     tian theology is that both in the West and in other parts of the world
     it has usually been acutely aware of the dangers, and has developed
     many creative yet faithful ways of avoiding them, without avoiding
     the challenge of dialogue with secular understandings. Judaism and
     Islam too have, as Kepnes and Koshul show, learnt wisdom through
     their complex engagements with modernity. The constructive task is
     to bring that wisdom into dialogue with secular wisdoms (and, of
     course, the wisdoms of other religious traditions). Such mutual
     wisdom-seeking is already happening in many spheres. The distinc-
     tive impulse emerging from Koshul and Kepnes is towards the double,
     simultaneous intensity of both reasoning around scriptures and rea-
     soning across the scriptural–secular boundary. To do one without the
     other limits the resources of possible wisdom. To do both together
     in mutual enhancement and critique could well shape vital contribu-
     tions to the Islam–West encounter, since this would address two
     central, interrelated questions: (a) How might Judaism, Christianity
     and Islam best relate to each other so as to draw on their resources
     for understanding, peace and human flourishing? (b) How might a
     complexly religious and secular world such as ours negotiate settle-
     ments that allow for particular religious and secular identities and
     contributions to the public sphere, yet without allowing either reli-
     gious or secular domination?

3   The third part of the strategy is perhaps the most difficult: the shaping
     of Judaism, Christianity, Islam and the secular in ways that open them
     up to each other while at the same time renewing their core identi-

---

[22] For a discussion of universities in relation to the religious and the secular see chapter 7.

ties from their deepest sources. Scriptural Reasoning grew out of a Jewish group called Textual Reasoning, and it has stimulated the formation of Muslim Qur'anic Reasoning and Christian Biblical Reasoning groups. In other words, there has been a complementarity between going deeper into each other's scriptures and deeper into one's own. Yet the most sensitive issues of identity are raised here. Sustaining the double dynamic (triple if one adds engagement with the secular) is always risky and especially vulnerable to attacks by those who stand either for a more exclusive or for a less particular identity. However, I am most concerned about the secular side in this. It is as diverse as the religious, and is as vulnerable to ideological takeovers and exclusivisms. In a world where religions cause much conflict, a secular temptation is to try to exclude it from the public sphere. One challenge facing the secular is how to share the public sphere with the religions without expecting that the ground rules have to be secular – for example, by insisting on neutral ground. In other words, those who are secular, like those who are religious, have to work out what they bring to mutual ground and how to negotiate there. Such work is happening,[23] and seems to me to be vital for twenty-first century polity and civil society.

Developing Scriptural Reasoning Further

Scriptural Reasoning has been seen in this chapter as having a considerable contribution to make to Islam–West dialogue but also as needing to be developed further in order to do so. In conclusion I will draw together and supplement the suggestions for its further development that have been made at various points, presenting them as an agenda of bullet points.

- The main contribution of Scriptural Reasoning is as a flexible, wisdom-seeking practice. As such, it needs to be creatively adapted to as many participants, situations, issues and spheres of life as possible, as has happened with the scriptures within each of the traditions over the centuries and around the world.

---

[23] A good example of a secular thinker who is proposing for the US a polity that takes seriously the religions in the public sphere (and also explores key texts in the secular democratic tradition which might be considered candidates for potential scriptural and secular reasoning groups) is Jeffrey Stout, *Democracy and Tradition* (Princeton University Press, Princeton, NJ and Oxford, 2004); cf. Talal Asad, *Formations of the Secular: Christianity, Islam, Modernity* (Stanford University Press, Stanford, CA, 2003).

- In each setting it needs to build up collegiality on 'mutual ground' among Jews, Christians, Muslims and others through an ethos of affirmation, critique and collaboration directed towards each other's traditions and towards secular understandings and forces.

- That double thrust towards other Abrahamic faiths and towards the secular needs to be accompanied by a third towards enriched appreciation of one's own tradition of interpretation.

- The difficulties, inconsistencies and ambivalences found in scriptures can become occasions for learning to cope with differences and conflicts, such as how to sustain a tradition of vigorous argument, and how to have a faith that is intelligently interrogative and exploratory, oriented towards a future with God that is open to learning the incompleteness and inadequacy of present affirmations and imperatives.

- Each tradition has its wisdom of disagreement and dispute, from which far more could be learned. Within Christianity the nearest analogy to inter-faith engagement has been the ecumenical movement, attempting to heal divisions among Christian churches. At the least that shows the scale of what is required in order to deal with deep religious differences: long-term discussion and deliberation grappling with core questions; slow building up of forms of collegiality in diverse settings – local, regional, national, international; thorough study and academic support through research, teaching and education both of specialists and of as many clergy and laity as possible in a less specialist way; courageous leadership; and material resources. Within all this there has been a vital role for the inter-church interpretation of scripture, and it would be surprising if this were not the case in inter-faith relations too.

- In universities, where Scriptural Reasoning originated, there are major questions to be tackled about how the traditional 'guilds' of scripture scholars, philosophers, theologians and other specialists relate to it, and how it might be part of research programmes, curricula and pedagogy. There is also the possibility of Scriptural Reasoning being a catalyst in enabling some universities to develop as 'inter-faith and secular' and so provide 'mutual ground' where people of many faiths and none can respond collegially to questions raised by our multifaith and secular world.

- The relation between plain sense and figural interpretation (see Kepnes on Hagar) is fruitful and fascinating, and deserves greater attention. From a Christian standpoint, figural reading might be seen as the integrator of its understanding of history – past, present and future – but also often in sharp tension with Jewish, Muslim and secular understandings of history. Is it conceivable that figural reading might both be critically retrieved 'after modernity' and also serve to enable non-allergic relations among Jews, Christians, Muslims and the West in the twenty-first century?

• The broader question raised by figural reading concerns hermeneutics. To which hermeneutical thinkers should scriptural reasoners be apprenticed in order to develop further? One of the marks of Scriptural Reasoning to date has been the variety of its philosophical mentors. With regard to the Islam–West encounter, I would suggest that, among Christian thinkers, Paul Ricoeur holds great promise. He is a wide-ranging philosopher who has engaged deeply with the Bible, fiction, history and poetry as well as with hermeneutical theory; he has learnt from and critiqued premodern, modern and postmodern thinkers; he takes seriously both historical critical study of the Bible and questions about its meaning for today; and he has a magisterial book on the relation of self and other, *Oneself As Another*,[24] in which he offers a conceptuality that helps describe the complex identities explored by Kepnes and Koshul.

• The very idea of 'developing further' and contributing to Islam–West encounter might suggest an inappropriate linear progression and instrumentalizing of Scriptural Reasoning. There is a quasi-liturgical aspect to it in which attention is paid to these remarkable texts for their own sake and for the sake of the God to whom they witness. Indeed, the paradox is that the benefits may be greater if this is the core attitude. As a God-centred practice the most important thing for its future may simply be that more people from various walks of life join in studying together in this spirit.

• That suggests the ultimate orientation of Scriptural Reasoning towards relating more intelligently and wholeheartedly to God and being drawn more fully into God's good purposes for all creation. That, from Jewish, Christian and Muslim standpoints, is the key criterion for any further developments both in the study of scripture and in Islam–West encounter.

---

[24]   Paul Ricoeur, *Oneself As Another* (Chicago University Press, Chicago and London, 1992). For my interpretation of him in this regard see *Self and Salvation: Being Transformed* (Cambridge University Press, Cambridge, UK, 1999).

Part III

WISDOM IN THE UNIVERSITY

Chapter Six

KNOWLEDGE, MEANING AND THE WORLD'S GREAT CHALLENGES: REINVENTING CAMBRIDGE UNIVERSITY IN THE TWENTY-FIRST CENTURY

'The University now belongs to us, as do the times. What will we do with them?'[1] In this chapter I want to ask that sort of question about the future of the University of Cambridge in particular, and of universities in general. Having delivered the Lady Margaret's University Sermon for the Commemoration of Benefactors in November 2001 on the future of the University of Cambridge,[2] I aim in this chapter to take these reflections further, deeply conscious of how impossible a topic it has proved to be. I am also extremely grateful to the many people who have been willing to engage in

---

[1] Unknown speaker at the Harvard Commencement Day of June 2001, quoted in Peter J. Gomes, *The Good Life: Truths that Last in Times of Need* (Harper, San Francisco, 2002) p. 16.
[2] David F. Ford, *The Future of Cambridge University* (Cambridge University Press, Cambridge, 2002).

conversations, in some cases lengthy and repeated, about Cambridge University's future.[3]

Why This Topic Now?

It does seem a suitable time to approach this topic. There are good reasons to do so that are specific to Cambridge at this time, ranging through current debates about governance; the need to decide priorities while taking into account quite a large financial deficit; the planning now under way for Cambridge University's biggest ever fund-raising campaign to coincide with its 800th anniversary and a number of serious issues facing our colleges.

There are further reasons nationally, where the question of universities, and especially their funding, has — after a period of relative neglect for around ten or so years — been one of the hottest recent political issues, culminating in the White Paper on The Future of Higher Education published in January 2003.

Perhaps even more importantly there are reasons grounded in the whole situation of universities today, especially to do with knowledge and its role in our world. Cambridge University's new Centre for Research in the Arts, Social Sciences and Humanities (CRASSH) spent two years concentrating on the theme of 'The Organization of Knowledge'. In early 2003 CRASSH joined with the British Academy to sponsor a conference in Cambridge on 'Changing Societies, Changing Knowledge'. It was concerned with such matters as the knowledge or information society, the knowledge economy, regimes of accountability, and intellectual values in relation to all this, and it specially focused on universities. The accounts of what is happening in Britain and in other parts of the world made it clear that universities are in the process of transformations at least as extensive as in any previous period of their history. Responding well to these transformations is Cambridge's

---

[3]   For the longer conversations involved in reflecting upon some of the material covered in this chapter I would like to thank Markus Bockmuehl, Nicholas Branson, Christopher Brooke, Alec Broers, Mary Broers, Victoria Coulson, Deborah Ford, Gordon Graham, Malcolm Grant, David Harrison, Gordon Johnson, Melissa Lane, David Livesey, Anne Lonsdale, James Matheson, Tim Mead, John Morrill, David Newland, Onora O'Neill, Mica Panic, Ben Quash, Jem Rashbass, Anil Seal, David Thompson, Margie Tolstoy, Bryan Turner, Alan Windle, David Wilson, Richard Wilson, Joanna Womack, and Frances Young. I am also grateful for papers presented to the Durham Institute of Durham University at two conferences on 'The Future University' for representatives of British and German universities. Above all I thank Daniel Hardy, Tim Jenkins and Ben Quash for many hours of concentrated discussion, and Daniel Hardy in addition both for his three papers to The Durham Institute discussion and for his substantive comments on the text of this chapter.

most fundamental challenge as a university. The nature of the internal changes required of the university, as well as the ways it responds to national government policy, need to be inspired by a vision of what its core concerns as a major world university should be at this time. These are, I suggest, primarily to do with knowledge, its learning and teaching, its significance, its uses, its expansion and enrichment, and the institutional and collegial settings in which it best flourishes. I will return to this.

A Dangerous Vacuum

Perhaps the most disturbing thing to emerge from the CRASSH conference was how little fundamental thinking universities are doing about their own future.[4] It may seem astonishing that, despite the whole range of disciplines being affected by the current transformations, there is so little collaborative intellectual effort to understand them and respond to them. It is, of course, nobody's field, and all of us want to get on with 'our own work'. Perhaps the situation is something like that of the natural environment in the early twentieth century. Disciplines studied aspects of it, but it was only when the environment was seriously threatened that it became a collaborative concern.

We may be in an analogous situation with our intellectual environment now. Universities are vital parts of the intellectual ecology of our world. There are many powerful groups who have a strong interest in changing universities to suit their purposes, affecting that ecology in ways that are likely to have long-term consequences. The practical significance of what appears to be a case of collective irresponsibility in failing to think about ourselves with anything like the rigour that we show within and (increasingly) between our disciplines is that universities are far more vulnerable than they need be to others setting their agenda and shaping their life. The outside influences and pressures will of course continue and perhaps inten-

---

[4]   Gordon Graham, professor of philosophy in the University of Aberdeen, spoke of 'one huge and glaring omission, one topic and context in which academics have signally failed to engage in critical thought and for the most part shown themselves sadly lacking in independence of mind. I mean the subject of the university itself.' – 'Intellectual Values and the Knowledge Economy' (Paper delivered to the conference 'Changing Societies, Changing Knowledge', Selwyn College, Cambridge, 9–10 January, 2003), p. 1. Cf. Gordon Graham, *Universities: The Recovery of an Idea* (Imprint Academic, Thorverton, UK and Charlottesville, VA, 2002), the best overview I have found of recent university history and the current situation in Britain. Christopher Padfield of Cambridge University's Corporate Liaison Office, spoke of the 'severe deficit in thinking about a contemporary "purpose" for universities'. – 'Third Mission and Wealth Creation' (Paper delivered to the Selwyn conference), p. 4.

sify, and they can be good as well as bad. But if they meet with a virtual vacuum where there ought to be vigorous thinking, deliberation, advocacy and action, then we who have responsibility for universities in this generation risk failing one of the more justifiable accountability tests: that before future generations, who will convict us of failing to nurture and develop further for their benefit this precious inheritance.

My concern now is to take that accountability before future generations seriously in relation to Cambridge University. Some of what I say will apply to other universities, some will not, but what can be said in general about universities is beyond my brief here. I am only trying to make one contribution to a discussion about Cambridge University – a discussion at present occurring only sporadically. Most discussion understandably concentrates on single elements that are seen (and with some justice) as vital to a healthy future – leadership, governance, management, financial planning, salaries, fund-raising, business enterprise, access, the colleges, teaching, research policy, external partnerships, use of information technology, and so on. I will comment on a few of those, but my main concern is with the sort of ecology we have in which those are some of the niches.

Endowment and a Long-term Intellectual and Social Ecology

I spoke just now of accountability across generations. We have a long-term ecology. One of the most encouraging (and least reported) parts of the White Paper published in 2003 was its recognition of how crucial endowment is for long-term university flourishing and independence. Charles Clarke, the former Education and Skills Secretary, said in his speech in the House of Commons launching the White Paper: 'First of all, we should face up to the truth that genuine university freedom comes through building endowment, rather than any other device. Universities in this country need to build up their endowments.'[5] He admitted that recent history shows how problematic it is to rely too heavily on public money, and he promised incentives to encourage benefactions.

The message of the former Secretary of State is clear: there is a direct relation between our freedom and our endowments, so if we prize our freedom we ought to make building endowment a priority. Surely the forthcoming fund-raising campaign should be approached as a major step, with government backing, towards greater independence of direct govern-

---

[5]   Speech in House of Commons, 22 January 2003.

ment financial support? Should we even aim at independence? Given the British tax structure and the absence of the sort of culture of giving that allows US private universities to be world leaders, even with new incentives it appears to me unlikely that Cambridge could raise the estimated £2.5 billion of unearmarked endowment needed to make up for present government funding.[6]

Yet a large increase in general endowment (including endowment of colleges) would be an immense help in enabling Cambridge to be more independent and sustainable long term. In the immediate future it would make possible a much higher level of scholarship and bursary provision. The government is surely right to be concerned about access. The appropriate things for Cambridge to do are to continue our extensive policy of links with schools and encouragement of applicants from less well-off backgrounds; to be fair and non-discriminatory in its admissions procedures aimed at admitting the best students; and to try to ensure that no student to whom it offers a place has to turn it down for financial reasons.[7]

If we do move in the direction of greater financial independence, however, we need to do it not only because of what even Mr Clarke agrees is the unreliability of governments. Our motivation should be rooted in the ways in which the quality of our university and its colleges is closely related to a long-term intellectual and social ecology. Education is transgenerational. It takes place best in the context of arrangements that have been developed, tested and adjusted over generations. The intellectual values that are at the heart of education and research are extraordinarily long-term ideals and practices in our civilization: truth-seeking, rationality in argument, balanced judgement, integrity, linguistic precision, and critical questioning. Their cultivation is greatly assisted by lively traditions of practising them in physical and social settings designed for their flourishing across generations. Indeed, in recent times the reality that has most impressed itself upon me, from a great many angles, has been this: the thriving of those intellectual

---

[6]   Yet I am open to persuasion on this. A further factor is the way alumni view their relationship with the University. When I asked Kenneth Rossano to account for Harvard's success in fund-raising, he said that the key factor is undoubtedly the enthusiasm and dedication of alumni and the care Harvard takes to cultivate and organise them. The form of belonging has parallels to that of belonging to a church: it is seen as a lifetime commitment, with lifetime giving being part of that, all in the service of a body that must be enabled to benefit future generations in a similar way to one's own. It is likely that Cambridge's long-term future depends more on whether it can develop this sense of commitment than it does on tax incentives.

[7]   I would want to extend that also as far as possible to non-British students, so that we can attract some of the best students in the would. The Gates Scholarships have been one of the most important enrichments of the Cambridge student body in recent years.

values is intrinsically linked to quality of collegiality; and, because these socially-embedded values aim at knowledge and understanding that are cumulative, and in principle unlimited in breadth and depth, they are served best by long-term collegial settings dedicated to their practice. These values are continually under threat from many quarters; and endowment, which is a key material condition for their social embodiment over centuries, can enable them to be better sustained and to be protected against those who fail to value them or even undermine them. Our intellectual environment needs habitats that can grow oak trees as well as cabbages, and that can be protected against the chain-saws which are able to level a forest of oaks in one parliamentary afternoon.

Reinventing Cambridge University

The continuity of what is highly valued is not the only advantage of a long-term institution. An historian of the university, Dr David Thompson, has said that, looking at the history of Cambridge, we can see it marked by periodic reinventions of itself. It has in fact been very different in different periods. 'We have always attempted to change not by revolution but by reforms that have recapitulated and renewed those traditions which we have most valued.'[8] The foundational medieval pattern; Renaissance and Reformation learning; Newtonian mathematics and science; the greatest transformation of all in the nineteenth- and twentieth-century explosion of disciplines and subdisciplines in the arts, humanities, and especially the sciences and technology; and the new tradition of the enterprise or entrepreneurial university: all these are still with us in various ways. Our long-term history therefore should encourage us to be sensitive to transformations in knowledge and in society and to be willing to respond to them by further reinvention.

What about our present situation? I see a strong case for fresh reinvention. The core factors are intrinsic to the dynamism of knowledge and its use, and especially its relation to the people who discover it, teach it, learn it, interpret it, and apply it. I would suggest that Cambridge University, along with others, is being asked to meet four interconnected challenges simultaneously.

[8]   David F. Ford, 'The Future of Cambridge University' *op. cit.* pp. 3–4.

Four Challenges

Uniting teaching and research

First, can Cambridge be a place where teaching and research come together fruitfully?

The White Paper envisaged some universities that only teach. There are also many institutions and organizations that do only research, or that combine their research with things other than teaching.[9] But Cambridge, as its statement of core values emphasizes, does unite teaching and research, and that has become an increasingly difficult thing to do. If the university is to sustain it, meet the difficulties, and fulfil its immense potential then it needs first of all to renew its recognition of its worth.

I would summarize that worth in terms of the deep affinity and mutual reinforcement between the habits, values and orientations of good teaching and good research. Both require those intellectual values of truth-seeking, rationality in argument, balanced judgement, integrity, linguistic precision, and critical questioning. Both involve disciplined, patient attention to the natural or social world, to texts that always have a surplus of meaning, to alternative hypotheses or interpretations, to complexities that resist our simplifying, and to particularities that defy our generalizing. And each at its best releases new energy and offers moments of sheer joy. Most of us who are passionate about our fields have caught the passion from our teachers. Our own passion for teaching is certainly a matter of relishing the interaction with good students and passing on in gratitude something of what we have been given; but it is also a recognition that, besides the contribution to many spheres of life made by our students, those who continue in our own field as academics are likely to contribute to it far more than we ourselves. So any concern for future research in our field beyond our own individual contribution supports the wisdom of cultivating lineages of researchers who are also teachers.

But beyond the need for continuing to support new thought and research in specific fields, today's situation makes the case for the cross-fertilizing of teaching and research even stronger. With so many jobs being knowledge-intensive, and with continual change in knowledge, information and skills

---

[9]   In the USA 'there are over 3000 institutions of higher education. Only a few hundred are recognizably universities and of these not more than 200 are research-based. Moreover, even in the leading research based universities, most teaching is not done by researchers but by short-term contract workers (Jacob and Hellström, 2000).' – Gerard Delanty, 'Ideologies of the Knowledge Society and the Cultural Contradictions of Higher Education' (Paper delivered to the Selwyn conference), p. 9.

requiring not only habitual new learning but also the perceptive integration of the new with the old, there is a sense in which we are all researchers now. In a wide range of jobs and professions we need to be active seekers of knowledge and understanding, to be able to sift through vast amounts of data, to grasp significant patterns and make new connections, to test hypotheses, to propose solutions, to make judgements of fact and value, and to be able to do all that collaboratively as well as individually; and these are just the things that can best be learnt through apprenticeship to those who are at the forefront of their field – if they are willing, and enabled, to teach it.

Once the case for the uniting of teaching and research is granted, then the question has to be faced: how well is the marriage actually doing in Cambridge? The university does outstandingly well by all the criteria of research assessment and teaching quality. That is good, but surely they should not be its main measure, not least because those appraisal procedures do not take into account (and are even disruptive of) the interrelation of teaching and research. If we go by what is required for the symbiosis of research and teaching to meet the demands both of Cambridge's expanding and complexifying spheres of inquiry and of its students as lifelong learners and researchers, then we need to discuss and take action on a range of questions. Can we make it more attractive for researchers to spend some quality time teaching undergraduates? How can the colleges and faculties collaborate better? How might staff workloads be reduced? Could the Tripos courses encourage far more active learning and collaborative learning akin to research? How can postgraduate education be improved, and might postgraduates learn more through apprenticeship-like relationships? And what about the creative uses of information technologies? To visit the new Centre for Applied Research in Educational Technologies (CARET) is to glimpse how computers can enhance our face to face teaching as much as they do our research.[10]

[10]   I am grateful to Jem Rashbass, Director of CARET, for introducing me to the various areas of research and their guiding principles. At the CRASSH conference mentioned above, Steve Woolgar of Oxford University, who had headed a £3.5 million five-year ESRC project on 'The Virtual Society', researching with 76 social scientists from 26 universities the impact of electronic technologies on society, was cautious about the transformative claims being made for these technologies, while also being enthusiastic about their value. His conclusions included such principles as: that the impact and use of new technologies depends crucially on local social context; that these new technologies tend to supplement rather than substitute for existing practices and forms of organization; and 'the more global the more local'. In my own limited study of the field a crucial benefit appears to be that the relationship of 'richness' to 'reach' can shift so that both can be enhanced. This seems to be confirmed by the research at CARET, where the 'richness' of traditional Cambridge methods of intensive small-group face-to-face teaching can be enhanced by appropriate uses of technology, while at the same time the interaction of such groups with other groups, networks and sources is extended in 'reach'.

The list could go on; but the main point is that we have no reason to be complacent about this core value of uniting teaching and research. Cambridge's ways of doing things up to now have brought it to the top of many league tables, but those criteria have almost nothing to say about this marriage's vitality, daily life, and resourcing. We need to pay much more attention to this.

Interrelating fields of knowledge

The second challenge was brought home to me when serving for three years on Cambridge University's Personal Promotions Committee. Its members are required by the guidelines to read all the papers submitted about every candidate put forward for a personal professorship or readership by every faculty and department – physical sciences, biological sciences, technology, arts, humanities, social sciences. So one spends days reading through personal statements, CVs, faculty statements, faculty minutes, references in various languages, and overall assessments. It offers a quite extraordinary view of the University, and it is most impressive. One sits back in amazement at what is going on in the university. But one also cannot help asking the question: how is all this connected? What is the significance of these fields for each other? One finds that one is completely ignorant of major research going on in areas quite close to one's own. More seriously, it is clear that there could be all sorts of fruitful interconnections that are not being made. The explosion of knowledge and publication in all fields, and the development of new disciplines and subdisciplines, has not been matched by their interrelation.

So the second challenge is how to interrelate disciplines in appropriate ways and across a wide range. Universities surely have a special responsibility here. Top level work may go on in many settings – in industry, in think tanks, in specialized research institutes of many sorts; but universities that maintain a broad range of disciplines are a different sort of environment, one with greater potential for interaction and cross-fertilization. It is hard to say that even a fraction of this potential is realized. Can the university be developed in such a way that it deals better with this challenge? Can it avoid the dangers, of which Cambridge is acutely aware, such as that of losing rigour and depth in the quest for breadth and connections?

Cambridge has in fact been interdisciplinary in many ways for a long time and it has accelerated in recent years. Just read through the blue pages in the telephone directory and note in alphabetical order: the African

Studies Centre, the Centre for Brain Repair, the Cambridge Institute
for Medical Research, CRASSH, the Institute of Criminology, Development Studies, the Centre for Advanced Religious and Theological
Studies, the Centre for Family Research, and so on. That is only up to F,
and I have already left out some centres, and all departments and faculties,
many of which combine several disciplines.[11] (The Telephone Network
Directory offers the best single overview of the University: it should be
required reading for all new students, staff, and secretaries of state.) Yet
despite this, in comparison with the potential, the present provision seems
inadequate, and also somewhat arbitrary and precarious – largely because
most of those centres and institutes rely on raising outside, short-term
funds.

It is widely acknowledged that many of the most significant and exciting
possibilities in the advancement of knowledge and understanding are
interdisciplinary. If the opportunities are to be taken then there are
considerable implications for how Cambridge conceives itself as a university,
what its priorities are, the partnerships it cultivates, how it fundraises, and
how it organizes ourselves. This amounts to a further dimension of
reinvention.[12]

In November 2002 I attended the opening of the Cambridge Genetics
Knowledge Park. Its motto is 'genetics knowledge for the benefit of society'.
It has five dimensions: scientific; clinical; public health; commercial; and
ethical, legal and social (with three ethicists, based in the faculties of law,
social and political science, and history and philosophy of science). Its aims
are: bringing together communities; integrating genetics knowledge and
relating it to other fields; dissemination, education, and training; and contributing to policy and public health. From within the University, the Park
has drawn together 11 sets of disciplines and 10 institutes or units, and from
outside, other universities and bodies are collaborating. This is a daring
experiment in interdisciplinarity.

---

[11]   Continuing in the same incomplete manner, I would note: the Hutchison/Medical
Research Council Research Centre, the Centre for International Studies, the Isaac Newton
Institute for Mathematical Sciences, the Centre for Latin American Studies, the Nanoscience
Centre, the Institute of Public Health, the Scott Polar Research Institute, the Centre for South
Asian Studies, Strangeways Research Laboratory, and the Wellcome Trust/Cancer Research
UK Institute of Cancer and Developmental Biology.
[12]   Initiatives are always likely to arise out of the intensities of particular inquiries meeting
complex questions that break the bounds of single fields, but there is also a University level
to this intellectual ecology, and perhaps that will develop best by the University improving
its ways of accompanying reflectively its interdisciplinary initiatives, sharing what is learnt,
and encouraging new initiatives.

Contributing to society

But it is about more than interdisciplinarity, and leads into the third challenge facing the University. In November 2001 the Regent House approved the following statement: 'The mission of the University of Cambridge is to *contribute to society* through the pursuit of education, learning, and research at the highest international levels of excellence'. The higher education funding body, HEFCE, now has, besides the funding for teaching and research, a 'third stream' concerned with contribution to society, and especially the economy. Charles Clarke at the launch of the 2003 White Paper named three 'great missions' of universities: 'research, knowledge transfer and, perhaps most important of all, teaching'.[13]

The emphasis on teaching and research is encouraging; the restriction of the third dimension to knowledge transfer is worrying. Compare it with what the Cambridge Genetics Knowledge Park (which is largely government funded) is attempting. That is about knowledge transfer – to clinical practice, public health, and scientifically based business enterprises.[14] But it is also concerned with the *significance* of genetics as one of the major new factors in our world. Genetics affects how we understand what it means to be human and our relationship to all living organisms; through commercial

[13]   Speech in House of Commons, 22 January 2003.
[14]   The latter has become an important new dimension of Cambridge in recent years with science parks and new 'knowledge transfer' relationships between business and the University in 'Silicon Fen'. The government has also financed the start-up of the Cambridge Massachussetts Institute (CMI) linking the University with the Massachussetts Institute of Technology. The value of these to both the University and the national economy seems clear, but government, university and business partners need to beware of overstressing both the importance to date and the future potential of the sort of knowledge transfer that turns parts of universities into businesses or links them very closely with businesses, let alone making these the key drivers of university strategy. For an instructive Australian study see Simon Marginson and Mark Considine, *The Enterprise University: Power, Governance and Reinvention in Australia* (Cambridge University Press, Cambridge, 2000).

At the CRASSH conference mentioned above, Jeremy Klein of Generics Group, which works with a large number of universities in several countries on knowledge transfer and 'spinouts', offered a sobering study of the potential in the UK. He showed that for a short time there was a 'bubble' in the attractiveness of knowledge-based companies, but that the bubble has now burst, with many casualties. His study of areas where university-generated companies and partnerships have been successful in varying degrees suggested that the best-known successes might not be good guides for the future because their achievements were often due to a stage of development of particular industries that has now passed. The message was clear: universities should certainly continue to engage in knowledge transfer and partnerships, but they would do well to concentrate mainly on their core activities of teaching and research.

exploitation and intellectual property issues it affects the balance of power in our world; there are large public policy questions; at every turn there are ethical issues about the uses of our knowledge and associated techniques, often with life or death significance for individuals; and the implications of decisions and practices in this area can last for generations. So a responsible attitude to knowledge transfer, rooted in commitment to the flourishing of future generations, must move into issues of meaning, values, ethics, and long-term commitments. There are very few places in society where there is even an attempt to consider all those together. Part of the value of universities to society is that they can be independent places of debate and deliberation about such matters in the interests of the long-term ethical and intellectual ecology of our civilization.[15]

This point therefore extends far beyond genetics. The CVs of those candidates for personal promotion were to me a convincing refutation of any caricature of Cambridge as an ivory tower. These top academics have innumerable links with businesses, public and voluntary bodies, schools, the media, professions, and major spheres of national and international life. Activities range from advising, commenting and consulting to full partnership and leadership responsibility; and in many spheres they have what might be called a 'ministry of meaning'. A healthy university whose present members take on this range of responsibilities, and whose graduates cover an even wider range in every walk of life, should not have its contribution to society measured by the ridiculously crude metrics in use in public debate at present.[16] One further responsibility might be to come up with more appropriate methods of assessing this reality – because there should surely

---

[15] The independence is not only to allow an integral approach, debate of controversial issues, and long-term commitments; it is also important in allowing for 'blue skies' research and theorising. Part of academic work is to do with valuing knowledge for its own sake and allowing ourselves to be led where the questions take us. This 'moment' of singleminded pursuit of truth has to have its own integrity. It need not by any means exclude or be in competition with the further 'moment' that asks about significance and use, but it is important to maintain the freedom of the first moment – and even whole departments that are dedicated to it.

[16] As Onora O'Neill shows in her Reith Lectures (*A Question of Trust: The BBC Reith Lectures 2002*, Cambridge University Press, Cambridge, 2002), one of the problems with inappropriate and unintelligent criteria is that they act as perverse incentives, undermining or distracting from high quality performance and significant contributions. In relation to universities this is especially damaging in the area of contributing to society: no credit is given, for example, for involvement in schools, for a wide range of consultative roles, or even for many types of publication in print and other media that widely disseminate knowledge and understanding. I know of colleagues in other universities who are forbidden to contribute to textbooks or write articles that cannot be counted towards the Research Assessment Exercise.

be no objection to describing and evaluating it in categories that really fit.[17] And yet another responsibility might be to communicate the truth of what we do far more effectively than at present, and to become more confident, passionate and politically astute advocates for the value of universities.

In all this, however, we need to make sure that our third mission is in line with our primary commitments. Of the world's great challenges (a phrase I borrow from the mission statement of the university that is our closest partner, the Massachussetts Institute of Technology) the main ones for us must be how to teach, study and research in responsibility towards the long-term flourishing of our world.[18] In doing that our chief contributions are well-educated people and excellence in the pursuit of knowledge and understanding.[19] Yet once this is taken seriously, and once it is recognized that teaching and research involve responsibility for the wider significance and uses of knowledge and understanding, then it also needs to be recognized that there are few other great challenges in our world towards which universities do not have some responsibility.

In my own field of theology and religious studies, for example, we are both acutely aware how many challenges the world's religions pose at present, and how few universities are equipped to deal with them.[20] How might the questions of meaning, truth, and practice that arise within the religions, about the religions and between the religions be done justice to through academic disciplines in ways that are responsible towards those disciplines, towards the religious communities, and towards the future of our

---

[17]   Why might some British universities not join together to produce much more sophisticated metrics for many spheres of society that are now suffering under measurements, and associated ideologies, that, as Onora O'Neill has argued (in her Reith Lectures, see previous note), are often distorting and counterproductive?

[18]   One dimension of this that is often underemphasized is the role of universities in testing and evaluating knowledge and understanding, coming (often slowly) to a sense of what is most significant in a field, and what, for example, deserves to become part of undergraduate and graduate courses and textbooks. New knowledge and understanding is produced in a great many places in our society; there are far fewer places where this is sifted, refined, integrated, and passed on as part of a coherent discipline or set of disciplines.

[19]   One danger in the way Cambridge has developed in recent years through adding a great many lateral connections is that these core concerns cease to be central enough in its strategic planning.

[20]   Having spent time as a student or staff members in Irish, British, US and German universities, and more recently having had relationships with Dutch, Chinese, and Indian universities, I am convinced that the pattern in many British universities of combining theology with religious studies, allowing (at its best) for those who are members of particular faith communities, together with those who are not, to study, teach and research together, could be of considerable importance for the future of the field internationally. See below on what is appropriate for a world that is simultaneously religious and secular.

world? Analogous questions arise in other fields, and their global range reminds us that, if our excellence is to be measured by international standards, then so too the society to which our contribution is made ought to be world society. The 3843 non-British nationals who in 2001 were registered as students of Cambridge University must not be seen only as a contribution to Britain's balance of payments; they also represent a responsibility towards every continent, and one which we would do well to consider more deeply.[21]

Sustaining and reinventing collegiality

The fourth challenge, I would suggest, is the most critical of all for us at this time. In his thousand-page work, *The Sociology of Philosophies: A Global Theory of Intellectual Change*,[22] Randall Collins writes a comparative history and sociology of intellectual communities, ranging through ancient Greece, India, China, Japan, Islam, Judaism, Christianity, modern Europe and America. His key discovery is very simple. It is that at the heart of intellectual creativity is intensive, disciplined face-to-face conversation and debate between contemporaries and across generations. He marshals a large amount of data to show that this was so in the days before printing, it continued after printing, and it still holds true in an age of rapid travel, mass communications and computers. It is sometimes encouraging to have the intuitively obvious confirmed at length! So the fourth challenge is the sustaining and reinventing of forms of collegiality in which these intensive conversations within and across generations can flourish.

---

[21]   The global dimension of the transformations in universities is one that I am largely ignoring in this chapter, but it is of increasing importance. In particular there is the development of consortia of universities and a wide range of partnership arrangements. Cambridge is doing various things in this sphere, with universities ranging from the USA to China, but compared with many others it is not far advanced. The Humboldt University in Berlin, for example, has more than 100 partnership agreements with other universities. The White Paper is weak on this international dimension, and does not begin to do justice to the proliferation of high-powered consortia and agreements to cooperate. This internationalizing of higher education poses a problem analogous to that of international business corporations for any national government. On the specific issue of European Union students the White Paper (Section 7.53, p. 90) envisages EU students paying up to £3000 tuition fees like UK students, which would seem to involve breaking current agreements. With many German universities (where 99% of undergraduate provision of higher education is free) now offering courses through English, their attraction to British students is likely to increase greatly after fees increase in the UK.

[22]   Belknap Press of Harvard University Press, Cambridge MA and London, 1998.

In its colleges we have probably the most distinctive feature of Cambridge University. They are long-term environments of conversational culture centred on meals. (After this lecture many of you will have the delightful setting of a feast for dissecting what I have said – all those collegial knives!) Colleges gather together from different generations and from all disciplines *people* who are dedicated to learning, teaching and research. Knowledge inheres primarily in people, rather than in the storage facilities of books and computers. The problem of an aggregate of unrelated disciplines is not met by some comprehensive system of knowledge accounting for them all – even were that possible it would soon be out of date; rather it is to be met by developing further our collegial culture.[23]

Colleges allow for many patterns of conversation between undergraduates, postgraduates, Fellows and other members. Time and again undergraduates attest how important it is to be it close contact with students of different disciplines, and that the small-group teaching based in colleges has been their core learning experience. Beyond these advantages for members there is also the quality of hospitality that colleges make possible, especially towards academics from all over the world. A further benefit, in a situation where much research, 'knowledge transference' and 'ministry of meaning' work goes on in short-term groups formed around problems and projects, is that colleges both allow for short-term hospitality in interaction with other academics and also give a strong home base from which to go out. There is also the advantage of having 31 very different micro-environments in the university where different things can be grown and where new things can be tried and sometimes fail (without having too disastrous results).[24] And a sober look at the costs of all this in relation to benefits makes clear that they are extraordinarily good value for money. Yet there are pressures for these long-term, high-quality educational environments to be eliminated or greatly modified. Surely the response should be to face the criticisms, and to reform where necessary, but overall to make the case for the even greater appropriateness of colleges in today's situation?

The disappearance or serious weakening of our colleges would be an ecological disaster for Cambridge's education and intellectual life. The twentieth century was a period of unprecedented collegial creativity in

---

[23] Daniel Hardy has suggested in conversation the idea of a university as a 'corporate encyclopedia', but one that is interconnected not arbitrarily through alphabetical order but intrinsically through the collegiality of those pursuing different disciplines while being in conversation with each other and at times in collaboration.

[24] In different terms, the colleges have some of the features of an internal market in the university, with some competition for good students and fellows, and a determination to do well in the Baxter Tables that analyse their academic performance.

Cambridge – between the 1950s and 1970s 11 new colleges of diverse types were added.[25] Even so the colleges have been outstripped in many ways by the far more massive expansion of faculties and research institutes. We probably still need some new colleges – for which the land is there in north-west Cambridge. Most present colleges certainly need more endowment. But we also face a more basic challenge to collegial creativity. The critical question is: how might colleges realize better than they do at present the quality of collegiality required to foster interplay between teaching and research, interdisciplinarity, and contributions to national and international society? Inspiring our efforts at rediscovery and reinvention might be that historical panorama described by Randall Collins, whose core dynamic of intellectual creativity centres on exactly what colleges do best. And they are only one set of collegial niches in our environment. There are also all the faculties and departments, the centres and institutes, the longer and shorter term partnerships, and the numerous teams, groups, projects, societies, syndicates, lecture series, and one-off events. Collegiality needs to be valued and cultivated at all levels of the University.

But what holds all this together structurally? What about the institution of Cambridge University as a whole? The immediate implication of valuing collegiality is that we have to pay attention to our polity, governance and management. This has been much discussed in recent times, and the verdict must be that there is a great deal of unfinished business. Change in large institutions is one of the most difficult things to achieve satisfactorily. In a

---

[25]   Peter Brooke in a letter (22 January 2002) to me wrote:

Between the 1950s and 1970s we actually did found 11 new colleges in Cambridge – 11 of the 31 are either totally new foundations or converted institutions of that period; a very remarkable achievement. Let us observe two contrasts: of the other 20 colleges 14 are medieval academic chantries – founded to support (mostly) graduate students and pray for their founders and benefactors; two were late sixteenth-century puritan foundations – with purposes so little different from the pre-reformation colleges that the greater part of the statutes of Emmanuel was copied (almost word for word) from St John Fisher's for Christ's! – the seventeenth college was Downing founded (very oddly) by the Court of Chancery in 1800; and out of several nineteenth-century attempts, three survived, your own Selwyn, and Newnham and Girton. That is to say, there is no period except the mid-fourteenth century when founders have been so active as in the 1950s–70s. . . . Four pressures particularly inspired the flurry of foundations. 1. The needs of university teaching staff . . . 2. The urge to gender equality . . . 3. The urgent need to provide for research students . . . 4. Visiting scholars – a major feature of the Cambridge scene, brought here by the immense prestige of our labs and the best working University Library in Europe . . .

Cf. Christopher Brooke, *History of the University of Cambridge, 1870–1990* (Cambridge University Press, Cambridge, 1993) especially Chapter 18.

self-governing institution such as Cambridge it requires the sort of broad participation, mature deliberation, and persuasion that there is a better, wiser way that we obviously have not yet achieved. In between the extremes of those who resist any change and those who favour strongly centralizing solutions are, I think, most of us who might perhaps agree on the following: we are a large and expanding institution whose governance and management have not kept pace with the complexity of both internal and external factors, including money; we want a better balance between continuing self-governance, central leadership, and management; we see the need for strategic planning in which academic and financial considerations go together; we long for a renewal of the trust that has suffered in recent events; and above all we want any prescription to be clearly in the service of the flourishing of our long term environment of teaching and research, interdisciplinarity, contribution to society, and collegiality.

Is it beyond our ability to devise such a prescription and then apply it? The stakes are high, with the threat of government intervention, the danger of demoralizing our best administrators, above all the risk of failing to sustain this extraordinarily fruitful environment. If we succeed, besides the obvious benefits to the University and its mission, we might also have modelled a sort of healthy institution that our society desperately needs. There is a shortage of private, civil and state institutions that can combine self-government, leadership and management in the effective service of a long-term vision.[26] Even our national government is finding it extremely difficult to reform parliament, so one trusts that it will understand why we too cannot come up with an instant solution. While there is urgency, we should surely take some time for this process – I think it is ridiculous to suggest that Cambridge's world-class performance as a university is immediately threatened. But there does need to be a well-conceived process of intensive conversation, consultation, deliberation, and decision making that is aimed not only at governance but also at a vigorous articulation of the university's purpose and priorities.[27] This would be helpful in many other ways: in letting students and staff appreciate better what we are all part of, in

---

[26] Another encouraging feature of the White Paper is its concern for the universities as self-governing institutions and its commitment to reduce regulation where possible. If this were combined with generosity in enabling endowments to be built up then it is just possible to imagine a strengthening of universities as vital institutions of our civil society, against the trend of state centralising and detailed supervision in recent decades. On the latter see Gordon Graham, *Universities*, op. cit.

[27] One way of putting this is that we need to discover an appropriate form of collegiality at the level of the University as a whole.

advocacy to government and the media, in fund-raising, in strategic planning, and in renewing our confidence in what we are about. If we do not do this, the vacuum created by our irresponsibility and irresolution will surely be filled by others and by less well considered ideas – and even perhaps by coercion aimed at producing short-term results.[28]

Wisdom and its Traditions

There is, however, one further consideration which has a pervasive significance for all the topics I have discussed and not least for our corporate deliberations. I have frequently used the imagery of environment and ecology, which encourages an integral understanding that tries to do justice to complex long-term dynamics and their interplay. I have also stressed the inseparability of knowledge from questions of meaning, value, ethics, collegiality, and transgenerational responsibility. There is a term for the sort of understanding that attempts to think through such matters together, with a view to the better shaping of life. It is wisdom. This is not only desirable when we think about the University's future; it is also classically the most comprehensive ideal of education, beyond information, knowledge, practice, and skills. The goal is to unite knowledge and understanding with imagination, good judgement and decision making in life and work.

Wisdom is even becoming a research topic in various disciplines. There is a 'Berlin Wisdom Paradigm' developed at the Max Planck Institute for Human Development, and at the last meeting of the Syndics of Cambridge University Press that I attended we accepted for publication a 'Handbook of Wisdom' written largely by psychologists and educationalists. It is good

---

[28]   It might not be an understatement to say that Britain's greatest challenge in higher education at the national level is to rebuild the relationship between the government and the universities, now at a low ebb after decades of failure to engage in the sorts of trust-based consultation and dialogue that might build consensus. It would be worth attending to the ways in which the German government and universities go about building consensus, even though German universities are in theory far more dependent on their government. Using US universities as the main point of reference internationally has many advantages, but the role of the state in Britain has more parallels with Germany and other European countries. Given strong direction from the centre, consensus-building, together with respect for the differences between institutions, is the sensible way to have a long-term policy that has full cooperation from both sides.

to see an ancient concept taking on new dimensions, and I would suggest that universities also reappropriate it. The questions that we are facing are of such range, complexity and long-term significance that we need the resources of the deepest wisdom traditions, ancient and modern, religious and secular. Let me just say a little about that last pair.

Our November 2001 statement of core values makes one striking omission in comparison with the University's statutes and the statutes of most of our colleges: it fails to mention religion. It does mention 'sport, music, drama, the visual arts, and other cultural activities'. I want to suggest that, in this understandably sensitive matter, we face the reality of our university, our nation, and our world. None of them can be labelled simply religious; none can be labelled simply secular; all are both religious and secular. Nationally that has been acknowledged by this government in its policy that primary and secondary education be both religious and secular. At the global level, the fact that a large majority of the world's population is directly involved in one or other of the world's religions has come back into consciousness recently, after being eclipsed – at least in the West – for much of the twentieth century. But what about religion and Cambridge University? I want to make just two points.

The first is that we need to make sure that the space occupied by religion in the statutes and in the whole conception and life of Cambridge University over many centuries is not left empty. Matters like intellectual values, education, the uses of knowledge, and long-term responsibility toward human flourishing cannot be detached from frameworks of overall meaning and from our convictions about what it means to be human, about justice, peace, and the nature of a good society – from what Durkheim called the compulsions that order society, which he found exemplified especially in religion. Our religions situation has of course undergone changes, but to suggest that disappearance is the right description, to be reflected in disappearance from a description of the University's identity, seems to me not only untrue but unwise. To acknowledge the significance of religion in the University's identity, past and present, might not only be a matter of political correctness – or, in some eyes, incorrectness. It might also be the sign of a determination, as we try to orient ourselves to serve this and future generations better, to draw on the riches of religious as well as secular wisdoms. Often, of course, they are inextricable from each other – just think of how the Hebraic, Hellenic, Latin and Christian strands have intertwined in the Western civilization that has shaped Cambridge. Surely its reinvention as a global university for the twenty-first century should involve a collegiality to which both those who are wisely religious and those who are wisely secular are encouraged to contribute?[29] The devil, of course, is in the detail of deciding what is wise and what is not: but on the sort of issues with which we are concerned I suspect that usually divisions are not along confessional lines.

The second point is that, if we were to do justice to the religious and secular dimensions of this University, it might be salutary for the peace of this and future generations. We may now be on the verge of a war that is inextricable from a history of deep religious divisions. Those have been in the making for centuries, and are likely to take centuries to heal – if the world is not destroyed first. Long-term institutions with responsibility for the education of future generations need to be part of the healing if they can. It may be that when future generations assess Cambridge's contribution to public life in our time they will judge it at least as important that we educated the present Archbishop of Canterbury and Chief Rabbi as that we educated the Secretary of State for Education and Skills. Let us shape a University that might go on producing successors to all three.

Coda for St Valentine's Day

To conclude, here are some verses from the Song of Songs chapter 7:

> How graceful are your feet in sandals,
>   O queenly maiden!
> The curves of your thighs are like ornaments,
>   the work of a master hand.
> Your navel is a bowl well-rounded
>   that will never lack spiced wine.
> Your waist is a mound of wheat,
>   encircled by lilies.
> Your two breasts are like two fawns,
>   twins of a gazelle.
> Your neck is like an ivory tower.[30]

[29] Universities are one of the few settings where those of various religions and none can study together and engage with each other on topics of common concern. Many universities are dedicated to a secular ethos; others are confessionally religious. I would argue for the importance in the twenty-first century of there being some universities that are both religious and secular. Cambridge already has this character in fact, and would do well to acknowledge and sustain it.
[30] Translation draws on New Revised Standard Version, Revised English Bible, New International Version and New Jerusalem Bible.

An ivory tower![31] The other name for this poem is the Song of Solomon, the supreme biblical figure of wisdom. What if the imagery of an ivory tower were to go back to these origins? The resonances with academic life might then be with the passionate desire that motivates us at our best, the elusiveness of what we pursue, the ecstatic beauty of what we sometimes discover, and the abundant fruitfulness with which the Song is filled. And the figure of Solomon, to whom, besides the Song of Songs, the diverse wisdoms of Proverbs and Ecclesiastes are also attributed, might inspire in us a love of wisdom that is also a wisdom of love.

[31]   I am grateful to Chad Pecknold for drawing my attention to this first occurrence of the phrase. I am also grateful to Josh Robinson for research on the term, showing that its use meaning seclusion or separation from the world and its harsh realities seems to come from Sainte-Beuve in 1837. Sr Edmee Kingsmill SLG in a letter to me (4 February 2003) quotes Marvin Pope: 'One may wonder how many of those who use the term are aware of its original biblical application to milady's neck' (Marvin Pope, *Song of Songs: A New Translation with introduction and Commentary*, The Anchor Bible, Doubleday, New York, 1977, p. 625). It seems quite possible that Sainte-Beuve himself did not have the Song in mind when he began the modern usage.

Chapter Seven

FAITH AND UNIVERSITIES IN A RELIGIOUS AND SECULAR WORLD

Part One

Following in the wake of Rawls and Neuhaus, any number of theologians, philosophers, historians, and political theorists – led by major figures like Alasdair MacIntyre, Michael Sandel, Charles Taylor, and Stanley Hauerwas – have re-examined, debated, challenged, and at times rejected the premises of liberalism, whether in the name of religion, or communitarianism, or multiculturalism.

To the extent that liberalism's structures have been undermined or at least shaken by these analyses, the perspicuousness and usefulness of distinctions long assumed – reason as opposed to faith, evidence as opposed to revelation, inquiry as opposed to obedience, truth as opposed to belief – have been called into question. And finally . . . the geopolitical events of the past decade and of the past three years especially have re-alerted us to the fact (we always knew it, but as academics we were able to cabin it) that hundreds of millions of people in the world do not observe the distinction between the private and the public or between belief and knowledge, and that it is no longer possible for us to regard such persons as quaintly pre-modern or as the needy recipients of our saving (an ironic word) wisdom.

Some of these are our sworn enemies. Some of them are our colleagues. Many of them are our students. (There are 27 religious organizations for students on my campus.) Announce a course with 'religion' in the title, and you will have an overflow population. Announce a lecture or panel on 'religion in our time' and you will have to hire a larger hall.

And those who come will not only be seeking knowledge; they will be seeking guidance and inspiration, and many of them will believe that religion – one religion, many religions, religion in general – will provide them.

Are we ready?

We had better be, because that is now where the action is. When Jacques Derrida died I was called by a reporter who wanted to know what would succeed high theory and the triumvirate of race, gender, and class as the centre of intellectual energy in the academy. I answered like a shot: religion.[1]

Is Stanley Fish just noticing a passing fashion in some American universities when he describes a surge of intellectual energy around religion? It is the argument of this chapter that he is in fact identifying something more fundamental.

Religion was intrinsic to universities from their European medieval beginnings and through most of their history. It has also been complexly involved with them during the past two centuries since the beginnings of the modern research university marked by the foundation of the University of Berlin in 1810. Yet those centuries also saw a widespread secularization of universities, in the sense both of the elimination of religious control of universities and also of the increasing marginalization of religion in the spheres of ethos, curriculum, policy-making, 'mission', and focus of concern. At the same time, the rest of the world was not simply undergoing secularization. It was developing in complexly religious and secular ways and arriving at a variety of balances, blends and settlements in different parts of the world and spheres of life. I argue that this has led to a mismatch between universities and their contemporary context. Universities on the whole teach, research and relate to society as if the world were simply secular, or, at most, secular with some religious survivals. There is rarely the sense that, as Fish says, hundreds of millions of people (in fact, the vast majority of the world's population), including a great many students and academics, see reality differently.

Fish draws attention to academics in a range of fields who in various ways have been challenging the universities (and other areas of public life) about the ways in which religion is ignored, misconstrued, marginalized, privatized or dismissed. This should have consequences for the way in which universities are shaped with regard to religion. At least they should not be places where some ideological version of secularism is taken for granted. At best there should be universities that are complexly religious and secular in modes that reflect, reflect on, study, discuss and are responsible towards our religious and secular world in appropriately academic religious and secular ways. This chapter is an attempt to explore the latter best-case scenario. Part one of this chapter sets the scene by considering some key phases in university history.

[1] Stanley Fish, 'One University Under God' *The Chronicle of Higher Education*, January 7, 2005.

First, there is some historical discussion of universities in the medieval and early modern periods. Then the foundation of the University of Berlin is examined as the root of the modern research university, and its significance assessed in relation to the religious and secular. It is seen as a historical surprise not only in its academic character but also in the originality and fruitfulness of its religious and secular settlement. Finally, the subsequent influence and problems of the Berlin paradigm are traced briefly, and the case is made for the desirability of a new surprise in order to repair, renew and in some respects supersede the Berlin paradigm, the concern here being especially with its religious and secular settlement. Such a surprise would require the sort of intellectual and institutional creativity that helped to generate the University of Berlin.

In Part Two an attempt is made, in line with the work of Jeffrey Stout and others, to describe the public sphere in terms that allow for (and even make desirable) a university that might be called 'interfaith and secular'. One element of the envisaged religious and secular university is the responsibility of its various religious and secular constituencies to think through their own convictions and commitments in relation to the university, and to enter into debate with others. The university needs to learn from the various traditions of understanding, wisdom and values that are present within it, and each of these traditions therefore has the task of continually relating their best wisdom to that of others, in the interests of the flourishing of the institution, its students and staff, its academic disciplines, and its wider responsibilities to our world. Each particular tradition or blend of traditions has to face this challenge, and as a Christian theologian I propose a conception of the interfaith and secular university that grows out of Christian understanding. In particular, I explore some academic Christian approaches to universities from Berlin to Yale and then to Cambridge, asking how religious traditions can be best mediated academically in the twenty-first century. This conception of the university is offered as a contribution to a debate in which it is to be hoped that other Christians, those of other faiths and those of secular or agnostic convictions will also participate.

Two further introductory comments are in order. One is that the present chapter is part of an ongoing project concerned with the shaping of universities in the twenty-first century. That universities should engage better with the religious and secular character of our world is just one element of this. There are of course a great many other elements in the shaping of universities, most of which are far more obvious than the issue of the religious and secular. How should teaching and research be related? What about core intellectual values, interdisciplinarity, university governance, collegiality, public and private funding, the commodification of knowledge, and the balance of responsibilities towards the flourishing of society? Some of those are mentioned when relevant, but they are not the main focus of this chapter. Most of them are discussed briefly in the previous chapter, which might act as a complement and context for what is said here, but I also intend to treat some of them at greater length in future work.

The second comment is on the analogies used by Fish in the opening quotation. He compares the present focus on religion with four other concerns: high theory, race, gender and class. Those have not only generated the 'intellectual energy' noted by Fish. They have also led to radical mind- and heart-searching; much suspicion, accusation and polemic; rewriting of history; reconceiving of courses, curricula and whole disciplines; faculty and institutional crises; political movements, campaigns, conflicts and correctness; and deep divisions. That does sound like a description of what religion tends to produce too! One response might be to try, in the interests of peace and goodwill, to resist religion coming back on to the university agenda, since it is hard to see how it can be prevented from generating those results. Yet it may also be that a factor contributing to religion being often so lethal in our world is its widespread exclusion from the higher educational environment of a large number of leaders, key workers, opinion formers and teachers. If within our cultural 'ecology' there are few niches where the issues about, within and between religions can be thoughtfully studied, taught, researched and debated by people of all faiths and none, then we should not be surprised if both the religions themselves and the realm of public discourse are impoverished as a result. If one goes by what has happened with race, gender and class, then academics may not anyway have much choice about whether religion is on the agenda or not; what they may have some say in is how that agenda is handled. This chapter speaks to that concern.

Universities: the medieval heritage

In the magisterial opening chapter of the four-volume *A History of the University in Europe* of which he is the General Editor, Walter Rüegg sums up what he calls 'the essential outlines of an academic ethic in the process of formation' distilled into 'seven values which in the Middle Ages legitimated, in religious terms, the *amor sciendi* and the university which was its institutional form'.[2] It is worth quoting at some length, since he and the

[2]   Walter Rüegg, 'Themes', in *Universities in the Middle Ages*, ed. H. De Ridder-Symoens, vol. 1 of *A History of the University in Europe*, General Editor, Walter Rüegg (Cambridge University Press, Cambridge, UK, 1992–), p. 32.

other contributors together make a convincing cumulative case over the three volumes that have appeared so far for there being, despite huge changes, some continuity linking the university's medieval origins with at least some of its successors today. There is of course a large question as to how much continuity there is or should be, but at least his distillation based on the first three centuries of the existence of universities offers a benchmark against which to measure change and some categories through which to approach the task of saying something normative as well as descriptive about universities.

The seven evaluative propositions are:

1   The belief in a world order, created by God, rational, accessible to human reason, to be explained by human reason and to be mastered by it; this belief underlies scientific and scholarly research as the attempt to understand this rational order of God's creation.

2   The ancient understanding of humans as imperfect beings, and the Judaeo-Christian idea of a creature fallen into sin, and the proposition deriving from these ideas about the limitation of the human intellect, operated in the Middle Ages as driving forces impelling intellectual criticism and collegial cooperation; they served as the foundation for the translation of general ethical values like modesty, reverence, and self-criticism into the image of the ideal scientist and scholar.

3   Respect for the individual as a reflection of the macrocosm, or as having been formed in the image of God, laid the foundation for the gradually realized freedom of scientific and scholarly research and teaching.

4   The absoluteness of the imperative of scientific truth already led scholasticism to the basic norms of scientific and scholarly research and teaching, such as the prohibition of the rejection of demonstrated knowledge, the subjection of one's own assertions to the generally valid rules of evidence, openness to all possible objections to one's own argument, and the public character of argument and discussion.

5   The recognition of scientific and scholarly knowledge as a public good which is ultimately a gift of God had not, it is true, even before universities existed, prevented study and teaching for the sake of money. Nevertheless, there has been less interest within the universities in the economic use of scientific knowledge than there has been in the learned professions outside the university. This relatively smaller interest in the economic utilization of scientific knowledge has been an axiomatic value of the university.

6   *Reformatio*, which regarded one's own scientific efforts as the renewal
    of previously established knowledge and its further development 'in
    the cause of improvement', laid a disproportionate weight in the
    medieval university on already established patterns of thought and
    older authors. Nevertheless, these were not accepted without criti-
    cism; they were critically scrutinized to test their veracity as the basis
    of one's own knowledge. They were a stimulus to new ways of seeing
    things and to new theories . . . Scientific and scholarly knowledge
    grows in a cumulative process, by building on earlier knowledge. In
    this sense, the progress of knowledge is a continuous process of
    reformatio.

7   The equality and solidarity of scholars in confronting the tasks of
    science enable the universities to become the institutional centres of
    the scientific community. The acknowledgement of the scientific
    achievements of those who think and believe differently from our-
    selves and of those who are members of social strata different from
    our own and the readiness to correct one's own errors in the light
    of persuasive new knowledge, regardless of its source, permitted the
    rise of science . . . Indeed, the more highly equality was evaluated,
    and the more it was joined to the common responsibility for the
    increase of knowledge, the better the university fulfilled its
    obligations.[3]

I will return to these propositions in Part Two when developing a Christian theology for the university. At this point it is worth noting three points.
First, as regards the Christian tradition in which they are historically rooted,
twenty-first century as well as medieval Christians could affirm them. The
teachings – God as creator of a world order accessible to human reason;
human imperfection; humanity in the image of God; the appropriateness of
public argument and discussion to the absoluteness of scientific truth; scientific and scholarly knowledge as a public good transcending any economic
advantage it might bring; the cumulative and self-correcting process of the
growth of knowledge; and the equality and solidarity of those committed
to the pursuit of knowledge – would be likely to gain the assent of a broad
range of Christians in universities: conservative, liberal, radical, postliberal –
though not, perhaps, some postmodern.

Second, members of many other faith communities, especially those
of the Abrahamic traditions, but also others, would affirm analogous
doctrines.

---

[3]   Ibid. pp. 32ff.

Third, the practical implications of the propositions – rational investigation of the world; ethical values of modesty, reverence and self-criticism; respect for the dignity and freedom of the individual; rigorous public argument appealing to demonstrated knowledge and rules of evidence; the recognition of the pursuit of knowledge as a public good irreducible to economic interest; the need for continual self-criticism in the course of improving our knowledge; and the value of equality and solidarity – all these could be affirmed, even if justified in very different ways, by many agnostic or secular people in the academy.

The conclusion is, therefore, that even in its medieval form the university had the potential to embrace those of many faiths and of none, though this was not to happen fully in European universities for many centuries. Nor is this surprising when its history is understood.[4] The universities that grew up in the thirteenth century drew heavily on non-Christian sources. The influence of Greek and Roman civilization on the curriculum was enormous. In the liberal arts (the *trivium* of grammar, logic and rhetoric; the *quadrivium* of arithmetic, geometry, astronomy and music) each subject was dominated by non-Christian authorities or by Christians who had learnt most of what they knew from non-Christians.[5] In the 'higher' faculties of law and medicine the situation was similar. Roman law was the model for both civil and canon law.[6] In medicine the main authorities were Greek and Islamic, and Muslims and Jews were among leading medical practitioners.[7] In the remaining higher faculty, theology, the chief authority was the Bible. During the early centuries of Christianity in the Roman Empire the Bible had become the 'classic' at the centre of Christian education, but it was studied in ways that owed a great deal to Greek and Roman *paideia*,

[4]   For a survey of relevant research see J. M. Fletcher (ed.) *The History of European Universities. Work in Progress and Publications*, 5 *vols.* (University of Birmingham, Birmingham, 1978–81) and J. M. Fletcher and J. Deahl, 'European Universities 1300–1700: the Development of Research 1969–81, and a Summary Bibliography' in J. M. Kittelson and P. J. Transue (eds.), *Rebirth, Reform and Resilience: Universities in Transition 1300–1700* (Ohio State University Press, Columbus, OH, 1984), pp. 324–57.

[5]   See Gordon Leff, 'The *trivium* and the three philosophies', and John North, 'The *quadrivium*' in *A History of the University in Europe*, General Editor Walter Rüegg *op. cit.*, vol. 1, *Universities in the Middle Ages*, ed. H. De Ridder-Symoens, pp. 307–36; 337–59.

[6]   See Antonio Garcia Y. Garcia, 'The Faculties of Law', in *A History of the University in Europe*, General Editor Walter Rüegg, *op. cit.*, vol. 1 *Universities in the Middle Ages*, ed. H. De Ridder-Symoens, pp. 388–408; P. Koschaker, *Europa und das römische Recht* (Biederstein Verlag, Munich, 1966); S. Kuttner, *The History of Ideas and Doctrines of Canon Law in the Middle Ages* (Variorum Reprints, London, 1980).

[7]   See Nancy Siraisi, 'The Faculty of Medicine', in *A History of the University in Europe*, General Editor Walter Rüegg, *op. cit.*, vol. 1 *Universities in the Middle Ages*, ed. H. De Ridder-Symoens, pp. 360–87.

with close attention to grammar, logic and rhetoric, and this continued in the medieval period. As the new urban universities complemented and competed with the older monastic schools, one of their main innovations was to bring into the centre of intellectual debate a wide range of texts originating in classical Greece and Rome. Many of these texts came through Islamic channels, the most influential being by Aristotle. Debate about the reception of Aristotle, and in particular his influence on theology, were among the liveliest in the medieval university, with the work of Thomas Aquinas as a high point in the critical integration of Aristotle (and of other classical philosophical and scientific thought) with Christian theology. So within the medieval university it was not generally permitted that pagans, Jews or Muslims be there in person, but they had contributed a great deal to the whole range of subjects on the curriculum, and they constantly figured in debates.

The medieval university developed other patterns that have been repeated with variations in later forms of the university. Three are of special importance.[8]

First, there were the tensions between different fundamental goals: understanding and truth for their own sake; formation in a way of life, its habits and virtues; and utility in society – study oriented towards practical use and employment in various spheres of life. These tensions were there from the start and have continued into twenty-first century debates. They have always been closely linked to the negotiations between groups with an interest in higher education. The medieval university was in its various institutional forms the outcome of settlements negotiated between what were then called *studium*, *sacerdotium*, and *regnum*. It is part of the argument of the present chapter that the university in every period has had to be vigilant about doing justice to the legitimate claims of each of those spheres (or their analogies in other periods), and that one of the neglected tasks today is that of rethinking the claims of *sacerdotium*, which requires coming to new terms with the complexly religious and secular character of our period.

Second, the medieval university embodied another closely related set of tensions concerning its unity and diversity. It was unified in overall conception through theology but the liberal arts were rarely content simply to accept their subordination to theology, and the law faculty was also jealous of its independence. Perhaps more important, the integrating discipline of

---

[8] On these see *A History of the University in Europe*, General Editor, Walter Rüegg, *op. cit.*, vol. 1, *Universities in the Middle Ages*, ed. H. De Ridder-Symoens, especially Chapters 1, 2, 3, 4, 13.

theology was itself institutionalized in a plural way. Closely involved with most university theology faculties were the *studia* of religious orders, especially the new mendicant orders of Dominicans and Franciscans (to be joined in the early modern period by the Jesuits). The presence of these orders, called '*religiones*', and the often energetic disputes carried on by them and the 'secular' teachers (not members of religious orders) of the university meant that right from the start there was built into the university fundamental disagreement and dispute about what integrates it. Indeed, one key characteristic differentiating the first universities from monastic and diocesan schools was their institutionalization of dispute. It has continued to be in the nature of an institution with many disciplines, interests and responsibilities to have to ask constantly about what holds it together, with inevitable disagreement about what, if anything, that might be. The answers have ranged from 'nothing' (hence the French solution discussed below) to a particular substantive religion, ideology or worldview, and other options have included specific 'master-disciplines' (theology, philosophy, law, experimental science), and specific uses (service of church, state, economy). But at another level of integration there has been the creation of the institutional space within which these disputes could take place. This has taken many forms, and Rüegg's list of seven propositions (with my associated remarks above about their continuing validity) suggests a higher-level integration in terms of shared intellectual, ethical and social values and practices.

Third, there was the development of collegiality. This took many forms,[9] one of which, the university college, because of its ability to sustain a religious dimension even in the face of strong secularizing pressures, will be of special interest in discussing the University of Cambridge in Part Two. Colleges in universities in the fourteenth and fifteenth centuries were 'privileged institutions serving to guarantee their members, at the price of a degree of discipline, the best conditions for work and study, in other words, to constitute a student elite', and 'in France, England and Germany they were henceforth the place where the pedagogic model which was to exert the greatest influence upon the evolution of practices of secondary and higher education in modern Europe was elaborated'.[10]

So overall the medieval university proved durable in some vital respects, while also capable, as later centuries were to show, of considerable innovation and reinvention.

---

[9] See ibid. Chapter 4.
[10] Jacques Verger, 'Patterns' in ibid., pp. 61f.

Early modern European universities: expansion and decline

The early modern period (for my purposes defined as stretching roughly from 1500 till 1800) included times of great upheaval in Europe, beginning with the Reformation and Counter-Reformation and ending with the French Revolution. Intellectually, there was a huge range of new developments, such as the impact of humanism on medieval scholasticism, the invention of printing, increased use of the vernacular, the opening up of America and other parts of the world that helped change the perception of humanity and culture, Protestant and Catholic theologies in polemical relationship with each other, a new relationship to the past through scholarship and historical study, and a series of 'revolutions' (scientific, industrial and political) which were deeply related to new ways of thinking and forms of knowledge. The very term 'Middle Ages', applied to what had preceded it, marked out this time of innovation and self-conscious difference. What happened to universities during these three centuries? It is not possible here to summarize what is now a large and growing field in historical research,[11] but what follows is an attempt to name some of the main developments.

Overall this period has been summed up as a time for universities of differentiation, professionalization and an expansion whose vigour was not sustained.[12] As regards differentiation and professionalization, many kinds of institutions of further education grew up, covering secondary education, technology, and scientific research, and at the same time the universities were increasingly guided by market demands to produce graduates suited to the professions and other employment.[13] As regards expansion, this was closely related to religious dynamics of Europe, with a large number of both Catholic and Protestant foundations, the most remarkable single element perhaps being the extraordinary energy and success of the Jesuits in university foundation and transformation.[14] But the very achievements of the churches and their pervasive influence on universities meant that as the churches were increasingly challenged – both intellectually and politically – the future of universities themselves was at stake, since they were so closely identified as religious institutions. Especially in the eighteenth century there

---

[11] Cf. Ibid. vol. II, *Universities in Early Modern Europe (1500–1800)*, ed. Hilde de Ridder-Symoens, *passim*.
[12] Willem Frijhoff, 'Patterns', in ibid. p. 79.
[13] Frijhoff says this 'is perhaps the most striking characteristic of the period', ibid. p. 80.
[14] For a clear overview of the huge expansion see the lists and maps appended to Frijhoff's chapter, ibid., pp. 90–105. It helpfully shows the pattern of Protestant and Catholic institutions, including a separate map of the Jesuit universities.

were fierce struggles for power as increasingly powerful and centralizing nation states sought control over education. This was a period in which secularization seemed to many to mean liberation from forms of church domination that constricted academic inquiry, adaptation, innovation and access in unacceptable ways. The resistance of many universities both to new knowledge and to secularization marked them down for destruction (as in France), radical reform (as in Germany) or marginalization (as in England until a combination of the foundation of new universities and nineteenth-century reforms of Oxford and Cambridge led to the *sui generis* system that will figure in Part Two).

I now turn to the most influential event in the history of the modern university.

The Berlin surprises

It was by no means inevitable that an institution associated with strong religious roots and control such as the university should become the leading research and higher level teaching institution of the contemporary world.[15] The French in 1793 replaced universities with a combination of academies and specialist government *écoles*. The Prussians were considering something similar at the beginning of the nineteenth century. But the combination of an extraordinarily creative set of thinkers and organizational innovators, together with appropriate historical conditions, led to Prussia reorganizing its educational system with the university at the top. The university became not only the centre for formal credentials for state employment and a range of professions; it also had a good deal of academic autonomy, an increasingly differentiated set of specialist faculties, and what Collins calls a 'structural impetus to creativity', with professors expected to produce new knowledge.[16]

This was above all embodied in the foundation of the University of Berlin in 1809. The Berlin model spread in Europe far beyond Germany and also to America and elsewhere, and its key features are still characteristic of those universities that dominate intellectual life around the world.

What about religion in these universities? Collins[17] tells a largely linear story of secularisation: theological and ecclesiastical domination were ended

---

[15] For what follows cf. Randall Collins, *The Sociology of Philosophies: A Global Theory of Intellectual Change* (The Belknap Press of Harvard University Press, Cambridge, MA and London, 1998) pp. 640ff.

[16] Ibid. p. 643.

[17] Ibid. chapters 12–14.

as disciplines won their autonomy and the state presided over the creation of a new system in which religion eventually played almost no part. In Collins' history the result of the process is that niches in the intellectual ecology previously occupied by theology are now colonized by other disciplines, especially philosophy, and religion has effectively disappeared. This is akin to the secularization theory according to which modernity brings with it the irreversible decline of religion in most areas, especially of public life. But what if a more complex, dialectical story is told, leading to a different conception of the contemporary implications?

Collins does not mention the religious–secular debate that took place over the constitution of the University of Berlin. Hans Frei's account of this emphasizes the differences between Fichte (its first Rector), who wanted to exclude theology because it was not sufficiently '*wissenschaftlich*', and Schleiermacher (Fichte's successor as Rector), who was both supportive of *Wissenschaft* and argued for the inclusion of theology as drawing on various disciplines with the overall aim of the professional education of clergy. Schleiermacher resisted any overarching systematic framework or theory of *Wissenschaft* for the University of Berlin since this could not do justice to 'the irreducible specificity of Christianity at the primary level of a "mode of faith", a cultural-religious tradition, and a linguistic community'.[18] Frei comments that Schleiermacher's

> view won the day resoundingly. But that is in its way startling. Here was *the* university, the conception of which was most deeply influenced by a philosophical system, the idealist view of the rational and unitary character of study; the university, furthermore, that was to be the model for others in Western Europe and the New World. And it, of all institutions, found itself, from the start, unable to embody its own unitary idea, while the man who ended up defending both – the idea of the intellectual unity and supremacy of Wissenschaft and the university, and the actual as well as conceptually irreducible diversity of the institution of higher learning – was himself one of the leading idealists. It was a triumph of orderly eclecticism over system by a leading systematician. And he based the right of theology to a place in the university on the status of the ministry as one of the professions in the modern sense.[19]

Beginning from that account, the story of the historical surprise of the University of Berlin and its contemporary significance for us might unfold

---

[18]   Hans W. Frei, *Types of Christian Theology*, ed. George Hunsinger and William C. Placher (Yale University Press, New Haven, CT and London, 1992) p. 114 – this is Frei's redescription of Schleiermacher's position.

[19]   Ibid. p. 112.

differently. The continuing interplay of the religious and the secular, appropriately adapted to specific contexts, and refusing any overarching philosophy, ideology or religion, might emerge as part of its secret. Its genius was to create an institution that simultaneously did several things: it constructively drew on the two deepest roots of European civilization, the Hebraic and the Hellenic; it was sensitive to the context and needs (including religious) of its own society; it embodied creative responsibility for the future through teaching and research; it tried to safeguard freedom of intellectual inquiry and of belief; and it pioneered a type of environment in which a good deal of the most important intellectual inquiry and debate in both arts and sciences has continued to happen. One could also draw up the other side of the balance sheet, noting features such as the massive reliance on the state and its bureaucracy, the potential of disciplinary autonomy leading to fragmentation, the limitation of theology to a certain type of state-recognized Christianity, and the whole system's vulnerability to political manipulation (of which the Nazi and Communist periods were only the most extreme examples). In addition, there was the lack of an endowment: this was part of Wilhelm von Humboldt's original vision to enable the university to be more independent, but it was refused by the Prussian government.[20]

Overall, this was a 'modernization of the medieval structure of the university'[21] and might be described as a creative blend of ancient and modern wisdom (together with some blind spots). It refused the *tabula rasa* pure modernism of the French Revolution; it also avoided the pure traditionalism that continued to rule Oxford and Cambridge for some decades. It maintained fundamental continuity with the basic values of the medieval university as discussed above, while doing away with church control. Yet it can hardly be called a secular university – certainly not in the French sense. This was a university that trained clergy for the state church and so was deeply related to the religious nature of its society. I suggest that the best description is for it is: a 'religious and secular' university. In line with that, it had its own version of medieval diversity described above, due to Schleiermacher's insistence on the inclusion of theology.

Looking today at the Berlin paradigm, one sees various continuities and discontinuities. But as regards the question about how these institutions help equip students and their societies to cope with a complexly religious and

---

[20] See Walter Rüegg, 'Themes', in *A History of the University in Europe*, General Editor Walter Rüegg, *op. cit.*, vol. III, *Universities in the Nineteenth and early Twentieth Centuries (1800–1945)*, ed. Walter Rüegg, p. 12.
[21] Ibid. p. 14.

secular world, the view is disappointing. The dialectical tension between the religious and the secular was anomalous even in relation to Berlin's founding concept of *Wissenschaft*, and in changed historical circumstances the tendency has been towards letting the tension slacken in the direction of an embracing, normative secularism. Even where this has not happened the form of the religious has been restricted to certain forms of Protestant and Catholic Christianity, with very limited concern for the rest of Christianity or other religions. On the whole universities have been powerful supporters of secularization, whether in anti-religious or more neutral modes. This has generally meant (though arguably it need not have) that their attention to religious traditions, living religious communities, and to the questions raised by the religions, between the religions, about the religions, and between the religions and non-religious or mixed forms of understanding, belief and practice, has been marginal. They therefore fail to do justice to huge swathes of past and present human culture, experience, thought, ethics, politics, economics, art and practice.

This leaves the educated elites largely ignorant, naïve or misinformed about some of the most important dimensions of their own and other people's societies, and this inadequate and distorted view of reality is widely disseminated through the media, schools and other institutions that are largely led by university graduates. It also leaves the religious traditions impoverished in the realm of informed, critical and constructive engagement in the public realm that might help them think through their self-understanding and their participation in society. And within the academy it not only leads to theology and/or religious studies being a small department often relatively isolated from others; more seriously it also cuts universities off from sources of wisdom they need to meet their current challenges.

All of this may be considered acceptable in a situation of massive expansion of the system worldwide to cope with hugely increased demands for higher education. Why should universities be concerned about wisdom when there is so much to get on with producing new knowledge and applications of it, and training graduates with the appropriate competence in their fields? Part of the answer is that wisdom directs attention to the whole situation and its tendencies over time. Universities are a vital niche in the long term intellectual and moral ecology of our world. As the clichés put it, we are in an information revolution, a knowledge economy and a learning society. Leaders and key workers in most spheres are university-educated. What happens in this niche is therefore of great importance across generations. If in crucial respects the Berlin model is no longer engaging fruitfully with a major aspect of our global environment, its religious as well as secular character, then it requires correction.

Part Two

How might a university today be true to the core ideals of the Berlin paradigm, including its combination of the religious and secular, but in a way
that is appropriate to the repairs and renewal that paradigm now requires?
The constructive question with which Part Two opens results from the task
set by Part One: to envisage 'universities that are complexly religious and
secular in modes that reflect, reflect on, study, discuss and are responsible
towards our religious and secular world in appropriately academic religious
and secular ways'.[22] This first requires something to be said about the
description of our world as religious and secular.

Universities in a religious and secular world

Most nations in the world today cannot be labelled simply religious or
simply secular: they are *both religious and secular*. The fact that a large majority
(estimated at between four and five billion) of the world's population is
directly involved in one or other of the world's religions has come back
into consciousness recently, after being eclipsed – at least in the West, and
especially among intellectuals – for much of the twentieth century. Religions are very important in shaping the contemporary world, for worse as
well as for better, and this poses a massive challenge: how best to engage in
and resource the continual, complex debates and negotiations within and
among religious traditions, and between the religious and the secular. The
peace and flourishing of our world in the twenty-first century is likely to
depend to a considerable extent on the outcome of such debates, negotiations and settlements embracing the religious and the secular, the breakdown
of which frequently results in violence. At present most of the major areas
of conflict in our world have religious dimensions, and this seems likely to
continue.

I am here using the phrase 'religious and secular' in a fairly common
sense way. 'Religious' refers to what is identified with any particular tradition such as Judaism, Christianity, Islam, Hinduism, Buddhism or other faiths
of importance on the global stage. The 'secular' is what shapes human life,
especially in the public sphere, without religious affiliation. A religious and
secular society or university is one where both elements are present, and
this can be in very different proportions and also in very different relation-

---

[22] See above, p. 116.

ships with each other, including complex and often creative syntheses or hybrids. So they are not necessarily mutually exclusive terms, even though rhetoric from extreme positions identifying with one or the other often sets them in opposition. They are quite vague, requiring a good deal of further specification – in a discussion of Cambridge University, for example, it is important to do justice to the fact that the major religious influence has been Anglicanism, and that the secular influences have generally been far more concerned about the integrity, autonomy and quality of academic inquiry and teaching, or about non-discrimination in access and appointments, than about opposing religion *per se*. In French higher education, by contrast, the secular has been much more anti-religious and secularist in an ideological sense.

Common sense and vague meanings, besides inviting such specification, can also act as a stimulus to discussion aimed at developing the sense in particular directions, and this is especially important when the phrase is being used prescriptively as well as descriptively. In debates about universities there is bound to be a diversity of prescriptive recommendations for how the religious and secular should come together, justified in terms of different traditions. I will leave my own Christian prescription till later, but for now want to note, out of the large literature on the topic,[23] two helpful recent contributions to discussion of the religious and secular.

The first is Talal Asad's essays in *Formations of the Secular: Christianity, Islam, Modernity*.[24]

Is 'secularism' a colonial imposition, an entire worldview that gives precedence to the material over the spiritual, a modern culture of alienation and unrestrained pleasure? Or is it necessary to universal humanism, a rational principle that calls for the suppression – or at any rate the restraint – of religious passion so that a dangerous source of intolerance and delusion can be controlled, and political unity, peace and progress secured?[25]

---

[23] Some of the leading contributions include: S. Bruce, *God is Dead: Secularization in the West* (Blackwell, Oxford, 2002); J. Casanova, *Public Religions in the Modern World* (Chicago University Press, Chicago, 1994); G. Davie, *Religion in Britain since 1945: Believing without Belonging* (Blackwell, Oxford, 1994); A. Greeley, *Unsecular Man: The Persistence of Religion* (Schocken, New York, 1972); D. Martin, *The Religious and the Secular* (Routledge, London, 1969); P. Norris and R. Inglehart, *Sacred and Secular: Religion and Politics Worldwide* (Cambridge University Press, Cambridge, 2004); B. Wilson, *Religion in Secular Society* (Penguin, London, 1966). For a helpful recent survey see Judith Fox, 'Secularization', in John R. Hinnells (ed.), *The Routledge Companion to the Study of Religion* (Routledge, London and New York, 2005) pp. 291–305.
[24] Talal Asad, *Formations of the Secular: Christianity, Islam, Modernity* (Stanford University Press, Stanford, CA, 2003).
[25] ibid, p. 21.

Asad is sensitive to the inadequacies of the conceptual binaries closely related to that of religious and secular – non-modern and modern, non-West and West, belief and knowledge, imagination and reason, fiction and history, allegory and symbol, supernatural and natural, sacred and profane. Yet he also refuses to reduce one to the other. Neither is an essentially fixed category and each has a shifting historical identity, but

> there were breaks between Christian and secular life in which words and practices were rearranged, and new discursive grammars replaced previous ones. I suggest that the fuller implications of those shifts need to be explored. So I take up fragments of the history of a discourse that is often asserted to be an essential part of 'religion' – or at any rate, to have a close affinity with it – to show how the sacred and the secular depend on each other.[26]

It is such recognition of their mutual dependence and interplay that I find illuminating in approaching the phenomenon of the contemporary university, an institution whose self-image is often exclusively in terms of one side of the binaries – secular, modern, Western, knowledge, reason, history, symbol, natural and profane. Asad opens a conceptual space, supported by social anthropological and historical research and reflection, within which the university can be rethought in religious and secular terms.

The second is Jeffrey Stout's book *Democracy and Tradition*,[27] which discusses the place of religious arguments in the public sphere in the USA. Stout opposes Rawlsian (contractarian) and Rortyan (pragmatic) liberals and others who see no place for religious arguments in the democratic arena; but he also opposes anti-liberal thinkers such as Alasdair MacIntyre, Stanley Hauerwas and John Milbank who resent what they see as secular liberal success in dictating the terms of public debate and social cooperation to the exclusion of religious traditions and the virtues that are carried within them. For Stout secular discourse is simply a recognition that in a pluralist society with many beliefs and worldviews ways are needed to discuss matters of common concern and these cannot be in the terms of only one group. Such benign, pragmatic secularity seems the only way to have a pluralist society without coercion, and says nothing about the decline of religion or the disenchantment of the world – indeed all the participants in such discourse could well be committed within particular religious traditions, and, given sensitivity and practical wisdom, might bring tradition-specific elements into the discussion.

[26] Ibid., pp. 25f.
[27] Jeffrey Stout, *Democracy and Tradition* (Princeton University Press, Princeton, NJ, and Oxford, 2004).

For my purposes here, two elements in Stout's position are most important. The first is the prescriptive picture he gives of a public sphere that is both religious and secular (the latter being my phrase to describe his conception of a secularity that is open to explicitly religious as well as secular contributions). He does not extend his position from the political sphere into higher education, but his vision is well suited to the conception of universities that I am advocating in this chapter. Its key ingredient is recognition among groups in a society that we are mutually accountable for our institutional arrangements and how we behave towards each other;[28] that we owe reasons to each other when we take stands on important issues (including reasons that are only fully justifiable within our own tradition); and that we need to cultivate the sort of conversation that includes understanding others in their own terms across the boundaries of enclaves. The conception of tradition this involves is of an enduring social practice – thus embracing, for example, modern democracy as a tradition with its own classics and characteristic virtues. The modern university likewise represents a tradition, and one that, in my interpretation, calls for the sort of corrective Stout tries to apply to American democracy, countering both anti-religious secularist attempts and neotraditionalist attempts to dictate terms. So Stout can portray his democratic, political ideal in ways that are directly applicable to a secular and religious university:

> All democratic citizens should feel free, in my view, to express whatever premises actually serve as reasons for their claims. The respect for others that civility requires is most fully displayed in the kind of exchange where each person's deepest commitments can be recognized for what they are and assessed accordingly. It is simply unrealistic to expect citizens to bracket out such commitments when reasoning about fundamental political questions.[29]

(For 'political' I would read 'higher educational'.)

> . . . [I]t is possible to build democratic coalitions including people who differ religiously and to explore those differences deeply and respectfully without losing one's integrity as a critical intellect.[30]

(For 'democratic' I would read 'academic'.)

The second key element is Stout's own practising of what he preaches. He makes it clear that he is not part of a religious tradition, nor does he

---

28   Ibid., pp. 184f.
29   Ibid., p. 10.
30   Ibid., p. 91.

identify with the positions of Rawls and Rorty. Yet repeatedly he demonstrates his understanding of the latter pair and of religious thinkers and
others in their own terms. It is especially unusual to find a secular academic
who has taken the trouble to become literate in theology. Indeed he makes
a most perceptive contribution to internal Christian theological debates
about Christianity and the secular. He both holds Christian thinkers accountable in relation to their own tradition and also shows how that very tradition
has rich resources for arguing in favour of the sort of religious–secular
coalition favoured by Stout on other grounds.

The urgency in Stout's argument comes from his reasoned perception
that the common good of the USA and its relations with the rest of the
world are at risk because of the impoverishment of its democratic culture.
The anti-religious secularists offer a thinned out public discourse that
cannot engage deeply enough with groups or issues; the neotraditionalists
withdraw into enclaves; powerful groups identify their own interests with
those of society, and serve them; and the energies of neither the modern
democratic tradition nor the religious traditions are mobilized effectively
for the common good.

The urgency in my argument comes from a similar concern for the
health of universities, and the societies (including religious traditions)
towards which they are responsible. Let me risk a few general judgements,
which would of course have to be nuanced in different countries and contexts. Powerful cultural, political and economic forces compete to dominate
universities and compromise the richness of education, the integrity of
thinking and research, and core values such as 'truth-seeking, rationality in
argument, balanced judgement, integrity, linguistic precision, and critical
questioning'.[31] There are numerous academic enclaves, but across their
boundaries common discourse has thinned out, and there is a lack of mutual
accountability and lively conversation. Institutions, academic disciplines and
educated elites are especially ill-equipped to handle the challenges of a
religious and secular world. What I am proposing here concentrates largely
on one dimension, the need to contribute to a renewal of universities
through a coalition (in Stout's sense above) of wisdom traditions, both religious and secular, in order to cope with their task of understanding, teaching
and researching in a religious and secular world. I approached that in Part
One through considering European university history and especially the
single most influential model for contemporary research universities, that of
the University of Berlin. Now I will explore what such a coalition might

---

[31]   See above, Chapter 6, p. 97.

involve today, especially for Christian thinking, if the challenge of the opening question is to be met adequately.

Challenge to the Berlin tradition: the negotiable university today

Part One began to describe some of the current problems of the Berlin model of the modern research university. It is worth briefly articulating the questions raised by these before asking, with special reference to the combination of the religious and secular, about how to address them.

I would identify six key areas in which there are major questions. First, can there be appropriate forms of interdisciplinarity and communication across fields in a situation of increasing fragmentation, with multiplication of disciplines and sub-disciplines? Second, can teaching and research be combined in the same institution so that both benefit? Third, what, if anything, should be attempted in the way of all-round educational formation of students? Fourth, what sort of collegiality among academics and students is desirable and possible? Fifth, who controls the university, and through what sort of instruments and polity? Sixth, what are the appropriate contributions to society, both national and international, of the university?

Any one of those areas would require one or more books to itself if it were to be dealt with adequately, and that underlines the great complexity of the issues. If one just focuses on major world class universities that sustain teaching and research across a wide range of fields it is likely that in any given institution all six of these will be in play together, with many interconnections between them. The contemporary university (like many other organizations) is a site of constant negotiation and renegotiation in relation to such matters and all the practicalities that they entail. In this 'negotiable university' it is vital what informs the negotiations. They are easily taken over by immediate pressures and short-term considerations. How might other considerations be appropriately formative? In the terms used in Part One, how might the 'seven evaluative propositions' identified at the heart of the academic ethic be kept in play? Or how might the three fundamental goals of truth, formation and utility be balanced and their claims given due attention? If, as I would argue, the seriousness of the issues suggests the need for a response as creative and comprehensive as the Berlin surprises at the start of the nineteenth century, how might this be arrived at?

In what follows I discuss the need for an intensive, wisdom-seeking conversation comparable to that which helped generate the University of Berlin; the need for contributions by diverse wisdom traditions; the importance that these traditions be academically mediated; the character of that mediation in relation to Christianity; and something of what is required in the conversation and negotiation.

Responding to the challenge

In general terms it is unlikely that the challenge will be met unless three dimensions come together: a favourable political, economic and cultural context; material provision for institutional renewal; and convincing ideas about reshaping the university.[32] It is not appropriate here to comment on the first two dimensions except to say, first, that with regards to the need both to meet the challenge facing universities, and specifically to relate the religious and secular more satisfactorily within them, the present situation in many Western countries seems more favourable now than for many years; and, second, that there appear to be many resources and increasing demand for higher education. The critical lack seems to be of appropriate conversation producing ideas that might inform the negotiations: the external conditions are there for major developments and even innovations, but universities themselves have not generated the sorts of ideas and visions that might meet their new situation creatively.

Under pressure from continual change in all major areas (including advancement of knowledge), the major players in the academy (both academics and administrators), as in government and business, find it hard to think fundamentally enough about universities – there are always more urgent matters. The result is that most strategies are variations on 'more of the same'. There has been an extraordinary vacuum in fresh thinking about universities that deals with the range of matters mentioned above,[33] and this is a major obstacle to creative reshaping. How might this vacuum be filled?

Berlin points to the need for intensive discussion over some time. The conception of the University of Berlin was generated through intensive conversation, debate and controversy over many years. Remarkably creative

---

[32] Randall Collins, *The Sociology of Philosophies, op. cit.,* pp. 623ff.

[33] With regard to Britain, for example, Gordon Graham, professor of philosophy in the University of Aberdeen, has spoken of 'one huge and glaring omission, one topic and context in which academics have signally failed to engage in critical thought and for the most part shown themselves sadly lacking in independence of mind. I mean the subject of the university itself.' – 'Intellectual Values and the Knowledge Economy' (Paper delivered to the conference 'Changing Societies, Changing Knowledge', Selwyn College, Cambridge, 9–10 January 2003) p. 1. Cf. Gordon Graham, *Universities. The Recovery of an Idea* (Imprint Academic, Thorverton, UK and Charlottesville, VA 2002) for an overview of recent university history in Britain.

philosophical, theological, scientific and literary networks interacted with each other. Chief among these were three.[34] One was centred in Königsberg, associated with Kant, Hamann and Herder. In 1769 when Goethe was 20 he met Herder and later found a position for Herder in Weimar. The ducal court of Weimar and the nearby university at Jena became the second centre. 'By the 1790s, Jena-Weimar had become a hotbed of rival groups, each with its own journal: Goethe and Schiller's *Die Horen,* the Romantic circle's *Athenaeum,* a little later Schelling and Hegel's *Kritisches Journal der Philosophie.*'[35] The third centre was Berlin. Fichte moved there after he was accused of atheism in Jena, and Schleiermacher, a theologian and preacher at the Prussian court, was also there. After the foundation of its university, Berlin outstripped all the others as an intellectual centre. It is crucial that this was not only about excellence in specific fields; nor was it only about interdisciplinarity; it was also about leading thinkers engaging with each other and with the government explicitly on the subject of university reform. Fichte delivered his *Lectures on the Scholar's Vocation* in 1794; and in 1808 during the French occupation his *Addresses to the German Nation* placed educational reform at the centre of his vision of future German greatness. Kant's last published work in 1798 was *The Conflict of the Faculties,* discussing the relation of the philosophy faculty (which for him included the arts, humanities, mathematics and the natural sciences as well as logic, metaphysics and ethics) to the 'higher faculties' of theology, law and medicine, and arguing for the overarching importance of the philosophy faculty as regards truth.[36] Schelling's *Lectures on the Method of University Study* were delivered in 1802–03, and Schleiermacher, Hegel and others in their circles also addressed the topic. What we see here is a discourse that was decisive

[34] Collins, *The Sociology of Philosophies op. cit.,* pp. 623ff.
[35] Ibid., p. 627.
[36] Now the philosophy faculty consists of two departments: a department of *historical cognition* (including history, geography, philology and the humanities, along with all empirical knowledge contained in the natural sciences), and a department of *pure rational cognition* (pure mathematics and pure philosophy, the metaphysics of nature and of morals). And it also studies the relation of these two divisions of learning to each other. It therefore extends to all parts of human cognition (including, from a historical viewpoint, the teachings of the higher faculties), though there are some parts (namely, the distinctive teachings and precepts of the higher faculties) which it does not treat as its own content, but as objects it will examine and criticize for the benefit of the sciences. The philosophy faculty can, therefore, lay claim to any teaching in order to test its truth, Immanuel Kant, *The Conflict of the Faculties* (1798), in *Religion and Rational Theology,* trans. and ed. Allen W. Wood and George Di Giovanni (Cambridge University Press, Cambridge, 1996), p. 256.

in shaping the University of Berlin, and which was internalized within the new university through the overarching role of a philosophical faculty that related to all disciplines. It was a discourse that embraced deep differences in politics, philosophy and religion. It led to a university that was not simply according to one person's vision, yet still had a clear conception of its identity – an identity strong enough to leave its imprint on all the leading universities of the twenty-first century.

Is there any possibility of the twenty-first century vacuum being filled in a comparable way? Many conditions would need to be fulfilled, but one essential is that there be contributions from different traditions of wisdom and understanding, each of which has risen to the challenge. Because of the comparative neglect of living religious traditions in universities, not just as subjects of study but also as sources of wisdom for the university, special challenges face the religions to contribute to the renewal of universities and the universities to enable this to happen. If the religious communities do not try to contribute when what is at stake includes matters of truth in relation to other concerns, formation of people who play key roles in society as well as in religious communities, and the appropriate uses of knowledge and know-how, then they have abdicated key responsibilities. Christianity, which played such a major role in the origins and development of universities, is particularly responsible for attempting this, and the rest of this chapter is largely about what might be involved in doing so.

Christian rethinking of the university in the university: from Berlin to Cambridge via Yale

Part One gave an account of the seven core values of the medieval university. The teachings underlying them were: God as creator of a world order accessible to human reason; human imperfection; humanity in the image of God; the appropriateness of public argument and discussion to the absoluteness of scientific truth; scientific and scholarly knowledge as a public good transcending any economic advantage it might bring; the cumulative and self-correcting process of the growth of knowledge; and the equality and solidarity of those committed to the pursuit of knowledge. Each one of those has continued to be thought through, and it is a massive task to rethink them in relation to the university too. This must be done in academically mediated ways for it to carry conviction in the university. There is no space here to develop their content, but it is crucial for each tradition that it has suitable institutional contexts in which to do that.

The University of Berlin was a renewal of the medieval model that embodied all those teachings, but with considerable innovation, not least in the nature of its religious and secular settlement. Schleiermacher, perhaps the greatest Christian thinker of the nineteenth century, managed to bring about a setting for academic Christian theology outside the sphere of official ecclesiastical control, and he also successfully resisted Fichte's conception of the monolithic university controlled by the idea of *Wissenschaft*. So in principle he opened up the university to a negotiated pluralism of irreducibly different frameworks. Yet by the time of Harnack a century later we find a Christian theology that no longer has the capacity to re-envision the university or to allow for Christianity's distinctiveness within it. In his conflict with Karl Barth one of the central issues is the *Wissenschaftlichkeit* of theology. Barth with justice accuses Harnack of imprisoning Christianity within *Wissenschaft*, not allowing it, for example, to affirm in faith what is not demonstrable according to academic historical criteria.[37]

What of Barth himself, perhaps the greatest theologian of his period, in his relationship to the university? He was deeply critical of Schleiermacher's theology, but for most of his life was a student or teacher within the German-language university system that owed so much to Schleiermacher. There is a paradox that this strongly ecclesial thinker did not do most of his theology within a church institutional setting. Nor did he try to re-envision the university. He was always uneasy within the university but, unlike Schleiermacher and Harnack, did not make a major institutional contribution to it.

It was left to Hans Frei, who was born in Berlin and went on to become perhaps Barth's most influential interpreter in the United States, to analyse the relationship of the thought of Schleiermacher, Harnack and Barth to the Berlin university model.[38] Harnack gives decisive priority to *Wissenschaft* over Christian particularity;[39] Schleiermacher treats them as autonomous equals to be correlated but not systematically integrated; Barth gives priority

---

[37]   See M. Rumscheidt (Ed.), *The Barth-Harnack Correspondence* (Cambridge University Press, Cambridge, 1972); Hans W. Frei, *Types of Christian Theology, op. cit.*, pp. 116ff.

[38]   Hans W. Frei, *Types of Christian Theology, op. cit.* especially Chapters 4 and 6, Appendix A and Appendix B.

[39]   Yet it is striking that Harnack 'played a leading role in the rejection of the proposal to transform the faculty of theology into a faculty or department of the science of religion' (Frei, ibid., p. 116). One of his reasons was that 'departments of religion encourage dilettantism' (ibid.). The alternative to a religion department in danger of dilettantism is one which takes a range of religions seriously in their full particularity and allows for both critical and constructive engagement with them in a setting that enables fundamental dispute – what is described below as theology and religious studies.

to Christian particularity but still engages in *ad hoc* correlation in ways that bring various academic disciplines into play. The question between Barth and the university is whether such a distinctively Christian theology can be accommodated within the Berlin paradigm without the latter protesting (which Harnack did in its name) that the integrity of its *Wissenschaft* is being violated. In fact, Berlin and other German universities have proved hospitable to Barth-like theologies, however much it is intrinsic to their advocates to be suspicious of the institution that houses them. Schleiermacher's eclectic settlement has proved its ability to embrace in academic freedom very different types of theology. It has been a continuation of what I described in Part One (there with reference to the medieval university) as a higher level integration creating institutional space for fundamental dispute.

Yet Frei wrote in Yale, a very different university setting. It has a seminary, Yale Divinity School, and a very separate graduate School of Religion. This represents a deep division in American academic life between what is often called theology (tradition-specific religious thought, constructive as well as critical) on the one hand, and, on the other hand, religious studies (the study through various academic disciplines of various religions as phenomena without allowing constructive discourse by participants in them upon questions of their truth, beauty or practice). He himself tried to bridge the divide, partly by his study and practice of hermeneutics and partly by relating his own theology more to the social sciences than to philosophy. He also attempted, without much success, to bring the two Yale institutions closer – trying, in my terms, to provide institutional space for fundamental dispute. This was the setting that helped to sharpen his perception of the tensions inherent in the Berlin settlement.

Yale is wrestling with a problem that individual German universities have mostly avoided. The classic form of the Berlin model in the area of religion is to have scholarly and theological engagements with Protestant and Roman Catholic Christianity alone, and some German universities have separate faculties for these. This made some sense as a settlement relating to the position of religion in nineteenth-century Germany, but it has grave problems in the twenty-first century. At present theology is mostly still divided along lines arising from the sixteenth century Reformation, while some German universities have developed 'science of religion' or 'history of religions' approaches (an equivalent to what in the Anglo-American universities is called the study of religion or religious studies) which are rooted in the Enlightenment and the nineteenth century. Yale juxtaposes these two strands, with the difference that its Divinity School embraces a broad range of mainstream Christian traditions. It recognizes the desirability of doing justice to Christian particularity and to a range of other religions.

This might be seen as a settlement suited to America until roughly the last quarter of the twentieth century, but since that time the thinking that Yale itself has produced has pointed up its problematic aspects.[40] On the one hand, if one tradition, Christianity, is encouraged within a non-confessional university to develop its theology and practice in both critical and constructive ways, why not encourage an analogous academic engagement with Judaism, Islam, Hinduism and others rather than having them only considered under the heading of 'religious studies'? On the other hand, why divide just one tradition, Christianity, between the Divinity School and the School of Religion? Is there any academic rationale, other than limiting 'academic' to something like a Fichtean concept of *Wissenschaft,* for the institutional separation of theology and religious studies in a university setting? Or might it be possible to work out something analogous to Schleiermacher's Berlin settlement, but now accommodating not only one religious tradition but several?

That is in fact the general direction of piecemeal reforms over many years in a number of universities in various countries, especially in Britain: to combine 'theology and religious studies' in order to be able to engage with matters of wisdom, truth and practice as well as meaning within the various traditions. In a religious and secular society one can plausibly make a case for a secular university or for a religious university, but it would seem to be irresponsible not to have some universities that are 'religious (or interfaith) and secular', on condition that both sets of traditions are academically mediated in appropriate ways.[41]

The ethos of an interfaith and secular university

In such a setting it is important to have an academic department focused on theology and religious studies that can take account of the religious and the secular in a way that allows for wisdom, truth and practice. But it is even more important that this be the ethos of the whole university with regard to the religions. It might then become an example of the public space Jeffrey Stout envisages (see above), where participants can draw on religious commitments and traditions and explore differences 'deeply and respectfully without losing one's integrity as a critical intellect'. Within such

---

[40]   Cf. Hans Frei, but especially David Kelsey, in particular *Between Athens and Berlin: The Theological Education Debate* (Eerdmans, Grand Rapids, MI, 1993).
[41]   For a discussion of what is involved in this see David F. Ford, Ben Quash and Janet Martin Soskice, *Fields of Faith: Theology and Religious Studies for the Twenty-First Century* (Cambridge University Press, Cambridge, 2005).

an environment it is possible to imagine the conversations, deliberations and negotiations occurring that might lead to wise reform and renewal of universities, alert to the fundamental goals and key current issues of universities and also to the richest available religious and secular understandings.

If the origins of the University of Berlin are paralleled, the most creative thinking is likely to be done in small groups that engage intensively with each other. Desirable elements in the ethos of such groups include willingness to offer insights from one's own particular field while also engaging across the boundaries of it, both giving and receiving intellectual hospitality; sufficient trust to risk developing ideas about big topics that transcend anyone's field; recognition that this is an exercise aimed at wisdom, by whatever names it may be called, and needs to take into account the long term intellectual and social environment of the civilization within which universities with a global reach are set; trying to embody in the process and ethos of discussion something of the quality that is desired in the reformed university; and devoting time and energy to a project that is hard to categorise in a time allocation survey and needs to take as long as the complex task requires – which may be many years.[42]

---

[42] Mike Higton's University of Exeter 2004 Boundy Lectures *Thinking about the University* (unpublished) make a perceptive plea for such elements. In the third lecture, 'Being a University', Higton makes a well-argued case for university-wide conversations:

> If we are serious about being a learning institution – about *being a university* – then we need to ask about the kinds of conversation which hold the whole University together. Not simply the individual and – let's face it – still peripheral conversations which occasionally flicker between one School and another, but the question of what kind of conversation we're involved in as a whole. And the frightening thing is, I'm not sure it makes much sense to try to describe the University that way. I'm not sure there's *anything* much approaching a common conversation. In conversational terms, we're not a *university,* we're a polyversity (even if not yet, I think, a polytechnic): all too much of the time we're a group of very disparate disciplines working in mutual isolation, united more by bureaucratic procedures and by financial constraints than by any form of conversation. So, as well as needing interdisciplinary conversation in order to deepen the forms of learning in which we are involved, I want to suggest that we are in desperate, desperate need of cross-university conversation, and that we are in desperate need of a cross-university conversation that is actually one which might shape our learning – in ways other than bureaucratic. And, as far as I can see, there is only one candidate for such a conversation – only one field of inquiry in which all of our disciplines have some kind of stake, some kind of interest. And that, speaking very broadly, is *ethics.* If I can put it this way, all of our disciplines have some kind of stake in thinking about the common good – whether it be thinking about the ends our work serves, or about the good of the society we're in, or about the flourishing of our students and staff, or about their responsibilities (pp. 65f. of unpublished typescript). By 'the University' Higton means the University of Exeter.

Participants in such conversation are likely to be inspired to engage more deeply with their own tradition as well as with others. The intellectual benefits of this for Christianity are potentially considerable, as they have been in many past encounters across boundaries. The opportunities for prophetic wisdom are also considerable, not least in dealing with perhaps the most fundamental challenge to universities today: the commodification of knowledge and education, as higher education becomes a globalized business. This may be the key difference between the Berlin model and the twenty-first century world class university: Berlin was national, funded by the state and, in its religious even more than its secular dimensions, serving the state's interest. Berlin itself suffered traumas through two ideological takeovers, by National Socialism and by Communism. But now it is not so much the domination of nation, race or class that pose the threat but money and the requirements of the global economy. What is Christian wisdom on that? There are no ready-made or easily found answers to this or the other pressing questions confronting universities, and it is very unlikely that they will be worked out (let alone realized) by Christians alone or by any other group alone. Mike Higton may be right in seeing the imperative for cross-university conversation being driven above all by the need for ethical discernment.[43]

Stanley Fish was quoted at the opening of Part One saying that, after high theory, race, gender and class, religion is becoming the new centre of intellectual energy in the academy. This, if true, is not necessarily good news, and he may also have missed the significance of money and money-making. But I have tried to show in this chapter that by taking religion seriously, to the extent even of conceiving themselves as 'interfaith and secular', universities have the opportunity to enrich the wisdom on which they can draw at a pivotal time in their history, to redress an imbalance in their over-secularized 'ecology', and to fulfil a responsibility both towards a fascinating field of thought and study and towards a twenty-first century world in which, for better and for worse, the religions are likely to continue to be widely and deeply formative.

[43] See previous note.

Part IV

THEOLOGICAL
INTERPRETATION OF
THE BIBLE

Chapter Eight

DIVINE INITIATIVE, HUMAN RESPONSE, AND WISDOM: INTERPRETING 1 CORINTHIANS CHAPTERS 1–3

The topic of divine initiative and human response is vast, and is related to most *loci* of Christian theology, in particular many that have provoked most controversy. In relation to one key sub-theme in the topic, that of grace (as one term for God's initiative), Christoph Schwoebel indicates its scope:

> In the Christian tradition 'grace' sums up the relationship of the triune God with creation. It depicts this relationship as grounded in the freedom of God's love and as directed towards the perfecting of God's communion with creation. Since God overcomes the contradiction of his will by sin and evil, grace includes God's judgement on sin for the benefit of the sinner. Christian doctrine, worship, and life are shaped in all their dimensions by the way in which grace is understood. Since the concept of grace determines our understanding of divine action and its relationship to human action it is a highly contentious concept. The history of Christian doctrine and pastoral practice could well be written as a history of debates on the interpretation of grace.[1]

---

[1] 'Grace', in *The Oxford Companion to Christian Thought*, ed. Adrian Hastings, Alistair Mason and Hugh Pyper (Oxford University Press, Oxford, 2000), p. 276. In this entry Schwoebel helpfully describes the history of the debates, including those between Augustine and Pelagius, Thomists and Scotists, Protestant Reformers and the Council of Trent, Calvinists and Arminians, Jansenists and Jesuits, and Enlightenment 'autonomy' and twentieth-century Christian theologians such as Tillich, Barth, Kueng and Rahner. The latter part of the story includes a great deal of agreement between Protestants and Roman Catholics on matters that have deeply divided them.

In this chapter I will take the opening chapters of 1 Corinthians as my way into this huge and complex topic. My ideal is threefold.[2]

First, I want to attempt a fresh reading of the chapters in relation to divine initiative and human response.

Second, I do not want to pretend that 'freshness' means ignoring the fact that the chapters have been read by many others century after century, just as the theme of divine initiative and human response has been thought through repeatedly in the history summarized by Schwoebel. There can be no 'innocent' reading of this text, and the best antidote to inappropriate preunderstandings is to try to be as aware as possible of the history of the reception of this text and of the doctrinal disputes. That could be a lifetime's labour, but fortunately there are some who have already devoted years to it. Of these, I will take as my main accompaniment the massive commentary by Thiselton.[3] Several reasons make this an attractive aid: it is recent; it summarizes a huge amount of previous scholarship and theology; it pays attention to the reception of the letter in Christian theology over the centuries (both in the course of commenting on specific verses and in separate excursuses on each section of the letter);[4] and its author is not only a perceptive commentator on the text according to contemporary practices in the 'guild' of New Testament scholars but also, unusually, has a rich understanding of philosophy, hermeneutics and systematic theology. Some years ago Frances Young and I attempted a combination of translation, scholarship, hermeneutics and theology with reference to 2 Corinthians (which involved close attention to 1 Corinthians too), and the present chapter is also to be read as continuing the concerns of that study.[5] So whatever freshness might be achieved tries not to ignore what has been said already.

---

[2]   For the purposes of this short chapter I take the first three chapters somewhat arbitrarily – a more natural unit in terms of the letter would probably be the first four chapters.

[3]   Anthony C. Thiselton, *The First Epistle to the Corinthians: A Commentary on the Greek Text* (Eerdmans, Grand Rapids, MI and Cambridge, UK; Paternoster, Carlisle, UK, 2000).

[4]   Thiselton's account of the reception history of 1 Corinthians had to be abbreviated because the book was already over-long. Whether because of this or simply due to the unmanageable vastness of the task, he mostly draws on the 'usual suspects' of the theological tradition such as Origen, Athanasius, Augustine, Aquinas, Luther, Calvin, Barth. This is helpful, but also serves to whet the appetite for a fuller account that might draw more than he does on lesser known biblical commentators and theologians; on those who have used the letter in ethics and spirituality, in meditations, in liturgy, and in hymns, poetry and other arts; and on a range of different ecclesial traditions.

[5]   Frances M. Young and David F. Ford, *Meaning and Truth in 2 Corinthians* (SPCK, London 1987; Eerdmans, Grand Rapids, MI, 1988). The chapters on the economy of God, Paul's authority, and God in 2 Corinthians are most relevant to the present discussion.

The third ideal is at least to indicate what it might be like not just to interpret what Paul wrote but to take his letter as a formative contribution to doing theology today. This involves going beyond his plain sense and becoming as deeply immersed in scriptures, in the practice of Christian faith, and in contemporary events in our time as he was in his. It is not just about saying what Paul said but doing something analogous to what he did, as he simultaneously and intensively grappled with scriptures (usually the Septuagint), the Gospel, God, his vocation, the shaping of Christian communities in a largely unsympathetic world, and the immediate urgencies of community living.

A Classic Illustration

The first three chapters of 1 Corinthians are an excellent example of a text that can be used to support classic mainstream Christian affirmations about the relation of God to human beings.

The chapters are utterly theocentric, with the word 'God' not only frequently mentioned but often in an emphatic position. The priority of God's initiative is insistently repeated.[6] The greeting opens by attributing Paul's calling as an apostle of Christ Jesus to 'the will of God' and ends with 'grace to you and peace from God our Father and the Lord Jesus Christ' (1: 3). There is then a thanksgiving 'because of the grace of God that has been given you in Christ Jesus' (1: 4), attributing their gifts, faithfulness, and calling to God. I will have more to say later about 1: 17–25 on the cross, but one thing is very clear: Paul takes it as the pivotal divine initiative. It is 'the power of God', used by God to make 'the wisdom of the world' foolish and to save those who believe. The Corinthian Christians, not many of whom were of high status, are seen as owing everything to God's choice of them, and 1: 30–31 sums up this divine initiative and the corresponding call to human recognition of it: 'He is the source of your life in Christ Jesus, who became for us wisdom from God, and righteousness and sanctification and redemption, in order that, as it is written, "Let the one who boasts, boast in the Lord"'. The following two chapters continue this radical emphasis on divine initiative. Paul's original proclamation to them is described as given 'not with plausible words of wisdom, but with a demonstration of the Spirit and of power, so that your faith might rest not on human wisdom but on the power of God' (2: 4–5).

---

[6] E.g. 1: 1, 3, 4, 8, 9, 18, 21, 24, 27–31; 2: 5, 7, 9, 10, 12; 3: 6, 7, 9, 10.

This then leads into contrasting with human wisdom the wisdom of God, whose priority is seen in having been 'decreed before the ages' (2: 7), and whose depths are searched out by 'the Spirit that is from God' (2: 12) that teaches believers. Chapter 3 works out the initiative of God in ministry in the church, and phrase after phrase drives home the point: 'the Lord assigned to each' (3: 5), 'God gave the growth' (3: 6), it is 'only God who gives the growth' (3: 7), 'we are God's servants . . . ; you are God's field, God's building' (3: 9), 'according to the grace of God given to me . . .' (3: 10), 'you are God's temple' (3: 16). The chapter's climactic accumulation of possessives explicitly wraps up everything ($\pi\acute{\alpha}\nu\tau\alpha$) in relation to God: 'For all things are yours, whether Paul or Apollos or Cephas or the world or life or death or the present or the future – all belong to you, and you belong to Christ, and Christ belongs to God' (3: 21b–23).

If one then looks through these chapters seeking indicators of human response they are equally fruitful. In the greeting the saints 'call upon the name of the Lord' (1: 2), the thanksgiving shows the Corinthians exercising gifts of speech and knowledge, and waiting for the revealing of Jesus Christ. The rest of the letter, beginning with 1: 10, 'Now I appeal to you . . .', is a plea for the Corinthians, with their divisions and other problems, to respond in line with the gospel that Paul proclaimed. In these chapters there is a particular concern about right and wrong boasting: right boasting recognizes the priority of God; wrong boasting takes the credit for oneself through human wisdom, power or status. Paul gives his way of proclaiming the gospel as an example of aiming at a faith that rests 'not on human wisdom but on the power of God' (2: 5). There are two specially vivid examples of the combining of divine initiative and human response, the first more cognitive, the second more in activity. In Chapter 2 there is the wisdom that God reveals through the Spirit 'so that we may understand the gifts bestowed on us by God' (2: 12). In Chapter 3 the initiative of God noted above elicits ministry variously described in the metaphors of planting, watering, and building, and there are rewards according to the work done.[7]

---

[7]   There are various points in these passages where questions of translation and/or interpretation are closely bound up with issues to do with the relationship of divine initiative to human response. I find Thiselton's handling of each of these cases convincing. For example, he emphasizes the non-immanence of the Holy Spirit in human beings in 2: 10–16; and his translation of θεοῦ γάρ ἐσμεν συνεργοί (3: 9) is 'for we are fellow labourers who belong to God', in preference to more synergistic renderings such as 'we are labourers together with God' (AV), 'we are God's fellow workers' (New American Standard Bible), or 'we are God's co-workers' (New American Bible).

The above two-sided analysis can easily be thematized with reference to classic theological discussions and a range of problems about God's grace and human freedom generated from it. Paul here exemplifies (and of course was a crucial inspiration for) basic doctrinal issues that were continually debated over the centuries. The lessons I would draw from these chapters read in the context of the rest of scripture and the history of Christian theology would include the following: God is so radically and comprehensively originative that divine agency is not in the same category as human agency;[8] this means that they should not be seen as competitive on the same level, and many of the apparent problems and contradictions are due to inadequate understanding of this – Karl Rahner's neat summary of this principle of non-competition is that human freedom increases in direct ratio to involvement with God's free self-giving.[9] The practical outcome is that human agency is best when it simultaneously recognizes its utter dependence on God's grace and also is responsively active in calling on God, thanking God, boasting in God, exercising gifts of God, and so on. The other side of human agency is that it can go badly wrong – for example, by wrong boasting, failing to acknowledge God's priority in practice, and trusting inappropriately in human wisdom, status and leaders. Paul's own letter, with its passionate appeal to the Corinthians to respond in certain ways, is itself evidence against any conception of divine initiative that is predestinarian, predeterminative, or otherwise appears to eliminate the significance of human responsibility – he is equally insistent on both God's comprehensive priority and the urgency of the Corinthian response.

A further refinement comes through examining how the chapters not only differentiate the divine from the human in non-competitive ways but also unite them, reidentifying each in the process. Jesus Christ is the obvious key to this. His name is linked time and again as closely as possible with

---

[8] This involves discussions of the meaning of God's transcendence and of the nature of language. 'Agency' is not a category within which both 'divine initiative' and 'human response' can be embraced, since agency is only analogously predicated of God – or, alternatively, if God's agency is taken as definitive, it is only analogously predicated of human beings.

[9] Karl Rahner, *Foundations of Christian Faith* (Darton, Longman and Todd, London, 1978), p. 79; cf. in American theology the brilliant analysis by Kathryn Tanner in *God and Creation in Christian Theology: Tyranny or Empowerment?* (Blackwell, Oxford, 1988).

God.[10] Simultaneously he is linked as closely as possible with believers. They are 'in Christ' (1: 2, 4, 30; 3: 1), they call on his name (1: 2), they are in his fellowship (1: 9), they are being saved through the message of his cross (1: 18, 21–3); Christ is to them God's power (1: 24), wisdom (1: 24, 30), righteousness, sanctification and redemption (1: 30); they 'have the mind of Christ' (2: 16), their church is built on the foundation of Jesus Christ (3: 11), and they 'belong to Christ' (3: 23). In terms of later doctrine, the 'grammar' of this double connection recalls the Chalcedonian identification of Jesus Christ with God and with humanity. But Chalcedon was also integral to the development of Trinitarian doctrine, and the Spirit of God too plays a vital part in these chapters. The Spirit of God is manifest in Paul's proclamation as 'a demonstration of the Spirit and of power' (2: 4). God's depths are searched by his Spirit, and through his Spirit he reveals hidden wisdom and teaches believers to 'understand the gifts bestowed on us by God' (2: 12–13), resulting in them having 'the mind of Christ' (2: 16). Believers are God's temple, indwelt by God's Spirit (3: 16).

So, through reference to Jesus Christ and the Spirit of God, there is a reidentifying of God through revelation and also a reidentifying transformation of those humans who are believers.

The decisive, distinctive focus of this double reidentification is the cross of Christ. It is the core of Paul's proclamation (2: 2), and has implications for understanding all the key terms mentioned already. It does not make sense to 'the wisdom of the wise' (1: 19) and redefines wisdom. It also redefines power, so that the whole notion of God's initiative needs to be thought through with reference to the weakness of the cross (1: 18, 24–5): a divine initiative that is subject to human initiative. It turns human standards of wisdom, power, and status upside down in the church (1: 26–31). It contradicts the use of manipulative means of communication and argument

---

[10]   For example, 1: 1: '. . . apostle of Christ Jesus by the will of God . . .'; 1: 2–3: 'To the church of God that is in Corinth, to those who are sanctified in Christ Jesus . . . who in every place call on the name of our Lord Jesus Christ, both their Lord and ours: grace to you and peace from God our Father and the Lord Jesus Christ'; 1: 4: 'I give thanks to my God always for you because of the grace of God that has been given you in Christ Jesus . . .'; 1: 9: 'God is faithful; by him you were called into the fellowship of his Son, Jesus Christ our Lord'; 1: 23–4: '. . . we proclaim Christ crucified . . . Christ the power of God and the wisdom of God'; 1: 30–31: '[God] is the source of your life in Christ Jesus, who became for us wisdom from God, and righteousness and sanctification and redemption, in order that, as it is written, "Let the one who boasts, boast in the Lord"'; 2: 1–2: '. . . I did not come proclaiming the mystery of God to you in lofty words or wisdom. For I decided to know nothing among you except Jesus Christ, and him crucified'; 2: 16: '"For who has known the mind of the Lord so as to instruct him?" But we have the mind of Christ'; 3: 23: '. . . and you belong to Christ, and Christ belongs to God'.

in proclaiming the Gospel (1: 17; 2: 1–5). It is nothing less than 'God's wisdom, secret and hidden, which God decreed before the ages for our glory' (2: 7), so that it shapes the understanding of God and all reality, with implications that are endlessly rich; and living in accordance with its implications is the key mark of being spiritual (πνευματικός – 2: 13, 15; 3: 1) and having 'the mind of Christ' (2: 16).

Why is That Unsatisfactory?

That approach (which could be developed at great length) has its value, but is also unsatisfactory.

Basic theological doctrines must draw on a wide range of scriptural and other texts and factors in order to be convincing, and one advantage of what has been done in the previous section is that it allows these three chapters of 1 Corinthians to play a minor role in contributing to the long-running debate about divine initiative and human response and to related doctrinal issues in Christology, the doctrine of the Trinity, pneumatology and salvation. It is easy to dismiss such use of the text on the basis of the considerations to be discussed below, but its value also needs to be recognized. The need to coordinate a range of texts makes sober sense in arriving at balanced overall judgements. Concern for the 'ecology' of Christian understanding as a whole may mean that interesting things about specific 'plants' or 'micro-environments' are ignored. Or, to change the metaphor, if a text is used to illustrate the 'grammar' of divine–human relations then a good deal of its richness may necessarily be ignored. An important issue in Christian theology is how valuable such 'ecological' or 'grammatical' exercises are, and how they respond to the points raised in the rest of this section. Crudely stated, the previous section exemplifies a typical use of scripture in doctrinal or systematic theology when faced with a general topic such as 'divine initiative and human response'; but it also easily exasperates scripture scholars, historians, students of literature and rhetoric, hermeneuticists, sociologists, psychologists, certain constructive theologians, and those concerned with contemporary Christian practice and spirituality.

What are some of the reasons for their dissatisfaction? Primarily, that their contributions are ignored. I will now attempt a brief (and therefore not very refined) indictment on their behalf. The previous section moved from a plain sense reading of the chapters (mainly requiring philological knowledge) to conclusions about the topic, making reference beyond the text principally to the tradition of Christian doctrinal theology. This process of abstraction from the plain sense of the text in order to answer a general question did not ask about the original context of the chapters in the first-century Hellenistic world, in the life of the Corinthian church or in Paul's other letters. The history of the period in which it was written seemed irrelevant, as also were the identities, psychologies and other characteristics of the author and the readers. As regards the text of 1 Corinthians, its genre was not an issue, and neither was its relationship to rhetorical conventions or philosophical traditions. Its intertextual relations with the writings it quotes as scripture (especially the text of the Septuagint) did not affect the interpretation offered. The letter is clearly one part of a dramatic engage-ment between Paul and the Corinthian Christians, but the particularity of the drama was of no interest except as material for statements illustrating general conclusions about divine–human relations. Even the final two para-graphs, with their comments on the reidentifying of divine and human participants and on the radical implications of the cross, seem to be domes-ticated within classic doctrines or left hanging with plenty of possible implications but none worked through. Overall, the dense particularity of the text in context has been thinned into becoming something like a proof text for theological concepts, and any potential for application in new his-torical circumstances is unfulfilled. Even the millennia-long Christian tradi-tion during which the text was repeatedly interpreted and applied in diverse ways has been thinned to certain orthodox doctrinal conclusions without regard for their context and development. In short, justice has not been done to the triple particularity of scripture, tradition and life today.

A Constructive Suggestion: Doctrine as Wisdom

Is it possible to do justice to that triple particularity and also to the need for more general statements that attempt to cover such a range and make such interconnections that they are inevitably 'thin' in relation to the 'thick-ness' of each particular? Or, in the jargon of information technology, is it possible to combine 'richness' with 'reach'?[11] Given the description of ele-ments above, I would make the following constructive suggestion.

Theology at its best is an attempt to discern and draw on the wisdom of scripture and of tradition in ways that contribute to wise understanding and living before God today. The long tradition of Christian thought about divine initiative and human response is one example of such an attempt,

---

[11] For a discussion of richness, reach and related concepts see Philip Evans and Thomas Wurster, *Blown to Bits: How the New Economics of Information Controls Strategy* (Harvard Business School Press, Boston, 2000).

and one should not underestimate the contribution of rigorous conceptual thought. Yet it inevitably abstracts from scripture, tradition and life in order to make its general statements. This is dangerous if one forgets the vital connection of the statements with the triple particularity. It only stays healthy if that vital connection is continually nourished by fresh engagement with that particularity. The previous section rightly criticized the section above it for failing to engage thoroughly enough with each of the three particularities. That sets the challenge for the rest of this chapter: to indicate, at least illustratively, how, in relation to 1 Corinthians 1–3, the understanding of divine initiative and human response can be enriched by taking fuller account of the particularities.

Enrichments

The four illustrations to be offered will all relate to the theme of wisdom: first, exploring the meaning of wisdom in 1 Corinthians and trying to face its challenge today; second, seeing Paul's interpretation of scripture in line with this; third, trying to learn a wisdom of unity and peacemaking from Paul's way of engaging with the Corinthians; and fourth, asking about contemporary analogies of the Corinthian community as a fellowship of 'nothings' (τὰ μὴ ὄντα, 1: 28) who are a sign of the wisdom of God.

Wisdom and its challenge

Is 1 Corinthians anti-intellectual? That is an important question in relation to divine initiative and human response. Its language, strongly contrasting divine and human wisdom and their forms of communication,[12] can easily be (and often is) interpreted as rejecting the use of human intelligence and

---

[12]   For example, 1: 17 '. . . to proclaim the gospel, not with eloquent wisdom, so that the cross of Christ might not be emptied of its power'; 1: 20: 'Has not God made foolish the wisdom of the world?'; 1: 25: 'For God's foolishness is wiser than human wisdom . . .'; 1: 27: 'But God chose what is foolish in the world to shame the wise . . .'; 2: 1: 'I did not come proclaiming the mystery of God to you in lofty words or wisdom'; 2: 4–6: 'My speech and my proclamation were not with plausible words of wisdom, but with a demonstration of the Spirit and of power, so that your faith might rest not on human wisdom but on the power of God. Yet among the mature we do speak wisdom, though it is not a wisdom of this age or of the rulers of this age . . .'; 2: 13: 'And we speak of these things in words not taught by human wisdom but taught by the Spirit . . .'; 3: 19: 'For the wisdom of this world is foolishness with God'.

wisdom in matters of faith. This would mean a competitive view of human intellectual activity and divine revelation, whereas the 'Classic Illustration' above suggested a non-competitive view. Thiselton takes the problem very seriously and carefully examines the key passages and the often conflicting interpretations of them to arrive at a decisive judgement, that 'It is not wisdom as such which Paul attacks, but that which is status-seeking, manipulatory, or otherwise flawed in some way which diverts it from the purposes of God.'[13] Paul constantly strove for wise argument. His respect for reason precludes any anti-intellectualism as such.[14]

'Wisdom' (σοφία) is used by Paul in several senses,[15] the two main ones being for worldly wisdom in a negative sense and for divine wisdom. There are two major points to note in order to appreciate what he is saying.

First, everything points to him taking up the theme because it was a favourite of the Corinthians. Sixteen of the nineteen uses of σοφία in the letters undisputedly by Paul occur in 1 Corinthians 1–3 as he appeals to them to stop quarrelling and responds to the issues that divide them, among which are claims to wisdom. So he is listening carefully to what they are saying and trying to give fresh content to their terminology in a vivid, contrastive way. 'Paul wishes to redefine and thus to rescue an important term.'[16]

---

[13]   Thiselton, *The First Epistle to the Corinthians, op. cit.*, p. 165.

[14]   Ibid., p. 208. Cf. Thiselton's translation of 2.2: 'For I did not resolve to know anything to speak among you except Jesus Christ, and Christ crucified.' That is a somewhat awkward translation, but its intention is to stress the positive resolution to speak of Christ crucified:

> Whether or not he spoke of anything else would be incidental; *to proclaim the crucified Christ, and Christ alone, remains his settled policy.* He did not take a vow of excluding everything else, whatever might happen, but he did make a commitment that nothing would compromise the central place of **Christ crucified** . . . These observations, together with what we know of the rhetorical background at Corinth, release Paul of any hint of an uncharacteristic or obsessional *anti-intellectualism*, or any lack of imagination or *communicative flexibility*. His settled resolve was that he would do only what served the gospel of Christ crucified, regardless of people's expectations or seductive shortcuts to success, most of all the seduction of self-advertisement (Thiselton, *The First Epistle to the Corinthians*, pp. 211–2, emphasis in original).

See also p.149 on the value of rhetorical analyses of the letter:

> First, Paul does not despise a judicious use of the resources of trained thought in the wider world of his day. Second, this emphasis helps to counter a widespread scepticism among some church people about the extent to which Paul would give such detailed attention to words, phrases, and sentences as biblical specialists tend to suppose.

[15]   '. . . there is a different shade of meaning in the word σοφία (and σοφος) every time it occurs.' – C.K. Barrett, *Essays on Paul* (SPCK, London, 1982), p. 7.

[16]   Thiselton, *The First Epistle to the Corinthians*, p. 230.

Second, the redefinition and rescue are achieved by 'the wisdom of God', centred on the cross. This is a framework that does not make sense, is 'foolishness', within the Corinthian conception of wisdom, but that by no means implies that it is unreasonable or anti-intellectual. It is 'the mystery of God' (2: 1), 'God's wisdom, secret and hidden, which God decreed before the ages for our glory' (2: 7); it is 'What no eye has seen, nor ear heard, nor the human heart conceived, what God has prepared for those who love him' (2: 9, quoting Isaiah 64: 4, 52: 15 and Sirach 1: 10). This is the wisdom that created the human mind and everything else, and whose long-term purpose is unimaginable glory and love. This is the only framework within which the cross makes any sort of sense. It takes for granted the wisdom of Sirach, Proverbs, Isaiah, Jeremiah, and Job,[17] and in these three chapters especially uses quotations that stress the transcendent difference and unfathomability of God's wisdom over against what human beings find for themselves. There is no denial of the wisdom literature's encouragement to seek wisdom passionately; the emphasis, however, accords with that literature's more fundamental emphasis on God as the source of wisdom and therefore on right human wisdom having its beginning in 'the fear of the Lord'.[18] In Paul's letters the practical affirmation of the passion for a wisdom and understanding in line with the purposes of God is Paul's own lively intelligence – arguing, reasoning, interpreting scripture, carefully crafting language, and trying to shape a community and a way of life that realize the wisdom of God. It exemplifies the non-competitive coexistence in his scriptures of wisdom as gift of God and wisdom as actively sought by human beings in response to God's invitation and command.

The challenge of this message of the wisdom of God is therefore immense: it is to receive a radically transforming and freely offered gift that leads to appreciating the deep purposes of God; to be given the incomparable dignity of being chosen by God, having the 'mind of Christ', and being God's temple filled with God's Spirit; and to be promised a future of 'glory'. The intellectual side of that is to think in line with the purposes of God, inspired by the Spirit that 'searches everything, even the depths of God' (2: 10). That 'everything' ($\pi\acute{\alpha}\nu\tau\alpha$) recurs in 2.15,[19] and in the daring conclusion

---

[17] 1 Cor. 3: 19 is the only quotation from Job in the New Testament.
[18] In 2: 3 Paul says that he came to the Corinthians 'in fear and in much trembling', the attitude appropriate to the presence of God.
[19] 'Those who are spiritual discern all things, and they are themselves subject to no one else's scrutiny.' On the difficulties of this verse see Thiselton, *The First Epistle to the Corinthians*, pp. 271ff.

of Chapter 3.[20] Paul's 'everything' embraces God and the whole creation. How have Christians and others down the centuries taken that horizon seriously and come to wise understanding within it? Who are those besides Paul who have most to teach us as we think and live within it? What are the transformations of contemporary 'wisdom of the world' that are required? How do current Christian understanding and practice emerge from a critique that uses a framework that has freshly thought through the purposes of a God whose decisive revelation is Christ crucified? To answer such questions would be to try to do justice to the threefold particularity of scripture, tradition and life today.[21]

Paul's interpretation of scripture and its implications

Paul's interpretation of scripture is a large and complex topic, with many technical scholarly discussions about Paul's scriptural texts, his relation to Hebrew and Greek versions, his Jewish interpretive context, differentiation between Jewish-Christian and other readers of his letters, and so on.[22] For theological interpretation of Paul today this is one of the most fruitful areas if it is attempted with alertness to the threefold particularity discussed above. Paul indwells his scriptures – as Ulrich Luz says, 'For Paul, the OT is not in the first place something to understand, but it itself creates understanding'[23] – and himself writes letters that later Christians indwell as part

---

[20] 'For all things are yours, whether Paul or Apollos or Cephas or the world or life or death or the present or the future – all belong to you, and you belong to Christ, and Christ belongs to God' (3.21–23).

[21] In the immediate aftermath of Paul, if the Letter to the Ephesians is taken to be not by Paul but by someone trying to distil his thought for the next generation, Ephesians is a model of creative development of the tradition as regards wisdom. The wisdom of God's purposes gathering up 'everything in heaven and on earth' in Christ is set out right at the beginning of the letter as its horizon (Chapter 1, especially vv. 8–10; and note the prayer that follows in which the first request is for 'a spirit of wisdom and revelation . . .', v. 17); the cross is pivotal and is applied especially to the fundamental issue of the relation of Jews to Gentiles (Chapter 2); in Chapter 3 the proclamation of the Gospel by Paul is again linked to 'all things' and 'the wisdom of God' (vv. 9–10); and in Chapters 4–6 a stream of practical wisdom is offered to the recipients. For my reading of this in relation to a contemporary understanding, see David F. Ford, *Self and Salvation: Being Transformed* (Cambridge University Press, Cambridge, 1999), especially Chapter 5.

[22] Cf. D. Moody Smith, 'The Pauline Literature', in D. A. Carson and H.C.M. Williamson (eds), *It is Written: Scripture Citing Scripture* (Cambridge University Press, Cambridge, 1988), pp. 265–91.

[23] Quoted in Thiselton, *The First Epistle to the Corinthians*, p. 160.

of a canon that also includes his own scriptures. How one interprets scripture wisely within the horizon of the purposes of God and God's relation to 'everything' is perhaps the core issue for theology. That horizon itself makes any limiting of interpretation to 'what Paul meant at the time he wrote' arbitrary and unwise. What he wrote itself invites and even necessitates going through and beyond the 'plain sense' in his context in order to seek a 'wisdom sense' such as the present chapter is attempting to illustrate.

The seeking of this wisdom sense has implications for how divine initiative and human responsibility are understood. Much controversy, past and current, over such matters as scriptural revelation, the inspiration and authority of scripture, literal and other senses of scripture, and fundamentalism, is deeply related to conceptions of God's initiative and human response. The very notion of a community actively seeking a wisdom sense through ever-fresh engagement with scripture, tradition and contemporary understanding and life is problematic for those who think they have less mediated, less complex, less messy, less risky, less intellectually demanding, less 'human', and more clear and reliable ways of understanding scripture in order to arrive at the mind of Christ or the will of God for us now.

Towards a wisdom of unity

The chief practical concern of Paul in 1 Corinthians is the health and unity of a divided Christian community. His main strategy is to call them to go deeper into the heart of the gospel and to conform themselves to 'the mind of Christ' that is found there, a mind that is contradicted by their dissension. An immense amount could be said about this as a wisdom of unity, but I only want to draw attention to one dimension of what he does in the letter.

As already mentioned, he takes the terminology and concerns of the Corinthians and works intensively with them to produce an original reformulation of the gospel in terms of 'weak power' and 'foolish wisdom'. It is itself a rich and still provocatively relevant formulation, but as part of a wisdom of unity it may be just as important to learn how to do the sort of thing Paul was doing rather than just appreciate what he said in that context. What he did was to try to communicate with them in accordance with 'the mind of Christ', which entailed vulnerability (approaching them 'in weakness' – 2: 3), dealing with them on their terms, refusing manipulative techniques, and appealing passionately to them. There are of course many suspicious interpretations of Paul as exercising his authority (not least through using appeals to weakness) manipulatively and oppressively,[24] but if they are not found convincing then it is possible to read 1 Corinthians 1–3 as a gospel-informed practice of peacemaking. Studying the drama of his relationship with the Corinthians – and even trying to sort out the very different reconstructions of it – greatly enriches the sense of the significance and complexity of this practice. The very impossibility of being sure when Paul is quoting the Corinthians and when he is responding to them is a sign of how successful he has been at entering into their mind-set and taking seriously what they say.

Immersion in these particularities is the most promising way through to a wisdom that is likely to be expressed in maxims about, for example, going deeper into what is shared; close and critical attention to language and methods of persuasion; the combined importance of perceptive description, grateful appreciation, and confrontation; the vital role of the overarching framework; and the ability to enter vulnerably into the thought-world of the other.[25] The maxims are worth distilling, but these only remain living wisdom if they are constantly referred back to their drama of origin, and on to the later dramas of history and those we are part of today. The wisdom is not only in the maxims but it is in the maxims as ways of remembering and continually learning from the contingencies of history (whose interrelated particularities never recur but can be learnt from), and also as ways of helping to repair and redeem the present in the interests of a better future. Scholarly insights such as those into Paul's way of working through the Corinthians' terminology help to understand the quality of his wisdom and give a density and detail that can inspire analogous responses in other situations.

Again, as with the interpretation of scripture, there is mediation through the difficulties of the text and the complexities of history that has implications for the way divine initiative and human response are conceived. If God does not insist on his own terms but takes initiatives in richly and sensitively responsive ways (why, for example, do we habitually give priority to God's speech over God's listening?), then many conceptions of scripture,

---

[24]   For a discussion of Paul's authority and its critics see Young and Ford, *Meaning and Truth in 2 Corinthians, op. cit.*, pp. 207–34.

[25]   'Maxim' is chosen as a term that suggests a distillation of wisdom and avoids claims to inappropriate precision. The vagueness of a maxim is an advantage, allowing it to play a pivotal role in mediating between particularities: it is always open to further specification in relation to new texts and contexts. As suggested above, many problems in Christian doctrine are caused if its general statements are reified as precise knowledge claims rather than understood as maxims distilled from the triple particularity of scripture (and its contexts), tradition (and its contexts) and contemporary understanding and life (and their contexts) – maxims that require continually renewed engagement with those particularities if they are to remain living wisdom.

doctrine and the powerful agency of God need to be revised, as do also many ways of seeking unity and peace.

God chose the 'nothings'

More fundamental than the disunity and other problems of the Corinthian Christians was the amazing fact of them being called by God 'into the fellowship of his Son, Jesus Christ our Lord' (1: 9). It is especially amazing because God chose the 'foolish', the 'weak', the 'low and despised', the 'nothings' of the world (1: 27–8). The social composition and dynamics of the Corinthian church have been extensively studied and speculated about.[26] I would argue that the ultimate purpose in doing this is to increase in

---

[26]   For a fairly recent bibliography and an interpretation of 1: 26–31 see Thiselton, *The First Epistle to the Corinthians*, pp. 175–96; for an earlier summary and interpretation of the sociological and historical approaches see Chapter 7 'Church and Society in Corinth' in Frances Young and David F. Ford, *Meaning and Truth in 2 Corinthians*, pp. 186–206. That chapter concludes about such approaches that they

> . . . may lead one in a reductionist direction, or they may illustrate the incarnational nature of the gospel, always inextricable from particular conditioned situations. But they certainly call in question some ways of using the letters in theology. A gospel about a person involved in ordinary physical existence to the point of death, and which is then maintained through his 'body' in history in ways that include travels, dangers, arguments and money as well as forgiveness and hope in God – this is not likely to be done justice to by a theology which, for example, abstracts truth content from historical particularity or locates primary experience of God in the interiority of immediate consciousness. An essential ingredient for an adequate interpretation and theology must be social and cultural understanding, informed by the particularities of the Bible, history and tradition in order to come better prepared to the task of being faithful and innovative in the present situation.

> Peter Winch, discussing the problems faced by anthropologists trying to understand another society, concludes:

> My aim is not to engage in moralising, but to suggest that the concept of 'learning from' which is involved in the study of other cultures is closely linked with the concept of 'wisdom'. We are confronted not just with different techniques, but with new possibilities of good and evil, in relation to which men may come to terms with life. ('Understanding a Primitive Society', in *Rationality,* ed. Bryan R. Wilson (Basil Blackwell, Oxford, 1970), p. 106)

> Learning from a letter of Paul has similarities to such primitive societies, and wisdom is a good term for the sort of unsystematic, highly particular and nuanced appreciation, insight and assessment that may result. The 'hermeneutical gap' can be crossed, just as it is in the wealth of otherness and 'gaps' that make up any pluralist contemporary society, and the results of sharing in the common sense and unusual sense of another culture are not controllable or predictable (pp. 203–4).

wisdom.[27] But rather than, as in the previous three illustrations, largely focusing on 1 Corinthians and leaving the contemporary implications almost wholly in the interrogative mood, this fourth will conclude by continuing with the interrogatives but doing so through a specific contemporary community with which I am somewhat involved and which I see as a sign of God's wisdom in Paul's sense.

The L'Arche communities, in which those with and without mental disabilities live together, are now a worldwide network of over a hundred communities.[28] I do not wish to idealize them, any more than Paul idealized the Corinthian church, but 1 Corinthians 1: 26–31 has some important resonances with them. Those with severe mental disabilities come quite near to being 'nothings' in contemporary society.[29] Many people think they should not exist, and would want if at all possible to prevent this in the future by abortion. A long-term community centred on them, honouring them, and enabling them to be accompanied in their suffering, to celebrate life, to find meaning, to be respected, to make friendships, to have vocations recognized, to work and play, and to die with dignity: that does not fit in with what Paul would call the wisdom of the world. L'Arche calls into question the nature and role in our lives of health, wealth, education, status, success. It raises questions such as: How do we understand the human worth, dignity and fulfilment of ourselves and others? How do we cope with vulnerability, suffering, or death? How are power and weakness related? Whom do we value most, and why? What happens to our hearts and souls when we are opened up to friendships such as those in L'Arche? What might happen to churches, to other religions, to secular groups, or to social services if they were to learn and practise some of the wisdom being learned at L'Arche?

Most scandalous of all is L'Arche's recognition that those with disabilities are given to the world by God and blessed by him. This coexists with continuing brokenness and anguish. Many of those in L'Arche have suffered greatly, including being rejected by others as embarrassing, shameful and repulsive. Yet through all this, not only can they have gifts, vocations and love that are necessary to others; they even have a privileged role in God's purposes. To miss out on community and friendship with them is to risk

---

[27] See quotation in previous note.

[28] For a helpful introduction to the history and development of L'Arche and to the life of its founder, Jean Vanier, see Kathryn Spink, *Jean Vanier and L'Arche: A Communion of Love* (Darton, Longman and Todd, London, 1990)

[29] There are of course differences between countries and cultures, but L'Arche has not found anywhere its approach is not substantially counter-cultural.

missing God's strange way of bringing in the Kingdom of God through the weak, despised 'nothings'.

This is one sign of God's surprising, cross-centred wisdom that is analogous to what Paul found in the Corinthian church.[30] It raises similar issues about God's weak, responsive initiatives and the privileged vocations of the weak and despised whose abilities in a worldly sense leave no room for boasting.

Beyond the Categories of Initiative and Response

I hope that this chapter has shown that 1 Corinthians 1–3 has something to contribute to the discussion of divine initiative and human response. I want now to comment on some of the ways in which those chapters also complement and even qualify the very categories of initiative and response.

This should already have been apparent through the discussions above of Jesus Christ, the Spirit, wisdom and the cross. Each of those stretches and transforms the conceptuality of initiative and response, with the overall result that that pair end up seeming a rather inadequate instrument for dealing with the multifaceted richness of this text, of history, of contemporary life, and of God. It is possible to explore the stretching and transforming, as I have tried to do, pressing towards complementary concepts of divine response and human initiative, and trying to do justice to their differentiations, interrelations and simultaneities. But to what end? There can be a sense of overemphasizing one theme, and the history of bitter and often

---

[30]   The following core statement was part of the outcome of some meetings with members of L'Arche and theologians in which I took part between 1993 and the present:

> God,
> through the wisdom of the Gospel,
> meets the brokenness, anguish,
> and deepest desires of human bodies and hearts
> in a long-term community
> of mutual presence,
> service,
> and friendship.
> This is a sign of hope for all people.

For a collection of essays on L'Arche by some members of that group see *Encounter with Mystery: Reflections on L'Arche and Living with Disability,* ed. Frances M. Young (Darton, Longman and Todd, London 1997).

deadlocked disputes around it invites us to be less insistent on its centrality.

1 Corinthians 1–3 might be able to help a little further here. 'Initiative' and 'response' are primarily action words, with an accompanying implied emphasis on two distinct agents. Part of the transformative potential of the cross is that it needs to be considered in relation to suffering and death, neither of which is easily subsumed under the categories of initiative and response. Part of the transformative potential of 'wisdom' is that it is more cognitive than active in sense, and allows for a participation and sharing that need not insist on differentiation of agency. Spirit and Jesus Christ also resist being tied too closely to these categories. But besides those major qualifiers of our theme there are also some others that are less obvious. I will mention just three in conclusion.

Glory

'But we speak God's wisdom, secret and hidden, which God decreed before the ages for our glory' (2: 7). It is possible, as I did in the 'Classic Illustration' section above, to analyse this statement in terms of divine initiative and human response, and to go further and connect it to debates about predestination. But there is so much more. Glory evokes brightness, radiance, and an overflowing abundance of divine, human and natural life together, a sphere in which any competition between the divine and human is unthinkable. Here agency terms are transformed aesthetically and eschatologically.

Depths

'. . . for the Spirit searches everything, even the depths of God' (2: 10). Here is an image of immersion that similarly relativizes and supplements concepts of agency. To be given this Spirit (2: 12) and to participate in this searching is to be led to imagine oneself beyond an initiative–response framework. 'Depths' links with nature at its most overwhelming, in which we are entirely engulfed, and 'depths of God' is not about God as an agent over against us.

Belonging

Finally, there is the image of belonging. At the heart of the Corinthian problem is factionalism in which groups say: 'I belong to Paul . . . to Apollos . . . to Cephas . . . to Christ' (1: 12). Paul argues that this is against essential Christian identity in terms of the cross, the Spirit, and 'the mind of Christ' – it is 'all too human' behaviour (κατὰ ἄνθρωπον – 3: 3). But typically he takes the terminology of factionalism (in this case the idea of 'belonging' is simply the use of the genitive case – 'of Paul', 'of Apollos', and so on) and turns it around, culminating in the comprehensive statement of reality in terms of genitive relationships at the end of Chapter 3:

> So let no one boast about human leaders.[31] For all things are yours, whether Paul or Apollos or Cephas or the world or life or death or the present or the future – all belong to you, and you belong to Christ, and Christ belongs to God. (vv. 21–3)

The factional language is here outflanked, swamped, overwhelmed. Their oppositional boundaries are turned into a theological ecology of mutual belonging. This simple language (ὑμεῖς δὲ Χριστοῦ Χριστὸς δὲ θεοῦ) under-cuts beautifully any notion of competition, and it, together with 'glory' and 'depths', may offer us a salutary imaginative freedom when we become tied in knots by too single-minded a concentration on the language of initiative and response. It is, indeed, the language of love; and it is no accident that the wisdom of 1 Corinthians 1–3 leads eventually to the hymn to love in 1 Corinthians 13. And that wise follower of Paul, the author of the Letter to the Ephesians, gathered together the glory, the depths, the belonging, the Spirit, Jesus Christ, 'the power to comprehend' and 'the love of Christ that surpasses knowledge' in the prayer at the centre of the letter:

> For this reason I bow my knees before the Father, from whom every family in heaven and on earth takes its name. I pray that, according to the riches of his glory, he may grant that you may be strengthened in your inner being with power through his Spirit, and that Christ may dwell in your hearts through faith, as you are being rooted and grounded in love. I pray that you may have the power to comprehend, with all the saints, what is the breadth and length and height and depth, and to know the love of Christ that surpasses knowledge, so that you may be filled with all the fullness of God. (Eph. 3: 14–19)

---

[31] The NRSV translation here goes beyond the Greek which says 'in human persons' (ἐν ἀνθρώποις).

Conclusion: Affirmation, Critique and Transformation in Christian Doctrine and Scriptural Interpretation

This chapter has offered a reading of 1 Corinthians 1–3 suggesting conclusions about both doctrinal or systematic theology and biblical scholarship. In relation to theology it has tried both to take seriously the achievement of discussions focused on divine initiative and human response and also to offer a critique of them from the standpoint of those who engage with the threefold particularities of scripture, tradition, and contemporary life (and their contexts). One temptation of theology is to abstract from those particularities in ways that are not continually renewed, enriched and developed by them. This can lead to a petrification of theological doctrines, concepts, themes, problems, disputes, and methods. A temptation of biblical scholarship is to limit its horizon to one set of particularities, that of scriptural texts and their contexts, ignoring the summons of those very texts to engage with tradition and contemporary life, and missing the benefits of philosophical and doctrinal questioning, conceptualization and argument. I have suggested 'wisdom' as a helpful term for what is needed to supplement both. A wisdom interpretation of scripture combined with a conception of doctrine as wisdom encourages the two approaches to engage fruitfully with each other within the same horizon. But such general statements can become petrified (or even oppressive) abstractions unless they are, as has been attempted above, embodied in understanding that simultaneously draws on particular scriptures, particular doctrinal topics from the tradition, and attention to contemporary disciplines and life.

Chapter Nine

BARTH'S
INTERPRETATION OF
THE BIBLE

A student had prepared a paper on a christological issue he felt is evoked by a section of the *Church Dogmatics*. The first question was addressed to him by a peer. As frequently happens, it was in reality not a question but a charge, that he had seriously misconstrued the issue because he had misunderstood Barth's method.

The debate that ensued was as convoluted as spirited. It moved from one complex methodological issue to two others. It continued in white heat for a polarizing hour. Throughout the hour Barth peered over his spectacles (and his glasses), stroked and smoked his outsized pipe, sipped his Rhenish wine, and spoke not one word.

As the debate was beginning to move into a second hour, it suddenly occurred to one of the students that there was, as we say, a 'resource person' present, who might possibly be able to throw light on the issues and adjudicate the dispute. He turned and ricocheted the previous question to Barth.

After a full minute of heavy silence, Barth raised his head and above the welter of complex formal issues that had been strewn on the table: 'If I understand what I am trying to do in the *Church Dogmatics*, it is to listen to what Scripture is saying and tell you what I hear.'

What can be made of this simplistic, obviously heuristic ploy? I wish to suggest that it be taken seriously.[1]

To take seriously that statement and the many similar ones made by Barth in the course of his life is to take a way that leads through the whole of his theology and offers the opportunity for fruitful insights into its strengths and weaknesses. There are many other ways of understanding his work, especially the *Church Dogmatics*, as a unity, ranging from a straightforward following of Barth's own progress through the doctrines of the Word of

---

[1]   R. C. Johnson, 'The Legacy of Karl Barth', in *Reflection*, vol. 66, no. 4, May 1969, p. 4.

God, God, creation, and reconciliation, to taking the standpoint of his doctrine of the Trinity,[2] or of grace,[3] or of justification,[4] or of Christ,[5] or of the Holy Spirit.[6] There has also been an attempt to see Barth's political biography as the key to his theology and method,[7] and Richard Roberts suggests Barth's understanding of time as another pervasive and unifying theme of the *Church Dogmatics*.[8] Such diversity is necessary to illuminate Barth's rich thought, and my approach is more a supplement to others than a competitor. Yet it does have the advantage of engaging Barth over the one documentary authority which he accepted as a primary source and criterion of theology. I will try, while doing justice to his ways of arguing from scripture to theological statements, to clarify the key points at which decisions for or against his method and conclusions need to be made.

Barth's exegesis covers the whole Bible and displays a great variety of hermeneutical skills and principles, but my thesis, to be supported by the rest of this chapter, is that he uses one dominant approach which provides the structure of argument and much of the content of his whole theology. This is his interpretation of certain biblical narratives, notably the Gospels but also the creation stories and those Old Testament narratives to which he appeals in support of his doctrine of election. I shall trace this theme from his early works through the main doctrines of the *Church Dogmatics*, and I will then suggest that his procedure has much in common with literary criticism of the genre of realistic narrative. This parallel is appropriate because it throws light on Barth's distinctive insights, and helps to explain both the nature of his appeal to Scripture and his virtual lack of theological concern about historical criticism. Finally, I will raise critical questions about Barth's method.

[2]   e.g. E. Jüngel, *God's Being is in Becoming*, trans. John Webster (T&T Clark, Edinburgh, 2001).

[3]   e.g. G. C. Berkouwer, *The Triumph of Grace in the Theology of Karl Barth* (Paternoster, London, 1956).

[4]   e.g. Hans Küng, *Justification: The Doctrine of Karl Barth and a Catholic reflection, with a letter by Karl Barth* (Burns and Oates, London, 1964).

[5]   e.g. Hans Urs von Balthasar, *Karl Barth. Darstellung und Deutung seiner Theologie* (Cologne, 1962). (*The Theology of Karl Barth* (Holt, Rinehart and Winston, New York, 1971) is an abridged trans. of 1962 German edn.)

[6]   P. J. Rosato, *The Spirit as Lord – The Pneumatology of Karl Barth* (T&T Clark, Edinburgh, 1981).

[7]   F.-W. Marquardt, *Theologie und Sozialismus. Das Beispiel Karl Barths* (Kaiser Verlag, Munich, 2nd edn 1972).

[8]   R. H. Roberts, 'Barth's Doctrine of Time: Its Nature and Implications' in *Karl Barth: Studies of his Theological Methods*, ed. S. W. Sykes (Oxford University Press, Oxford, 1980), pp. 88–146.

I

Late in his life, in a rare piece of spiritual autobiography, Barth ascribed to the hymns of Abel Burckhardt, which he was taught as a child and which simply retold Gospel stories in local dialect, a naïvety in which

> there lay the deepest wisdom and the greatest power, so that once grasped it was calculated to carry one relatively unscathed – although not, of course, untempted or unassailed – through all the serried ranks of historicism and anti-historicism, mysticism and rationalism, orthodoxy, liberalism and existentialism, and to bring one back some day to the matter itself. (CD [*Church Dogmatics*] IV/2, 113)

Although Barth did little extensive interpretation of biblical narratives before writing the *Dogmatics*, this does suggest a thread worth searching for in his earlier work.

Barth's reaction against liberal theology during his pastorate in Safenwil was expressed through his new way of interpreting the Bible. His 1916 lecture 'Die neue Welt der Bibel'[9] set the tone for what was to follow, with its direct acceptance of the world of the biblical events as the revelation of God, and its insistence that the Bible interprets itself. There followed his exegesis of the Epistle to the Romans, in which this attempt to identify a hermeneutical circle within the Bible itself was focused on the two central events of the Gospel, the crucifixion and resurrection. This is true of the first and second editions of his *Epistle to the Romans*,[10] though with the major difference that in the first the emphasis is on the resurrection, whereas in the second (influenced by Overbeck, Dostoyevsky, and Kierkegaard) the paradoxical relation between the two events is stressed and 'dialectical theology' proper is born.[11] Barth's dialectical thought-form has the relation between the crucifixion and resurrection as its main exegetical basis. The crucifixion is a negation which is so radical in its judgement on everything human that time itself cannot contain the Yes of the resurrection. Between them the two events enclose the meaning of reality, the hermeneutical circle being between God's posing of the ultimate problem through the crucifixion and answering it himself in the resurrection.[12] The logic of this radical

---

[9] Eng. trans. in *The Word of God and the Word of Man* (Harper, New York, 1957).
[10] Bern, 1919, and Munich, 1922.
[11] For three meanings of 'dialectic' in Barth's thought at this time see H. Bouillard, *Karl Barth*, vol. I, *Genèse et Évolution de la Théologie Dialectique* (Aubier, Paris, 1957), pp. 73f.
[12] W. Lindemann, *Karl Barth und die kritische Schriftauslegung* (Hamburg—Bergstedt, 1973) is perceptive on this, esp. p. 30.

concentration on one story is carried through in the second edition's sustained attack on 'religion'. The main effect of this polemic is to make the very use of the word 'God' depend on that story. God is no longer someone Christians can assume they have in common with other religious people, even (or especially) within the Church. Since the crucifixion is seen to have an epistemological role in rebutting all claims to knowing God except paradoxically through itself and the resurrection, there is no longer any positive connection between the Gospel and religion or natural theology.

In the period between the second edition of the *Epistle to the Romans* and the first volume of the *Church Dogmatics* Barth's development in relation to my theme can be summed up under two headings. First, there was a move away from the expressionist style of the *Epistle to the Romans*, with its preference for non-mimetic, often mathematical imagery, towards a sober doctrine of the Word of God which more easily allows for faithful reflection (*Nachdenken* – thinking through in correspondence with what is given) of biblical narratives. This included a lessened emphasis on the 'infinite qualitative distinction' between God and humanity and more on their *relationship* through God's Word. This shift is clearly seen in the *Prolegomena zur Christlichen Dogmatik* of 1927,[13] where Barth offers a positive doctrine of God as Trinity whose Word is God himself (*Dei loquentis persona*) communicated in a historical event (*geschichtliches Ereignis* – *Chr D*, 230ff.), which is understood as revelation only through the biblical account.[14] This retreat from the paradoxes of the second edition of *Romans* led increasingly to the resurrection tone of the first edition becoming characteristic of his whole theology.

The second development was an intensification of the second edition's polemic against religion and natural theology. Barth parted company with his chief colleagues of the 'dialectical theology' group, and each break can be symbolized by an emotion-laden concept – the 'pre-understanding' (*Vorverständnis*) of Bultmann, the 'orders of creation' (*Schöpfungsordnungen*) of Gogarten, and the 'point of contact' (*Anknüpfungspunkt*) of Brunner. In each case the issue might be subsumed under the heading of natural theology, which Barth's developing doctrine of the Word of God was increasingly rigorous in excluding. The culmination of his attempts to find an autonomous basis for theology was his study of Anselm's ontological argument for God's existence. In *Fides Quaerens Intellectum, Anselms Beweis der Existenz Gottes*,[15] Barth interpreted Anselm as offering an *a posteriori* proof of God

13   C. Kaiser Verlag, Munich.
14   'Die Offenbarung steht, nein sie geschieht in der Schrift, nicht hinter ihr.' (p. 344.)
15   Munich, 1931. Eng. trans., SCM Press, London, 1960.

from his revelation.[16] This insight became the basis for Barth's exegesis which denied any vantage point outside the hermeneutical circle: God has given the proof of his own existence in his self-expression in history as told in the Bible, and so it is only the biblical stories which render his identity authoritatively.

II

Barth's doctrine of the Word of God in Volume I of the *Dogmatics* is less helpful in understanding his hermeneutics than might be expected. He engages there at great length in conceptual clarification and related polemics, with a strong emphasis on the divinity of the Word (an aspect discussed by Roman Williams).[17] This must, however, still be followed in each succeeding volume by exegesis which proves his doctrines anew from Scripture, so it is in those later volumes that he shows how he handles narratives in practice. From the point of view of hermeneutics, the two parts of the *Church Dogmatics* I are perhaps best read in retrospect when one can appreciate, for example, what Barth means by God's language being his act, how he supports his claims for the incomparability and universality of the biblical accounts, how he carries out his three operations for interpreting Scripture (observation, reflection, appropriation – see *CD* I/2, 719ff.), and, above all, the pervasive significance of his insistence that the form of revelation is inseparable from its content (e.g. *CD* I/1, 285), and that 'when the Bible speaks of revelation it does so in the form of narrating a story or series of stories' (*CD* I/1, 362).

Yet for an understanding of Barth's habitual use of Scripture his prolegomena do give one important indication: his doctrine of the Trinity. Eberhard Jüngel has given a masterful and concise account of the way in which Barth's hermeneutics and ontology coincide in this doctrine.[18] My concern, which Jüngel's study supports, is to point to the crucial fact that Barth describes the Trinity as an order in God expressed in the interrelation of crucifixion, resurrection, and Pentecost. The doctrine of the Trinity, says Barth, is a 'self-enclosed circle' (*CD* I/1, 436), and the Trinitarian God's characteristic proofs in the New Testament are indicated by Good Friday, Easter

---

[16]   See C. E. Gunton's illuminating comparison of Barth's and Hartshorne's interpretations of Anselm in *Becoming and Being: The Doctrine of God in Charles Hartshorne and Karl Barth* (Oxford University Press, Oxford, 1978).

[17]   R. Williams, 'Barth on the Triune God', in *Karl Barth: Studies of his Theological Method*, ed. S. W. Sykes (Oxford University Press, Oxford, 1980), pp. 147–93.

[18]   *Op. cit.*

and Pentecost, and accordingly His name indicated as that of the Father, the Son and the Holy Spirit (*CD* I/1, 437, cf. 380, 382, 430). This story is not simply seen as an indicator, however, for Barth insists repeatedly on identifying God in himself (*Deus in se*) with God in his revelation (*Deus revelatus*), for example: 'Revelation is of course the predicate of God, but in such a way that the predicate coincides exactly with God Himself.' (*CD* I/1, 343, cf. especially, 380.) This point is most comprehensively made by his understanding of the Trinity in terms of the *repetition* of the nature of God in three different ways. Since these ways are exclusively revealed in the events of Jesus Christ's existence (the Old Testament, as I show below, being included by typology), this inevitably gives a strong Christocentric bias to his doctrine of God.

The concentration of such immense significance in one story is an extreme case of what has been called the 'scandal of particularity' in Christian theology. In other theologians it is often softened by various forms of natural theology, but Barth devotes a section of his doctrine of the Trinity (*CD* I/1, 383ff.) to denying all claims to insight into the Trinitarian nature of God other than those appealing to 'the form which God Himself in His revelation has assumed in our language, world and humanity' (*CD* I/1, 399). So the main argument for the truth of the 'scandal' is the claim that as a matter of fact God chose to reveal himself in this unexpected but effective way. God's freedom to express himself in a particular way is therefore fundamental to Barth's conception of God. God is not primarily to be described in terms of general attributes such as omnipotence, omnipresence, justice, and so on, but these attributes have their content determined by the way in which God has in fact determined himself, as told in the Bible.

The demand that all statements about the nature of God be 'cashed' in biblical terms, and especially in terms of the Gospel's climactic events, dominates Barth's doctrine of God in the *Church Dogmatics* II/1. He says there that 'God is the One whose being can be investigated only in the form of a continuous question as to His action' (*CD* II/1, 61), and he champions the 'only' in another polemic against natural theology. Then in his account of the qualities (or perfections) of God the basic description of God as 'the One who loves in freedom' is consistently given its decisive content by reference to the story of Jesus, where the love of God is seen in what happened and the freedom of God is seen in God's own choice that it should happen in this way. As Barth says about God's omnipotence: 'we must recognize His capacity, His *potentia absoluta*, only in the capacity chosen by Him, in His *potentia ordinata*. We no longer need to reckon with the possibility that He could have acted differently' (*CD* II/1, 541). For Barth what is greatest is what God actually does, and so God's will, for example, is not infinite, for it 'fixes a sphere which it does not overstep . . . There is no outside this sphere' (*CD* II/1, 555f.). This sphere is for Barth articulated primarily by the biblical stories, which is why his exegesis and his theological statements are so tightly locked together.

Such a concentration of course threatens to 'objectify' God in history, and so Barth needs the all-pervasive affirmation of God's freedom and grace. In hermeneutical terms the function of God's freedom in his theology is to enable the biblical stories to be the all-embracing world of meaning. This is clearest in the doctrine of election, according to which God freely decides that a certain stretch of history will determine all other history by containing his own temporal self-repetition. There God's freedom answers the problem of the scandal of particularity in relation to eternity. It plays a similar role in relation to humanity, for in the Holy Spirit God chooses to address all people through one particular man, and to do this using the biblical accounts. Barth's most general expression of this freedom of God with humanity is his concept of the *analogia fidei*. His objection to natural theology and the *analogia entis* is that they try to see God's relationship to the world as structurally fixed and discernible apart from God choosing to speak. The *analogia fidei* points in contrast to the fact that God is always a free personal presence, who is there to be invoked and who uses particular analogies to give knowledge of himself in ever new events (knowledge for which the *analogia entis* searches in the nature of the analogies themselves).[19] In relation to my theme it is important that Barth insists that his use of the term 'analogy' is 'not . . . a systematic but an exegetical decision' (*CD* II/1, 227). The exegesis concerned focuses yet again on the crucifixion and resurrection. The reason why there can be no calculation of the degrees of similarity and dissimilarity of God *vis-à-vis* the world is that God freely both veils and unveils himself in his revelation, and in neither case is it a matter of quantity.[20] Rather, it is a matter of two events, the crucifixion and resurrection which take place in an 'ordered dialectic' (*CD* II/1, 236) and definitively indicate the nature of God. So Barth concludes the section in which he deals with analogy with an explicit concentration of 'the limits and the veracity of our knowledge of God' on the crucifixion and resurrection of Jesus Christ (*CD* II/1, 254). Thus his doctrine of analogy is tailored to fit this one story, and so of course repudiates more general theories; and his own generalizing is by means of the freedom of God – his fatherly freedom to express himself completely through a particular man's history, and his

[19]   Cf. E. Jüngel, 'Die Möglichkeit theologischer Anthropologie auf dem Grunde der Analogie, Eine Untersuchung zur Analogieverständnis Karl Barths', in *Evangelische Theologie*, no. 10 (Oct. 1962).
[20]   On the identification of veiling and unveiling, cf. *CD* I/1, 380.

further freedom to offer to humanity through the Holy Spirit the knowledge of this all-embracing reality.

III

What Barth offers in his doctrine of God can therefore be seen from my viewpoint as a 'metaphysics of the Gospel story', a thoroughgoing attempt to understand the eternal God through a temporal history. This makes his understanding of time and of the relation of time to eternity crucial for the whole of his theology (especially the perennially central theological problem of immanence and transcendence), which Richard Roberts deals with.[21] My concern now is to draw on selected volumes of the *Church Dogmatics* to illustrate in what ways Barth's three main doctrines of God, creation, and reconciliation are dependent on his use of biblical narratives.

My first example is the doctrine of election in the *Church Dogmatics* II/2, which is part of his doctrine of God and has been called the heartbeat of his theology.[22] His main point is that Jesus Christ is to be identified on the one hand with the God who elects and rejects and on the other hand with those who are elected or rejected by God. The place where this unity is decisively demonstrated is the history of Jesus Christ. Right at the beginning of his exposition Barth confirms the account I have already given above by seeing Scripture as rendering the history which 'plays out' (*abspielen*) in time the 'primal history' (*Urgeschichte*) in God himself (*CD* II/2, 8ff.). The doctrine which follows shows how Barth embraces within the Christian story both the Old Testament and all other history. The basic contention is that God has expressed himself fully and frankly in Jesus Christ. This means that there is no fear of God having any side to his nature which conflicts with what can be seen in Jesus Christ, nor is there a need to search anywhere else for a key to the character of God and of history: what God has actually decided is absolute, and is 'the principle and essence of all happening everywhere . . . a work which still takes place in all its fullness today' (*CD* II/2, 183). Hence Barth's insistence that a general idea of providence or world order be subordinated to that of this particular election, for God orders all things with this in mind. Hence too his qualified argument in favour of supralapsarianism over infralapsarianism, in the course of which he makes an uncompromising statement of his counter-intuitive claim about the biblical narrative world:

[21] *Op. cit.*
[22] Von Balthasar, *op. cit.*, Eng. trans., p. 145.

According to the Bible, the framework and basis of all temporal occurrence is the history of the covenant between God and man, from Adam to Noah and Abraham, from Abraham and Jacob to David, from David to Jesus Christ and believers in Him. It is within this framework that the whole history of nature and the universe plays its specific role, and not the reverse, although logically and empirically the course of things ought to have been the reverse. (*CD* II/2, 136)

This appreciation of God's freedom to surprise us by expressing universal truth in a personal and particular way is at the root of Barth's rejection of most post-Enlightenment worldviews (cf. *CD* II/2, 144). The latter insisted on finding more general frames of reference (whether universal history, a person's individual, social, religious, or political development, or some other frame) into which the biblical history was either fitted or not, whereas Barth sees God's acts as the context in which all other events are to be understood. The whole *Church Dogmatics* can be seen as an attempt to think through the implications of this for Christian faith, knowledge, and practice in all areas of life.[23]

Barth rarely tries in the *Church Dogmatics* to relate extrabiblical events systematically to his overall framework, although of course he makes many references to such events. It is usually the Old Testament which stands as his representative of world history, and his method of relating it to the New Testament is generally that of typology. In traditional Christian exegesis typology has been described as 'at once a literary and a historical procedure, an interpretation of stories and their meanings by weaving them together into a common narrative referring to a single history and its meaning'.[24] Typology stands between, on the one hand, allegory (understood as the description of one reality under the guise of some other which has suitable similarities) and, on the other hand, the description of earthly, personal existence in such a way that it does not 'mean' anything else – it just is what it is. The mark of typology is that the literal meaning or historical reality *both* is itself *and* at the same time points to another event or person of fuller meaning. In biblical exegesis its fundamental presupposition is the providence of God: that God does have a design, that the correspondences between various stages of the biblical history are not random but providen-

---

[23] Barth's ethics have aptly been labelled 'theological contextualism' (G. Outka, *Agape: An Ethical Analysis* (Yale University Press, New Haven, CT, 1972), pp. 229ff.), but are usually considered without appreciation of their distinctive hermeneutical context.

[24] Hans W. Frei, *The Eclipse of Biblical Narrative: A Study in Eighteenth and Nineteenth Century Hermeneutics* (Yale University Press, New Haven, CT and London, 1974), p. 2.

tial, and that God has the freedom to use the account of one event or person or history to point to the meaning of another.

Barth sharpens this belief in providence into a doctrine of election inclusive of providence. In exegesis this means that Barth, even more than the traditional typological exegetes (as my discussion of his doctrine of creation, below, shows) relates all Old Testament history to Jesus Christ. In the second part of the second volume of the *Dogmatics* his chief way of doing this is to do a literary analysis of stories which give instances of God's election and rejection (such as Cain and Abel, Jacob and Esau, Saul and David, Judas and Paul), and to interpret the elected and rejected as being in a binary opposition throughout Israel's history until this is resolved in Jesus Christ, who is the reality prefigured by both the elected and rejected. Jesus's crucifixion is understood as the only rejection in the full sense, and his resurrection shows God's election of this rejected man. Therefore all other rejection and election is relativized by Jesus Christ: both before and since him others can exemplify either state only as imperfect types. Barth's efforts to bring this structure to light in the Old Testament result in some remarkable pieces of exegesis, in particular on the sacrifices in Leviticus 14 and 16 (*CD* II/2, 357ff.), on Saul and David (*CD* II/2, 366ff.), and on 1 Kings 13 (*CD* II/2, 393ff.). Noteworthy in his method is the deliberate lack of any systematic connection between the exegetical assessment and the judgement of faith that it is in fact Jesus Christ who is prefigured. The exegesis only claims to show the *possibility* of a Christological interpretation (e.g. *CD* II/2, 364). Here, as elsewhere in the *Church Dogmatics*, literary analysis fulfils a role similar to that in some other systems of natural theology or apologetics as a *praeparatio evangelica*: it is a way of posing an enigma which faith in the Gospel answers. This is not surprising, since Barth has ruled out extrabiblical 'natural theology', and so his own version of it must be one appropriate to a literary authority. Yet, as it is only in faith that one can pass from discerning a correspondence to belief that here God prefigured his later action, this is not a natural theology which falls under Barth's own criticisms − that is, it does not infringe the freedom of God's self-revelation.

The climax of Barth's typological exegesis in his doctrine of election is reached in his section 'The Determination of the Rejected' (*CD* II/2, 449ff.). Here the concentration of all decisive meaning into the story of Jesus Christ is at its most intense. Barth's doctrine is that the determination of the rejected is 'that from being a reluctant and indirect witness he should become a willing and direct witness to the election of Jesus Christ and His community' (*CD* II/2, 458). What determines this is Jesus Christ as the rejected on Golgotha representing all others and making their ultimate rejection inconceivable: 'With Jesus Christ the rejected can only *have been* rejected. He cannot be rejected any more. Between him and an independent existence as the rejected, there stands the death which Jesus Christ has suffered in his place, and the resurrection by which Jesus Christ has opened up for him His own place as elect' (*CD* II/2, 453). In supporting these conclusions the only exegetical evidence Barth offers is an interpretation of Judas's role in the Gospel story: 'There can be no doubt that here at the very heart of the New Testament we are confronted by the problem of the rejected . . . And we meet this question at the same central place where the New Testament raises and answers the question of the elect' (*CD* II/2, 471). This way of posing the question at once limits the argument to the meaning and logic of the Gospel story. Barth sees Judas and Jesus standing opposite each other at the pivotal point of the story. Judas sums up the sin of the apostles, of Israel, of the world (*CD* II/2, 472), in his handing over (παραδοῦναι) of Jesus. Yet this sinful action coincides with Jesus's own will to be handed over for the sake of others, which is in turn identical with the Father's handing over of his Son in the Incarnation. Therefore in the one action of Judas the pattern of handing over represents the convergence of the intentions of Judas (and through him of all sinners), of Jesus and of the Father (cf. especially *CD* II/2, 502f.). This is the ultimate confrontation of God with evil, and what happens is that, through Jesus's obedience, the literal meaning of the event (sin) is given a new meaning (righteousness). The literal meaning still remains, but can now be seen to be no longer the final meaning: the story of Jesus's passion, death, and resurrection is now the all-embracing context in which to understand that sin has been taken up by God and the new resurrection life given in exchange. Barth demonstrates this only by employing typology which, by the discernment of patterns and types, can focus this universal meaning in particular events. He carries this method yet further in what follows, for he even sees grounds of hope for Judas's salvation not only in Jesus's substitutionary death and resurrection but also, as a result of that, in Paul's transition from being one who handed over Christians to punishment (this being a type of Judas) to being one who instead, after experiencing the resurrected Jesus, hands over the gospel to others (*CD* II/2, 478ff.).

It is clear, therefore, that the main hermeneutical support for his doctrine of election that Barth offers is a literary analysis of certain biblical stories in such a way as to find the will of God making sense of the interweaving of good and evil by creating the master pattern, Jesus's death and resurrection, in which the relation of evil to good is finally defined.

IV

The creation story of Genesis was in the traditional Christian scheme the beginning of the overarching story and accepted as an accurate account of what happened. With the growth of modern biblical scholarship and of sciences such as geology and biology this worldview became untenable for many people, and there resulted not only a crisis over how to understand Genesis 1 and 2 and how to conceive creation, but also a deep disorientation as regards the place of humanity in time and history. To Barth, a theologian who wished to avoid natural theology and apologetics, this situation posed a special problem in his doctrine of creation. He discusses it in his introduction to the first part of volume three and says that, after some perplexity, 'the relevant task of dogmatics at this point has been found exclusively in repeating the "saga" (i.e. of Gen. 1 and 2), and I have found this task far finer and far more rewarding than all the dilettante entanglements in which I might otherwise have found myself' (CD III/1, x).

Barth's definition of saga, in distinction from history and myth, is that it is 'an intuitive and poetic picture of a prehistorical reality of history which is enacted once and for all within the confines of time and space' (CD III/1, 81). It is part of the larger category of biblical narrative, and Barth says: 'It does not merely use narrative as an accepted form. It is itself narrative through and through. It has no philosophical system as an accompanying *alter ego* whose language can express abstractly what it says concretely. What it says can be said only in the form of its own narrative and what follows' (CD III/1, 87). The definition therefore tries to cover both the fact that there was a creation and the fact that it was an event of such a nature that only an imaginative story could convey its meaning. It is an idiosyncratic definition whose main purpose seems to be to avoid the term 'myth', which Barth reserves for imaginative stories conveying some abstract truth. Yet clearly many definitions of myth would include Barth's 'saga' without prejudging the issue of the occurrence of creation.

What status does this lead Barth to give to the details of Genesis 1 and 2? At the simplest level he takes the details seriously and reflects on them theologically, a favourite method being to connect what Genesis says (e.g. on water, on man and woman) with what is said elsewhere in the Bible. But this is by no means the most important procedure for his theological conclusions, for he has two main further strategies. The first is to interpret the sagas as having their chief meaning not in any information about creation (for it is an imaginative story) but in the sort of God they portray – their 'only content is God the Creator' (CD III/1, 78). It is this that lets Barth affirm the authority of the sagas, for they evoke a sphere outside which we cannot go to find a vantage point (*CD* III/1, 65), one which 'has a genuine horizon which cannot be transcended . . . (which is the divine will and utterance and activity)'. By construing the details of the sagas as pointing to the identity of their chief character, God, Barth is engaging in an essentially literary exercise. This is underlined by his insistence on the indispensability of the right use of one's imagination in order to gain knowledge from the sagas. He strongly attacks 'a ridiculous and middle class habit of the modern Western mind which is supremely phantastic in its chronic lack of imaginative phantasy' (*CD* III/1, 81), and says that 'Imagination, too, belongs no less legitimately to the human possibility of knowing. A man without an imagination is more of an invalid than one who lacks a leg' (*CD* III/1, 91). So here too there is the suggestion of literary appreciation as a *praeparatio evangelica*. Nor is the attack on the modern Western mind incidental, for it is by his concentration on the self of God that Barth opposes the Cartesian stress on the thinking self of the individual (Cf. *CD* III/1, 360ff.). The reversal of the post-Enlightenment philosophical orthodoxy is here too closely tied to Barth's method of exegesis, for it is only by knowledge of God, the self who is truly central (knowledge gained through biblical accounts), that anthropocentric distortions can be avoided.

Barth's second strategy is to interpret the sagas typologically. He sets them on the lowest level of a typological hierarchy: the sagas point to the history of the covenant of God with Israel which itself prefigures Jesus Christ. In all of this the final test of 'reality' is the story of Jesus Christ (e.g. *CD* III/1, 275f.). Thus, by this strategy too, little theological weight need be placed on the 'concreteness' of the saga: its function, besides helping in a minor way to render a picture of God (which needs the evidence of other parts of the Bible as well), is to provide material for a typological scheme in which it is the later parts of the Bible that are decisive.

This twofold strategy represents a considerable modification of the traditional position of creation in the overarching story. Traditionally the 'sense of a beginning' about creation was strong. Barth, by stressing not anything intrinsic to the sagas but rather their double correspondence with God's will and with the history of Jesus Christ, has relocated the sense of a beginning. It is now firmly in God's will (the doctrine of election) on the one hand, and in its historical expression, the Incarnation, on the other.[25] The first of these points to the beginning in the author of the story, the second to the beginning of the one story in which all other stories have their figural place. Since, as we have seen, Barth's doctrine of election is strongly Christocentric, this innovation in the traditional framework means placing

[25] Cf. his statements on the Virgin Birth in *CD* I/2, esp. pp. 182ff.

immense weight on the interpretation of the Gospels, to which I now turn.

V

It may seem strange that the problem of the historical accuracy of the Bible has not arisen so far, despite Barth's great reliance on biblical stories. My discussions of God, election, and creation give part of the answer: Barth is more concerned with the sort of God portrayed than with the verifiability of details in the stories. More important still, God's freedom is clearly such that if he chooses he may speak through the Bible despite any errors in it, just as he is able to take up and transform Judas's sin. Yet such general principles do not do justice to Barth's position on the role of historical verification. His whole theology pivots around two events in one man's life-story, the crucifixion and resurrection, and it is chiefly in relation to these that his attitude to history must be examined. Further, since few question the factuality of the crucifixion, the resurrection will emerge as the main issue as I now discuss some of the *Church Dogmatics* IV/1, where Barth presents the first part of his doctrine of reconciliation.

In this section of the *Dogmatics* Barth is clear about the importance of the historical factuality of the Gospels: 'It is a matter of history. Everything depends upon the fact that this turning as it comes from God for us men is not simply imagined and presented as a true teaching of pious and thoughtful people, but that it happened in this way, in the space and time which are those of all men' (*CD* IV/1, 247–248). Yet this history also has peculiar features:

> There is no question of appealing to His remembered form as it had necessarily appeared to His disciples before the verdict of the Holy Spirit was pronounced on His life and death, abstracted from the verdict of the Holy Spirit. In the editing and composition of the Evangelical narratives the interest and art and rules of the historian do not matter. What matters is His living existence in the community and therefore in the world. What matters is His history as it has indeed happened but as it is present and not past. (*CD* IV/1, 320)

Within this history there is also a distinction: 'The death of Jesus Christ can certainly be thought of as history in the modern sense, but not the resurrection' (*CD* IV/1, 336).

The crucifixion and resurrection are central to the very structure of this part. Sections 57 and 58 stress in an introductory way the importance of the history of Jesus Christ for reconciliation; Section 59.1 prepares for the next two sections of Section 59 on the crucifixion and resurrection; and Sections 60 to 63 build on the basis of what has been laid out in Section 59. In Section 59.2 the most revealing indication of how Barth interprets the Gospel story is an excursus (*CD* IV/1, 224ff.), which offers a literary analysis of the story from the beginning of Jesus' ministry to his resurrection. Barth's main point is that the pattern of the synoptic Gospels represents the pattern of Atonement. In his ministry Jesus emerges as alone and superior to his disciples and other people, who are judged by his presence and by their reaction to him. Then comes the contrast of the passion story in which the roles are reversed. Now Jesus is the object of what happens, he suffers rather than acts, and instead of judgement falling on other people it falls on him. This pattern of exchange is shown best by the Barabbas episode. Finally the third part of the story, the Easter narratives, tell that the same person, the judge who was judged, was acknowledged by God, was with his disciples again, and is still alive. Because his identity is known in his history, one must know that history in order to know him now. In all of this Barth makes no attempt at historical criticism or even at redaction criticism. The nearest he comes to the latter is in pre-empting it by noting that the events of the passion narrative are substantially the same in all the Evangelists. Therefore what count as historical facts for theological reflection are the events as described in the Gospels. Barth does not try critically to distinguish the history likeness of the Gospels from their reference to verifiable events. In other words he does not try to distinguish the story from a novel by historical methods.

Yet Barth does not think the Gospels are fiction, and so the most crucial question in relation to his whole method is raised: granted that the events of this story are not to be verified by referring them to whatever historical critics can reconstruct, does Barth suggest an alternative referent? He does: Jesus Christ alive now. Until we reach the third part of the story, the resurrection (*CD* IV/1, 227), there is nothing to suggest that the Gospel is not a novel or fictional short story. A novel too can render a character, and it might be impossible and unnecessary to be able to draw the line between fact and fiction in order to understand the character's identity and the story's general relevance. But in this story as it is told, the referent is not just a historical or imagined character but one who is alive now as the same person.

The question at once arises how this affects the historical status of the story. Barth's answer is that it makes the history 'significant in and by itself' (*CD* IV/1, 227), for now the story is simply the means of knowing someone who is present himself to speak through it: 'He speaks for Himself whenever He is spoken of and His story is told and heard' (*CD* IV/1, 227). Barth, by making the identity of Jesus Christ the referent, has created a closed circle of the accounts and the presence of Christ, in which any turning aside to check historical details is theologically superfluous. This is Barth's Christocentric sharpening of God's freedom to speak through the biblical text as it stands. No amount of historical reconstruction can make Jesus Christ any more willing to speak than he is already. Later, Barth states the same circle in its subjective aspect (*CD* IV/l, 314ff.). He answers the question of how to experience and prove this reality by saying that prayer is the way. This prayer is through Jesus Christ as portrayed in the Gospels, and again there is no room for any turning aside to assess the reliability of those accounts. The argument amounts to an assertion that this is in fact how the story 'works', or, in Barth's terms, to the affirmation of Jesus Christ's self-authentication by speaking for himself.

We can now see how fundamental for his hermeneutics Barth's conception of the resurrection is. It not only expresses the Father's affirmative verdict on Jesus's life and death but it also justifies two positions essential to Barth's whole theology. The first, as has already been suggested, is his taking of the Gospel narratives straightforwardly as his data for theological reflection. This means that the most appropriate handmaid for theology is literary reflection, especially of the sort that understands a character's identity through his words and actions and the encounters and events in which he took part. David Kelsey, in a pregnant half-chapter on Barth's use of Scripture, has well illustrated this in relation to Barth's interpretation of parts of the Gospel in the *Church Dogmatics* IV/2.[26] The climax of the first part of the doctrine of reconciliation in the *Dogmatics* IV/l can also be seen as intensive literary discussion, first on the meaning of the passion and crucifixion in Section 59.2 (with the excursus on Gethsemane, *CD* IV/I, 238ff., parallel to that on Judas, *CD* II/2, in its assessment of the convergence of the intentions of Satan, Jesus, and the Father), and then Section 59.3 on the complex continuity and discontinuity between the crucifixion and resurrection as together they express the natures of the Father and of the Son as a differentiated unity.

The second position that the resurrection makes possible is that of an inclusive Christology, one which embraces all humanity and all history in the meaning of this event. In the three part-volumes of the *Dogmatics* IV the resurrection explicitly plays this transitional role in moving from the one man Jesus to his universal significance. Barth describes the result of the resurrection as follows:

[26] *The Uses of Scripture in Recent Theology* (Fortress Press, Philadelphia, 1975), Ch. 3, pp. 39ff. Note Kelsey's embracing of Barth's interpretation of other parts of the Gospels besides the passion, death, and resurrection in a theory similar to mine.

But the fact that He is risen to die no more, to be taken from the dominion of death (Rom. 6:9), carries with it the fact that His then living and speaking and acting, His being on the way from Jordan to Golgotha, His being as the One who suffered and died, became and is as such His eternal being and therefore His present-day being every day of our time. (*CD* IV/1, 313.)

What this means for the 'hermeneutical gap' between the first and twentieth centuries is that he can call it a 'technical' issue (CD IV/1, 287ff.) which is not serious in theology because the situation has been revolutionized by answering positively the question: 'Supposing our contemporaneity with the Word of God made flesh, with the Judge judged in our place, is already an event?' (*CD* IV/1, 241). This reverses the commonly understood position: no longer is the interpreter autonomously standing in judgement over the records of past history, but instead the interpreter is himself being questioned by the living Christ, and the vital matter is not what status the interpreter will allow Christ, but 'How will it stand with us when we are alongside Jesus Christ and follow Him, when we are in his environment and time and space?' (*CD* IV/1, 293). This universalizing of a particular person and the events of his life is the ultimate expression of God's freedom to communicate himself in a way appropriate to himself and to humanity.

Barth's own label in the *Church Dogmatics* IV/2 for what he has contributed to the doctrine of the incarnation is 'actualization', which (as *CD* IV/2, 150ff. best explains) turns out to mean the sort of concentration of the event, or history, of Jesus Christ that I have described. How does this help him with the main traditional doctrine of the humanity and divinity of Christ? The brief answer is that both natures are defined from within the Gospel story, but interpreting it from different angles. Thus IV/1 uses the story to identify Jesus as the Son of God, seeing it as a description of the free self-humiliation by God for the sake of humanity, while IV/2 identifies Jesus as the Son of Man in whom humanity is raised to unity with God. Barth therefore does not want to talk about two natures in the sense of separate definitions of what is divine and what is human which then must somehow be reconciled in relation to Jesus Christ. Rather he holds that the primary datum is the involvement of God with humanity as told in this one story, that this story is God's own way of defining the two natures, and that therefore the story (and not any outside definition) must be allowed to dictate what true humanity and true divinity are. In other words, we have here another aspect of Barth's insistence that there is no higher viewpoint on God and humanity than this story. Expressed through traditional terminology, the *communicatio idiomatum* is seen as the whole event of Jesus's life from birth to resurrection (IV/2, 75); a definition of divinity in itself is ruled out by rejecting the idea of a λόγος ἄσαρκος (IV/2, 33ff. – i.e. the humanity of Christ is integral to the eternal nature of God through the act of election); and the only sure guide to what true human nature is is to be found in Jesus Christ, where it is of course in union with the nature of God, above all in the *communicatio operationum* (*CD* IV/2, 104ff.).

In all of this the resurrection again plays a vital role, for Jesus's obviously human history is recognized as an act of God only in the light of the resurrection (e.g. *CD* IV/2, 100, 107, 250, 299, 310), and the Gospels themselves are rightly understood only when they are seen to 'breathe the resurrection' (*CD* IV/2, 132). In an earlier volume Barth expressed the role of the resurrection in relation to the two natures most succinctly:

> What implications has it for the being of Jesus in time that He was in time in this way too, as the Resurrected? . . . The answer is that the particular content of the particular recollection of this particular time of the apostolic community consisted in the fact that in this time the *man* Jesus was manifested among them in the mode of *God*. (*CD* III/2, 447f.)

In the same section Barth suggests a new temporal concept as the mediator between time and eternity: the time of Jesus's resurrection appearances (*CD* III/2, 449; cf. *CD* II/1, 19f., *CD* IV/1, 301). It seems to me that Roberts is right when he finds no clear conceptual resolution of the relation of time to eternity in the *Church Dogmatics*, but I interpret Barth as suggesting that there can be no such resolution. Instead, there are stories of a man risen from the dead and in this person participating in and uniting time and eternity – something of such novelty that it can only be stutteringly indicated by a variety of unharmonized stories.[27]

How Barth, with this understanding, goes about describing the *distinction* between humanity and divinity in detail cannot be discussed here, but his main procedure should be noted. It is to see individuals as truly human when they are freely responding to God, reflecting back the freedom and love of God himself. The dominant pattern is therefore that of correspon-

[27] Barth's use of the time of the resurrection appearances to signify the concord between time and eternity is strikingly like Frank Kermode's literary critical use of Aquinas's concept of *aevum*, which is likewise used to resolve the dissonance: 'The concept of *aevum* provides a way of talking about this unusual variety of duration – neither temporal nor eternal, but, as Aquinas said, participating in both the temporal and the eternal' (*The Sense of an Ending: Studies in the Theory of Fiction* (Oxford University Press, London, 1966) p. 72). Kermode sees such a concept expressed today largely in novels or poems, and his comments on their imaginative and narrative resolutions of the problem are relevant to the way Barth understands the resurrection narratives to function in the Gospels.

dence or reflection, an ordered relationship in which the initiative rests with God, expressed in his grace, and human fulfilment is to be found in ever new responses of gratitude. In Jesus this subordination in love is shown to be part of God's own nature and so the individual has the privilege of being a participant in God through Jesus Christ. As regards hermeneutics the correspondence means that the sort of intensive discussion of the Bible's crucial paradigmatic events as offered by the *Church Dogmatics* is essential as a guide to appropriate forms of response.

VI

In the above analysis of some of Barth's hermeneutical principles in key parts of the *Church Dogmatics* I referred several times to the literary critical nature of Barth's approach. The literary genre that seems to be most fruitful as a comparative model is that of the realistic novel. Erich Auerbach's classic, *Mimesis, or the Representation of Reality in Western Literature*,[28] has already set parts of the Bible in a long tradition of realism in literature on which, he claims, they had a powerful influence. In England Dame Helen Gardner has endorsed Auerbach's insights into the New Testament in her criticism of Austin Farrer's exegesis of St. Mark's Gospel – his method, she says,

> does nothing to illuminate, and indeed evaporates, St Mark's sense of what we mean by historical reality, the 'Here and Now' of our daily experience, the 'Then and There' of memory, by which I do not mean detailed precision of testimony, but the deep sense of 'happening' . . . which has struck, and strikes, reader after reader.[29]

Besides, Hans Frei has recently made out a strong case that eighteenth- and nineteenth-century biblical hermeneutics failed to appreciate the Gospel's realistic form.[30] There were two main reasons for this. The first was that their 'history-likeness' (literal meaning) was confused with ostensive reference, the former was reduced to an aspect of the latter, and realistic reading of the text came to mean reading with a view to critical reconstruction of the events referred to. The second was the attempt to find the essential meaning of the stories either in the ideas they illustrated, or in the subjectivity of their narrators or readers. This too led to ignoring what the stories

---

[28]   Princeton University Press, Princeton, NJ, 1969. First published, Bern, 1946.
[29]   'The Poetry of St Mark', in *The Business of Criticism* (Clarendon Press, Oxford 1959), p. 118.
[30]   *Op. cit.*

said in irreducibly narrative form. Frei's suggestion that Barth is one of the few modern interpreters not to have this blindspot is the seed from which the ensuing interpretation has grown.

My simplest contention, therefore, is that Barth is one of the readers who sees in the Bible what Auerbach, Dame Helen and Frei see, and that therefore the sort of literary criticism the latter explicitly engage in might illuminate Barth's implicit principles. The realistic novel is, of course, the subject of many conflicting interpretations and theories, but as further support for the following necessarily condensed reflections I would propose *On Realism* by Peter Stern,[31] a work that both develops Auerbach's insights in a more theoretical way and also gives independently a sensitive account of the main problems and issues that I discern in Barth.

Barth, as I have shown, recognized that it is chiefly through stories that the Bible conveys its understanding of reality. He went further in insisting that this way of rendering reality is one in which form and content are inseparable. The portrayal of complexity, individuality and particularity as they unfold in a sequence of characters and events in interaction is not something that can be understood except by following the sequence attentively. The meaning is built up cumulatively and in an irreducibly temporal form, and amounts to a rich reality to which abstractions and generalizations cannot do full justice. This way of writing is what I mean by 'realism', and it is found in many novels and biblical narratives which render a world of meaning in terms of its characters and particularities, presenting it as they go along.[32] One problem which this parallel raises is the relation between fact and fiction, but before dealing with that it is neccessary to draw some more exact comparisons between Barth's method and that of literary realism.

The major thing in common is appreciation of what Stern calls the 'middle distance' perspective of realism. This is a perspective which is suited to the description of people in interaction, of 'individual lives informed by what in any one age is agreed to constitute a certain integrity and coherence'.[33] Barth does not see the Gospels as biographies of Jesus, but their portrayal of him by his words, acts, and sufferings and by the reaction of others to him is of great importance for his theology, and it is just these elements which in the first century were accepted forms of character-

---

[31]   Routledge and Kegan Paul, London, 1973.
[32]   Indeed a case can be made for the plurality of worlds offered by novels being the successors in Western culture to the one overarching biblical story; see C. A. Patrides, *The Grand Design of God: The Literary Form of the Christian View of History* (Routledge and Kegan Paul, London, 1972).
[33]   Stern, *op. cit.*, p. 121.

portrayal.[34] Furthermore, much of Barth's polemics can be interpreted as aimed at preserving the form of accuracy appropriate to a perspective which tries to describe people and events in the way the Gospels do. On the one hand he is suspicious of any 'generalizing' which gets so far away from the story as to blur its particularities. He attacks any perspective which fails to take the distinctive interrelationships, sequences, and identity-descriptions of the Gospels as the primary data for theological reflection – any meaning which can be formulated apart from the story's content and structure is ruled out. On the other hand he sees much historical criticism as having a perspective that misses the wood for the trees by coming too close. He is quite happy with contradictions and alternative accounts of the same events, but without a certain 'middle distance' agreement and reliability (above all in the sequence of crucifixion and resurrection) most of his theology would be baseless. The most dangerous enemy of the middle distance that Barth sees is, however, a third perspective, one which takes its stand in the Christian's subjectivity. Here the decisive meaning of the narrative is located not in a sequence of events that happened to Jesus (the point being primarily a rendering of the identity of Jesus by telling his story) but in the consciousness of believers who have had their self-understanding illuminated. Barth does not deny the change in self-understanding, but he insists that it is secondary, and that to focus on it is to miss the meaning of the narrative and to change the primary object of Christian theology from Jesus Christ to the believer. His concern is for the correct ordering of the Christian in relation to Christ. He sees the hermeneutics of Schleiermacher and Bultmann as his chief opponents here, but his criticisms go well beyond them to strike at what he saw as the post-Enlightenment tendency to let the self of the individual usurp the central place reserved for Jesus Christ. He also makes parallel criticisms of Roman Catholic theology for its Church-centred version of the same error.[35]

In this context too the resurrection is the key event. The resurrection appearance stories have a middle distance perspective on Jesus, and the resurrection itself is also, as would be agreed by most New Testament scholars, the main determinant of the Gospel writers' own perspective on their whole story. The purpose of the whole is to lead up to this news. For Barth the resurrection is also the place where God's own perspective is expressed – it is 'the verdict of the Father' on Jesus's life and death. So here in the resurrection we are given a God-guaranteed point of view which we must share

---

[34] See e.g. Graham Stanton, *Jesus of Nazareth in New Testament Preaching* (Cambridge University Press, Cambridge, 1974), esp. Ch. 5, pp. 117ff.

[35] Cf. Stern, *op. cit.*, p. 150.

if we wish to understand Jesus correctly. Barth is here claiming an insight into the structure of the Gospel story, into the way it is shaped so as to convey its message. There is a parallel with his way of supporting the doctrine of election by showing how God's verdict on the elect and rejected is expressed in the course events took. This is an important further accord with the insights of literary critics into realism. For literary realism is not just a matter of a certain sort of description, but it also involves realistic structures and assessments – literature that is not realistic can be produced (as by Kafka) by subjecting a realistic description to a non-realistic or fantastic assessment, as Stern shows.[36] Furthermore, as Stern says, 'The structures which display moral and legal assessments translate more readily from one language to another and one era to another than do the textures of descriptive passages'.[37] They therefore offer an irreducible minimum of realism which is least vulnerable to the problems of the hermeneutical gap, and Barth's use of them takes advantage of this. But as regards the resurrection, the main issue is whether that event can offer a realistic perspective on Jesus. Many readers, of course, see it as offering rather an unusual and fantastic one, and they, if they wish to attach decisive significance to him, often on the one hand interpret the resurrection as an event whose significance is not for Jesus himself but for his disciples (i.e. it was some sort of subjective event which does not let us say anything about the present state of Jesus), and on the other hand relocate the ending of Jesus's own story at the crucifixion (finding his primary significance either there or in his teaching or example or in some combination of these). Barth, however, sides with the mainstream Christian tradition in seeing the resurrection as the verdict which is the ultimate in realistic assessment because it is so not only in a literary sense but also through its being God's act in raising Jesus so that he can still be present as himself.[38]

This brings us again to the problem of fact and fiction. How can Barth both claim the resurrection as a historical fact (albeit only describable indirectly, through saga-like realistic stories) and also refuse to base his conclusion on ordinary historical investigation? There have been many analyses of Barth's position on the historicity of the resurrection (which changed between the *Epistle to the Romans* and the *Church Dogmatics*). One of the most acute on the validity of his arguments is that by Van A. Harvey.[39] Harvey's conclusions seem to me sound in so far as they show that Barth's

---

[36]   Stern, *op. cit.*, pp. 129ff.

[37]   Stern, *op. cit.*, p. 131.

[38]   Cf. here Stern's Ch. 3 about the expression of the transcendent in realism, and his remarks about the realism of assessment on pp. 140ff.

[39]   *The Historian and the Believer* (Macmillan, London, 1967), pp. 153ff.

arguments (*CD* III/2, 437ff.) do not succeed in establishing the resurrection to an ordinary historian's satisfaction. Yet Harvey is open to the objections that he has neither taken seriously enough the 'imaginative-poetic' status of the saga of the resurrection appearances in the *Church Dogmatics*, nor tackled Barth's claim for the uniqueness of the resurrection.

The first objection raises the whole problem of the relation of truth to fact and to fiction. This has been hotly debated, especially since the post-Renaissance rise of historical critical method.[40] The core of the problem is that there seems to be an inevitable imaginative element in reconstruction of events which tries to do justice to their many-faceted richness, and this can even lead to a historical novel expressing the truth of a person or period better than conventional history. Brian Wicker, commenting on our understanding of the Gospels, makes the same point: 'Perhaps it is only now, as a result of our long experience of reading novels, that is, narratives which once again combine the empirical and the fictional in a mode of narration more complex than either of these can be by itself, are we able to recover the true nature of narratives written before the split occurred.'[41] Any simple separation of fact from fiction is especially difficult when it is a matter of conveying a vivid character. How important is the verification of details when they are being used as part of a complex synthesis to portray an individual? Given that the rendering does not contradict known facts, but embraces them, of what might falsification consist, short of giving an alternative portrayal which would raise the same problem? Barth is well aware of the complex amalgam offered by biblical narratives and is committed to reflecting theologically on the whole synthesis, taking it in its integrity as literary work. As regards the Gospels, he recognizes that, since we have four versions, the authors and their traditions are engaging in creative reconstruction to some degree. But he also insists that they offer quite enough to identify Jesus unequivocally, and he centres his understanding of Jesus on the passion, death, and resurrection, where the agreement of the Gospels on the 'bare facts' is greatest. One thing that the fixing of the canon could be seen as saying is that we may trust that the rendering of Jesus given in these stories is the best available and so we may confidently begin our theological reflection from them. It seems to be the practical function of Barth's doctrine of Scripture to support such a view, enabling him to get on with the business of *Nachdenken*.

[40]   For an account of its origins, with a look forward to its continuation in discussions of the novel, see William Nelson, *Fact or Fiction: The Dilemma of the Renaissance Storyteller* (Harvard University Press, Cambridge, MA, 1973).

[41]   *The Story-shaped World – Fiction and Metaphysics: Some Variations on Theme* (Athlone Press, London, 1975), p. 105.

It seems to me therefore that Barth's principle is to trust that the Gospels do have a 'middle distance' reliability which is sufficient for theological truth and that when there is a choice between the Gospels and any other (inevitably partly imaginative) reconstruction he will always choose the former. He is willing to accept that the accounts of the resurrection appearances are in saga (imaginative but realistic) form, but he holds that they unanimously point to the continuity of Jesus's identity through death and that any reconstruction which denies this is contradicting all the sources and engaging in imaginative storytelling on its own account.

The second objection possible to Harvey's criticisms is that he does not explore Barth's distinctive claim for the uniqueness of the resurrection. It is here that Barth goes beyond any parallel in fiction or history, for, as I have already described, he is saying that the main character of this story is alive to confirm it. In other words, the identity of this person is defined by events which include one that allows him to be present now. I have shown how Barth supports this by elucidating the logic of the Gospels: they are told in a way which poses for the reader the problem of the present status of Jesus, and they offer a solution in the telling. This sets a unique epistemological problem, which can be stated as follows: the Evangelists *both* inescapably raise the question 'Did the resurrection actually happen?' *and* describe what is claimed to have happened in a way which makes verification inseparable from faith in the presence of Jesus.[42] Therefore the logic of the story converges uniquely with the necessity for faith; and Barth's theology includes here at its heart his literary insight.

VII

Having described what I consider the essence of Barth's hermeneutics of biblical narrative and offered a possible rationale for it, I now come to the task of criticizing it. The issues raised have been so vast that an adequate assessment would require at least a book, so for the most part I will be content with identifying the points at which important decisions for or against Barth may be made, and I will go into somewhat more detail only about the criticisms that spring from my literary parallel.

---

[42]   See esp. his remarks in *CD* IV/2, pp. 478f., and R. Smend's lengthy comment on its significance for Barth's whole theology in an article that is one of the best on Barth's hermeneutics, 'Nachkritische Schriftauslegung' in *Parrhesia, Karl Barth zum 80. Geburtstag* (Zürich, 1966), pp. 215–37.

One central question on which Barth is conscious of being opposed to most contemporary thought is that of the overarching story, or plot of history, whose author and chief character is God. There are many points at which one may diverge from him on this. Does Barth's God exist? Is Barth's combination of literal and typological exegesis the right way to understand the Bible? Is it also the right way to understand God's purposes in history? Even if one accepts affirmative answers to these three questions, one might still ask whether Barth's Christocentric concentration of the story is convincing. Can he do justice to world history, to other religions, to the importance of history since the resurrection? Or is his 'scandal of particularity' sharpened polemically beyond anything intended by the Bible?

Implied by some of these questions is the problem of Barth's rejection of natural theology. Might it not at the very least be desirable to combine his understanding of God through biblical stories with the granting of some theological weight to factors such as the natural and human sciences, historical criticism, and other religions? Two ways of posing this sort of question in Barth's own terms would be: 'is he limiting too dogmatically God's freedom to speak in various ways?' and: 'granted that the Genesis sagas used the cosmology of their time in understanding creation, might it not similarly be the task of a modern doctrine of creation to use contemporary cosmology and sciences rather than simply to reflect on Genesis?'

Historical criticism is an area where damning attacks on Barth have become usual. I have tried to moderate this by showing the coherence and plausibility of Barth's achievement. He grasped better than most exegetes in recent centuries the significance of realistic narrative form in the Bible. He then concentrated his reflection of this feature, shared by novels and historical writing. This raises a range of issues which his critics must not bypass, such as the relation of truth to fact and fiction, the role of imagination in knowing, the possibility that realistic narrative is the highest form of religious language about a God who acts in history, the way in which works of literature cross the hermeneutical gap, and the freedom of the Holy Spirit. Above all, by taking the resurrection as his main methodological principle he draws attention to its claim to uniqueness and to the decisiveness for the identity of Christianity of the question of the presence of the living Christ. None of this can be ignored simply because one finds that his statements about the historicity of the resurrection or of other events fall short of one's norms of historical proof. Yet on the other hand one must ask whether at the very least he ought to admit a criterion of historical falsification into his theology, and whether at the most he should accept that God is free to make historical reconstructions or the results of redaction criticism into data for theological reflection. Such a position would make his theology more complex (as would an admission of natural theology) but perhaps that would be the right result of trying to reflect a complex reality.

Barth's sustained attempt to avoid such complexity is in the interests of his powerful appeal to the centrality of the resurrected Jesus Christ. He is undoubtedly right that if his understanding of the crucifixion and resurrection is correct then this necessitates a revolution in our knowledge and existence. The characteristic 'tone' of his whole theology is a blend of astonishment and thanks: 'The statement "God reveals himself" must be a statement of utter thankfulness, a statement of pure amazement, in which is repeated the amazement of the disciples at meeting the risen One' (CD I/2, 65).

We are here facing the fundamental challenge of Barth's theology, his assertion that there is this extraordinary reality, the risen Christ, whose presence is endlessly rich and fruitful for understanding and for all of life. Barth's main concern is to state this clearly and to work out its implications, and this involves his distinctive theological method centred on biblical narratives. The critical question of the complexity of reality arises as Barth claims that the presence of Christ carries with it a complete world of meaning defined, in the way I have described, by stories. I suspect that it is in wrestling with the problems of presence and completion that one faces the deepest theological problems in the *Dogmatics*. They arise in his anthropology (CD III/2) where the biblical material must be squeezed hard to produce a universal definition of humanity traceable to Jesus Christ. They arise in his orientation of all world history to the one history of Jesus Christ, and in the accompanying doctrines of election and creation which use typology to create an unprecedented totality of correspondences. They arise in the questioning of commentators such as Wolfhart Pannenberg, Jürgen Moltmann, and Robert Jenson about whether Barth attaches proper importance to history since the resurrection or whether the resurrection for him marks history's essential completion.[43] They have arisen in other forms too in this chapter, and their common factor is that in my terms they suggest a weakness in Barth which is closely related to his strength.

What I refer to is Barth's tendency to load the story of Jesus Christ with significance in such a way that it twists under the strain on its main character. A good example is his treatment of Judas in II/2, referred to above. In his eagerness to see all rejection enclosed in Jesus's death and overcome in his resurrection, Barth presses the typology of Judas with Paul so as to support

---

[43] Note that Barth can say that the resurrection, Pentecost, and the *Parousia* are only different forms of the one event (CD IV/3, 293).

the possibility of an ultimately favourable verdict on Judas. Yet the two grim New Testament versions of Judas's death clearly make no attempt to remove in this way the sting of finality from Judas's fate. Barth is intent on enveloping Judas in salvation whatever his crime (e.g. Judas is 'wholly elect', *CD* II/2, 104) and in doing so not only tries to know more of God's purposes than can be elicited from the story but also does violence to its realism, which does not let any general understanding of salvation gloss over Judas's final responsibility for his action. The literary analogy of Barth's approach here is a genre which has been dominant in German fiction and which Stern contrasts with the realistic novel. This is the *Entwicklungsroman* or *Bildungsroman*, which is centred on one person's development and of which Stern says that in it the hero eats up the background – the whole world yields before him and is organized around him (*CD* II/2, 104). One can appreciate Barth's great temptation to this sort of interpretation, for he does believe that all creation is ordered around Jesus Christ. Yet the Gospels do not reflect this in the manner of an *Entwicklungsroman*, but are stubbornly realistic. So Barth's tendency is to interpret them as more Christocentric than they are and so upset the realistic 'ecology' of responsible and free agents in interaction.[44] It is no accident that such a flaw should appear in the doctrine of election which integrates so much of Barth's theology. He is straining to put in place the keystone of his structure, the Christocentric interpretation of election which will let it retain the importance it had for Calvin while avoiding the objectionable aspects of 'double predestination'. But the story will not quite fit, and so he uses typology in a way that obscures the literal, realistic sense.

Barth's tendency, here as elsewhere, is to try to peep over God's shoulder, to claim an overview which is not in keeping with the humble *Nachdenken* of the story. His danger is that in his astonished gratitude for God's self-expression through one set of events, he will absolutize them and play down the possibility of God using different and new combinations. This leads to a clear statement of what he considers essential, but risks impoverishment at other levels. Søren Kierkegaard wrote:

> If one does not maintain strictly the relation between philosophy (the purely human view of the world, the *human* standpoint) and Christianity, but begins straight away, without special penetrating investigations of this relation, to speculate about dogma, one can easily achieve apparently rich and satisfying

---

[44] Another suggestive instance is his interpretation of ἐσπλαγχνίσθη in *CD* IV/2, 184ff., where the reality of other people's suffering becomes 'secondary' in relation to that of Jesus.

results. But things can also turn out as with marl at one time, when, without having investigated it and the soil, people used it on any sort of land – and got excellent results for a few years, but afterwards found that the soil was exhausted.[45]

I have used realistic novels as a purely human standpoint and given some examples of their value in explaining what Barth is doing. That has had the effect of making the logic of Barth's theology more comprehensible and more amenable to discussion and criticism. It also suggests ways in which Barth's theology needs to be more open and comprehensive. This is not at the level of the rendering of Jesus Christ, but at the level of general conclusions drawn from this. Above all, there is the question as to whether story-language should have the virtual monopoly Barth gives it, or whether Barth's way of concentrating on it, for all its value, also overloads it, and is restrictive.

Yet already one can imagine Barth's self-defence, asking us to consider whether gratitude might not be the continuation appropriate to a perfectly complete event. Might it not be, he asks, that one event, one person, is so astonishingly rich that the significance of all subsequent history might consist in becoming more and more thankful for it in thought, speech, and action?

[45] *Journals and Papers*, III (Indiana University Press, Bloomington and London, 1970), p. 3253.

Part V

THINKING FURTHER –
THEOLOGICAL TOPICS

Chapter Ten

THE GOD OF BLESSING WHO LOVES IN WISDOM

> May God grant me to speak with judgement,
>   and to have thoughts worthy of what I have received;
> For he is the guide even of wisdom
>   and the corrector of the wise.
> For both we and our words are in his hand,
>   as are all understanding and skill in crafts . . .
> For wisdom is more mobile than any motion;
>   because of her pureness she pervades and penetrates all things.
> For she is a breath of the power of God,
>   and a pure emanation of the glory of the Almighty;
>   therefore nothing defiled gains entrance into her.
> For she is a reflection of the eternal light,
>   a spotless mirror of the working of God,
>   and an image of his goodness.
> Although she is but one, she can do all things,
>   and while remaining in herself, she renews all things . . .
>   (Wisdom of Solomon 7:15–27)

Jesus increased in wisdom . . . (Luke 2:52)

If any of you is lacking in wisdom, ask God, who gives to all generously and ungrudgingly, and it will be given you. (James 1:5)

The passage from the Wisdom of Solomon above might be read as a commentary on, or even footnote to, the prayer in its opening lines; but it is also an implicit claim that the prayer has been answered, and it gives part of the answer. The cry for wisdom echoes through the scriptures and especially in the intertestamental period, and it is taken up again in the early church and in both Western and Eastern traditions of Christian theology. If one were to select from the scriptures and Christian tradition just one term to characterize what theology is seeking, a strong case could be made for wisdom. It is not in competition with other terms such as understanding, reason, knowledge, doctrine, thought, truth, reflective praxis, or many others; but, in its various classic and contemporary forms, wisdom can be argued to do fuller justice to the multifaceted nature of theology than do the alternatives. It is also a term with a long history of being applied to God as a key attribute, and it therefore poses sharply the question of how the nature of theology is related to the reality of God. Therefore it may be that rethinking the significance of wisdom in theology and in the doctrine of God will prove worthwhile.

This chapter will interpret Eberhard Jüngel's thought about God as a form of wisdom theology that is acutely aware of the responsibility of theology continually to think afresh both its own practice as thought and speech and its content as engagement with God. The implication is that Jüngel's contemporaries and successors are being invited to take up this responsibility and rethink his (and others') thinking and speaking in order to seek further wisdom of God. It would not do justice to Jüngel simply to repeat what he has written. There is an imperative of continually renewed thinking. The challenge he offers is to do something analogous to what he has done so as to give a further theological testimony to the God of super-abundant wisdom who, as the Letter of James reminds us, is willing to be generous in response to our petition for it. Such wisdom-seeking theology is thus part of what he describes as 'unser Leben als einen Akt der Anrufung Gottes zu leben'.[1]

Engaging with Jüngel as a Wisdom Theologian

To describe Jüngel's theology is to cover many of the defining characteristics of Christian theology understood as the seeking of wisdom. Yet at the same time (and this is to be expected according to his own account of the nature of theology and the ceaselessly fresh thinking it requires) each characteristic can also be opened up further, supplementing, complementing and sometimes critiquing what he says.

---

[1]   E. Jüngel, *Gott als Geheimnis der Welt: Zur Begründung der Theologie des Gekreuzigten im Streit zwischen Theismus und Atheismus* (Mohr Siebeck, Tübingen, 1977), p. 531; English Translation (E.T.) transl. D.L. Guder, *God as the Mystery of the World: On the Foundation of the Theology of the Crucified One in the Dispute between Theism and Atheism* (T. and T. Clark, Edinburgh, 1983), p. 387: 'to live our life as an act of calling on God'.

God and God's Word of the Cross

Utterly fundamental is his primary orientation to God and a concern to think all reality in relation to God. Jüngel is supremely a theologian of the word of God, the radical initiative of God in coming and addressing humanity. The language of coming, address, event, freedom, interruption, mystery, and so on, is deeply rooted in the revelation of a God whose word precedes and elicits thought. And what thought! *Jüngel is above all a thinker in response to the word of the cross, the word of the God of love.* He is committed to the long, slow processes of thinking and to thinking about thinking. It is no accident that two of the five sections of *Gott als Geheimnis der Welt* are about the problems and possibilities of thinking of God in recent centuries.

How might this intensive, sustained thought, simultaneously immersed in scripture, in Christian tradition, and in a wide variety of modern Christian and non-Christian thought, best be described? I want to explore the possibility of seeing it as *a creative development of the Christian wisdom tradition.* I will discuss how it makes sense to describe Jüngel as a contemporary wisdom theologian and then how wisdom might open paths beyond where Jüngel has travelled.

A contemporary genre of wisdom theology. First, consideration of wisdom might begin to do justice not only to the individual strands in Jüngel's theology – the scriptural interpretation, the wrestling with classic doctrinal issues, the philosophy, the ethics, the politics, the hermeneutical sophistication, the preaching, the teaching – but also to his way of uniting these together.

What is the genre of his theology? He is no systematic theologian in the modern sense. If one were to take Wolfhart Pannenberg as an example of truly systematic theology, the differences with Jüngel are as striking in form as much as in content. Even Karl Barth's *Church Dogmatics* exhibits an architectonic integration of doctrines (so well described by Jüngel) that may disavow the adjective 'systematic' but yet exhibits a level of overall structural integration that Jüngel does not try to imitate.[2] This refusal of modern forms of cognitive systematicity is in line with his distinctive theological approach. It is not that he is unsystematic in his thinking – there is ample evidence of deep and rigorous involvement with systematic theological and philosophical works. It is rather that the theological content to which he is trying to do justice never seems to allow him to stop there – he moves through

---

[2]   K. Barth, *Church Dogmatics*, 4 vols. (T. and T. Clark, Edinburgh 1956–75).

systems and beyond them, thinking in exploratory ways along paths that resist cognitive overviews or summary statements.

Better, there are summary statements, but they do not tend to take systematic form. They are more likely to be essays that leave one addressed and gripped by a few big thoughts that have the capacity to go on being generative, liberating the reader's own thought in response. This is even more the case with his preaching and lecturing. It is very much part of wisdom traditions that they value the oral, and that the event of mutual engagement is intrinsic to the learning that needs to happen.

The difficult test case for this understanding is *Gott als Geheimnis der Welt* which is the main focus of this chapter. Yet my reading of that extraordinary work is that it is also Jüngel's richest wisdom so far. Its form is *sui generis*, suited only to Jüngel's particular task and content, moving with an inner logic from the aporetic statement of the challenge of speech about the death of God in modernity through the 'Denkbarkeit Gottes' and 'Sagbarkeit Gottes' to the 'Menschlichkeit Gottes'. Throughout there is no doubt about the key focus on 'the word of the cross'. But that very phrase is juxtaposed in its scriptural setting of Paul's first Letter to the Corinthians with a radical concept of Christ crucified as 'the wisdom of God' (1Cor. 1–2). This invites us to see Jüngel's project in his largest single work as the thinking through of a distinctively Christian idea of wisdom. Like Paul, he challenges other forms of wisdom, especially that of modern atheist philosophers and of modern theologians who have failed to keep the word of the cross at the heart of their thinking. More positively, he thinks rigorously the reality of a God who is most decisively defined by his own coming to be united in Jesus Christ with death for the sake of life. Cognitively, this is extremely demanding – Jüngel's long wrestle with Hegel is especially important here. But wisdom, above all this wisdom of the cross, can never be simply cognitive. It is simultaneously love. So Jüngel's thought is constantly straining to do justice to the language of love showing, as it were, 1Cor. 13 to be coinherent with 1Cor. 1 and 2.

What we have here can therefore be seen as a new enactment of Paul's reconceiving of wisdom in the face of the crucified Jesus Christ. Reaching further back in the Bible it might be seen as analogous to the Book of Job. There the wisdom of Job's friends is tested, questioned and found wanting in the face of Job's suffering, and of his interrogation of them and of God. This is the wisdom tradition's own self-transcendence through grappling with the most profound realities of historical existence and of the mystery of God's involvement with them. There are resonances with Jüngel's own often lonely way in late twentieth-century theology and his conception of theology is as radically rooted in the initiative of God as is that of wisdom in Job 28. The locus in twentieth-century theology that most frequently comes to mind in reading Jüngel on God is the fourth volume of Karl Barth's *Church Dogmatics*. There we find a comparable attempt to do justice to the cross and to the obedience and love of Jesus Christ as intrinsic to the being of God in his action in the world, and in *Church Dogmatics* IV/3 we also find Barth's most thorough engagement with the wisdom tradition in his interpretation of Job.

Jüngel might be seen as offering a doctrine of the Trinity that has learnt the lessons of Barth's journey from *Church Dogmatics* I/1 to IV/4. How might Barth have rewritten his doctrine of the Trinity in Volume I/1 had he returned to it after working out the rich economic Trinity implied by the Christological sections of Volume IV? Jüngel's own journey from *Gottes Sein ist im Werden* to *Gott als Geheimnis der Welt* might give some hints;[3] but his achievement in the latter is more than a commentary or supplement to Barth (and there are more references to Luther than to Barth, and almost as many to Descartes, Kant, Hegel and Heidegger). It is the achievement of a genre of theology (which I am describing as a development of the wisdom tradition) deeply appropriate to the centrality of the crucified Christ and to simultaneous immersion in the Bible and in the modern world. It is far more concerned to make rich yet rigorous connections, both positive and critical, between scripture and modernity than it is to conform to the genres that have often been employed to order more strictly cognitivist approaches in theology and philosophy. It is a genre suited to being drawn into the sort of demanding 'Nachdenken' practised by Jüngel himself, and therefore to a learning of theology that has to travel a certain route (including many apparent detours) in order to do more than arrive at conclusions. *There is a pedagogy of thought here in which the journey is part of the conclusions*, and in this inseparability of the process of being taught from the position arrived at there is also something of the wisdom tradition. Jüngel does call it a 'Studienbuch'.[4]

It is striking that a characteristic 'result' of Jüngel's theological thinking is often the distillation of thought into a maxim, thesis or phrase. *Gott als Geheimnis der Welt* is studded with these rich condensations of theological understanding. '*God is more than necessary*';[5] 'the essence of the addressing

---

[3]   E. Jüngel, *Gottes Sein ist im Werden: Verantwortliche Rede vom Sein Gottes bei Karl Barth: Eine Paraphrase* (Mohr Siebeck, Tübingen, 1966), E.T., *The Doctrine of the Trinity: God's Being is in Becoming* (Scottish Academic Press, Edinburgh, 1976).

[4]   Jüngel, *Gott als Geheimnis der Welt*, p. xvi.

[5]   Ibid., p. 30: '*Gott ist mehr als notwendig.*' (E.T., p. 24.) This expands into three fundamental propositions: '(a) Man and his world are interesting for their own sake. (b) Even more so, God is interesting for his own sake. (c) God makes man, who is interesting for his own sake,

word is approach through interruption';[6] 'God *is* in the midst of the struggle between nothingness and possibility';[7] 'the word of the cross is the self-definition of God in human language, which implies a definition of man';[8] 'analogy is the addressing event of gripping freedom';[9] 'the being of God . . . realises itself *in the midst of such great self-relatedness as still greater self-lessness,* and is as such *love*';[10] 'revelation is the becoming present of an absent one as absent'.[11] Such statements have a remarkable capacity not only to summarize lengthy discussions but also to overflow them and go on being generative of fresh thought in different contexts. They have, in other words, something of the fruitfulness of classic wisdom formulations in both challenging thought to stretch itself in many directions at once with reference to their original context and also being open to new connections in other contexts. In this they exhibit something of the new eventfulness that Jüngel ascribes to the Holy Spirit. His own treatment of the Spirit is biblical and classically Western in its emphasis on love,[12] but there is scope for an equally biblical, and more Eastern, identification of the Holy Spirit with wisdom too.

Word as Wisdom. Yet in fact Jüngel says very little indeed explicitly about wisdom. I do not want to discuss why that might be, interesting though the question is. Rather, having tried to make a case for Jüngel's theology being *de facto* a form of wisdom, I want to suggest some ways in which the more explicit recognition of wisdom might open further paths in continuity or at least in intersection with his. It is a brief thought experiment that asks: what if Jüngel's favourite term 'word' were to be thought through as 'wisdom'? It is not to suggest that they are interchangeable, only to

interesting in a new way.' (Ibid., p. 43; E.T., p. 34.) Here the use of 'interesting' ('interessant') as a key category invites its development by reference to the biblical understanding of wisdom as simultaneously to do with human exploration of the world and divine revelation.

[6]   Ibid., p. 221: 'Das Wesen des ansprechenden Wortes ist *Annäherung durch Unterbrechung*.' (E.T., p. 165.)

[7]   Ibid., p. 295: 'Gott [*ist*] mitten im Streit zwischen Nichts und Möglichkeit.' (E.T., p. 217.)

[8]   Ibid., p. 312; E.T., p. 229.

[9]   Ibid., p. 399: 'Die Analogie ist das ansprechende Ereignis fesselnder Freiheit.' (E.T., p. 292.)

[10]   The complete sentence reads: 'The basic hermeneutical structure of Evangelical talk about God, namely, the analogy as the still greater similarity within such a great dissimilarity between God and man, is the linguistic-logical expression for the being of God, which being realises itself *in the midst of such great self-relatedness as still greater selflessness,* and is as such *love*.' (E.T., p. 298.) '. . . das Sein Gottes, das sich als *die inmitten noch so grosser Selbstbezogenheit immer noch grössere Selbstlosigkeit* vollzieht und insofern *Liebe* ist'. (Ibid., p. 408.)

[11]   Ibid., p. 478; E.T., p. 349.

[12]   See especially ibid., pp. 512–14; E.T., pp. 374–6.

recognize that in scripture and tradition they overlap and interweave, and that a theology which does not recognize this is in danger of impoverishment in certain respects.

The biblical roots of this suggestion should not need much elaboration. In the Septuagint λόγος (logos) and σοφία (sophia) are frequently linked. In the New Testament there are strong wisdom associations both in Jüngel's favourite text referring to 'the word of the cross' from 1Cor. 1 (see above) and also in what is perhaps the key passage on the logos for the whole Christian tradition, John 1:1–18. The Prologue of John has many scriptural references, the most obvious being to the book of Exodus – concerning tent-pitching (cf. Ex. 25:8–9), seeing the glory of the Lord (cf. Ex. 24:15–16), the law (the whole Sinai story), and grace and truth (cf. the Hebrew pair *chesed* and *emet* in Ex. 34:6). But it also interweaves a range of wisdom texts. Personified Wisdom 'existed before the creation of the world' (Prov. 8:22–33), and was with God (Sir. 1:1). Wisdom was active in the creation of the world (Wis. 9:9), and is said to be better than life (Prov. 8:35) and like light (Eccl. 2:13). Wisdom came into the world and was rejected (1Enoch 42:2). However, she set up her tent among the people (Sir. 24:8) and dispensed glory and grace (Sir. 24:16).[13] The resonances with wisdom literature continue throughout the Gospel of John.[14]

At the very least all this is an encouragement to think through Jüngel's word-centred account of God asking: is it appropriate to bring in more of the meanings associated with wisdom? That would be a massive task, too great for the present chapter. It is possible to speculate that some aspects of his theology would be modified or corrected – for example, the role of language in his theology might be more closely interrelated with the non-linguistic, and his doctrine of creation might be developed more fully.[15] But for now I will concentrate on the way in which his use of 'word' is closely linked to 'event' and 'act', emphasizing the address character of language, its coming as an interruption, with the 'word of the cross' as the supreme interruptive event.

[13]   M. W. G. Stibbe, *John* (Sheffield Academic Press, Sheffield, UK, 1993), p. 23.
[14]   For two surveys strongly in favour of interpreting John's Gospel in wisdom terms see B. Witherington III, *Jesus the Sage: The Pilgrimage of Wisdom* (Augsburg Fortress, Minneapolis, 1994), Chapter 8, and S. H. Ringe, *Wisdom's Friends: Community and Christology in the Fourth Gospel* (Westminster John Knox Press, Louisville KY 1999). Cf. M. Scott, *Sophia and the Johannine Jesus* (Sheffield Academic Press, Sheffield, UK, 1992); E. Schüssler Fiorenza, *Jesus: Miriam's Child, Sophia's Prophet – Critical Issues in Feminist Christology* (Continuum, New York 1994); E. A. Johnson, *She Who Is: The Mystery of God in Feminist Theological Discourse* (Crossroads, New York, 1994).
[15]   Cf. John Webster's comments: J. Webster 'Eberhard Jüngel' in D. F. Ford (ed.), *The Modern Theologians. An Introduction to Christian Theology in the Twentieth Century*, Second edition (Blackwell, Oxford, 1997), pp. 63f.

This account of reality characterized as eventfulness centred on a God who is the event that happened in the death of Jesus, with the doctrine of the Trinity as the conceptualization of the passion history of God,[16] is immensely fruitful for a contemporary theology, as Jüngel's work demonstrates. But it has its limitations, especially if pursued single-mindedly. Wisdom draws attention to dimensions of reality less amenable to categories such as event, address and interruption. It is concerned with those, but also with complex connections, continuities, developments over shorter and longer timescales. It is about the shaping of life as a whole, the communities, structures, patterns, environments and contexts that help it flourish, and the habits and practices that support such flourishing. 'Word' can of course be linked to all those dimensions; but wisdom, both in scripture and Christian tradition, is more congenial. Of Jüngel's own dialogue partners in *Gott als Geheimnis der Welt*, the most obvious sources of complementarity here are Aristotle, Augustine, Aquinas, Hegel and Heidegger, and to the wisdom of each of them he in turn represents a prophetic challenge.

Yet perhaps the most fruitful in the long term might prove to be Dietrich Bonhoeffer, who from within Jüngel's own Lutheran tradition identified in one of his earliest works the theological issues connected with the categories of act and being.[17] Bonhoeffer went on wrestling with these issues and it is in the late wisdom-like writings in his *Ethics* and *Letters and Papers from Prison* that he reaches towards a creative solution, above all in his way of relating the ultimate and penultimate.[18] This mature answer to the problems posed by his early work combines utter immersion in history (the penultimate) with radical emphasis on eschatology (the ultimate), and both understood as inseparable from God's uniting with the world in Jesus Christ. Jüngel brilliantly appropriates Bonhoeffer on the non-necessity of God, secularity, and the God who lets himself be pushed out of the world on to the cross; but the question is whether the dynamic interrelation of ultimate and penultimate (the latter being especially associated by Bonhoeffer with wisdom),[19] which is partly intended by Bonhoeffer as a corrective to

---

[16]   Cf. Jüngel, *God as the Mystery of the World*, p. 371; German text: p. 508.

[17]   D. Bonhoeffer, *Akt und Sein: Transzendentalphilosophie und Ontologie in der systematischen Theologie* (Dietrich Bonhoeffer Werke, II, Chr. Kaiser München, 1988); E.T., *Act and Being: Transcendental Philosophy and Ontology in Systematic Theology* (Fortress, Minneapolis, 1996).

[18]   This is treated in D. Bonhoeffer, *Ethik* (Dietrich Bonhoeffer Werke, VI, Chr. Kaiser München, 1992); E.T., *Ethics* (Collins, London, 1964 [based on the sixth German edition, 1963]) Cf. P. Janz, *God, the Mind's Desire* (Cambridge University Press, Cambridge, UK, 2004).

[19]   My own use of wisdom is as much to do with eschatology as history, and is especially concerned with their interrelation.

tendencies in his own tradition's word-centred theologies, is adequately reflected in Jüngel's thought.[20] Bonhoeffer in his later work succeeds in moving beyond the interruptive and the limitations of the word as address and event. This not only fulfils the potential of his earlier work on act and being but also learns lessons from many sources: his wrestling with concepts of personhood; his dissatisfaction with Lutheranism's treatment of natural life and secular goodness; his critique of Barth on revelation; his experience of forming and living in a Christian community; his ongoing dialogue with Roman Catholic and Anglican thought and practice; his own immersion in the ambiguities of history; and, through all those, his interpretation of scripture. *It is therefore his life together with his thought that stands as a wisdom critique of Jüngel's favoured conceptuality, not so much contradicting what Jüngel says as opening it up to other dimensions, and so drawing it simultaneously deeper into the penultimate contingencies of history and ordinary life and more comprehensively into the possibilities of the Kingdom of God.*[21]

Jüngel and Scripture

Scripture has occurred several times already above. Jüngel is a passionately scriptural theologian. He was well trained in biblical scholarship and hermeneutics as well as in dogmatics (Fuchs, Ebeling, Vogel) and has always been dedicated to the unity of exegesis and dogmatics. In *Gott als Geheimnis der Welt* he sums up the basic hermeneutical principles of evangelical theology, in being guided always by 'the reality of the biblical texts', as follows: 'the place of the conceivability of God is a Word which precedes thought'.[22] His own thought as it has striven to correspond to the Word has become increasingly rich in its appreciation of scripture, especially the significance of kerygmatic address, metaphor, parable, and historical narrative. I want to suggest further possibilities of this appreciation, gathered together loosely under the heading of wisdom.[23]

---

[20] This is a genuine question, perhaps to be answered positively by Jüngel's increasing concern for the natural, and his affirmation of the world as interesting for its own sake as well as made interesting in a new way by God.

[21] The theological programme of Jürgen Moltmann (who did important early work on Bonhoeffer) might be read as being at least in part set by Bonhoeffer in such terms.

[22] Jüngel, *God as the Mystery of the World*, p. 155; German text: '. . . der Ort der Denkbarkeit Gottes [ist] ein dem Denken vorangehendes Wort' (p. 206).

[23] So far as I am aware, despite my characterization of much of his theology as wisdom, Jüngel has never engaged at length with the biblical wisdom literature; though what I have in mind in what follows is not limited to what scholars might include under the biblical genre of wisdom.

The core issue is the nature of the thought that, through engagement
with the biblical texts, best corresponds to this Word. The biblical texts are
in many genres, moods, voices and so on, and the thinking that corresponds
to them needs to be sensitive to this. How is this best done? Theologians
adopt many strategies. As regards the role of theological concepts in relation
to biblical texts I would situate Jüngel somewhere between Barth and
Pannenberg. Barth accompanies his doctrinal exposition with detailed exegesis and frequently shapes his whole exposition around a narrative or
parable or book of scripture (the use in *Church Dogmatics* IV of the gospel
pattern of the life, death and resurrection of Jesus Christ, and, within that,
of the parable of the Prodigal Son, and of the Book of Job, is the most
striking example). Pannenberg rarely does extended exegesis, and his references to scripture tend to subsume it into his concepts and arguments with
relatively little concern for its genres or other distinctive features. Jüngel in
Gott als Geheimnis der Welt is constantly drawing on scripture and is alert to
particular features, yet still rarely immerses his thought for long in a specific
text, let alone in the intertextuality of several texts. The danger with this is
that thinking about theological issues leads him to distil concepts from
scripture (often with extraordinary perceptiveness), but that this movement
into concepts leaves the texts behind without encouraging reengagement
with them. *The fully formed concepts easily take on a life of their own in relation
to each other rather than with reference to the life and complexities of the texts.* The
result is that argumentative discourse dominates other genres, cutting itself
off from their capacity to question such conceptual distillations and generate
alternative interpretations.

I would, if there were space, want to argue for a more radical immersion
in scripture even than Barth achieves – one in which the intertextuality of
scripture and even a new appreciation of the possibility of interpreting
scripture in multiple senses becomes the atmosphere of theological thought,[24]
whose concepts are constantly being opened up afresh by renewed engagement with scriptures. This immersion in the Bible as a canon invites *inter-
textual and multilevelled interpretation* that respects its genres and other
particularities. But there are also other 'immersions' that invite the interpreter's involvement and that likewise constantly open up any theological

---

[24]   For a superb example of contemporary justification and practice of exegesis that finds
multiple senses in scripture see P. Ricoeur, 'The Song of Songs. The Nuptial Metaphor', in
A. LaCocque, and P. Ricoeur (eds.), *Thinking Biblically. Exegetical and Hermeneutical Studies*
(University of Chicago Press, Chicago and London, 1998). Cf. on figural interpretation, discussing with remarkable scholarly and theological perception the figural reading of scripture
(with special reference to Origen, Auerbach and Hans Frei), J. D. Dawson, *Christian Figural
Reading and the Fashioning of Identity* (University of California Press, Los Angeles and London,
2002).

concept or doctrine, often destabilizing them or exposing their limitations as attempts to do justice to scripture. I think of *the Bible's own immersion in history* in all its complexities and contingencies, and the fruitfulness of apparent detours through the bewildering variety of historical, sociological, economic, cultural, psychological and other factors. Such factors help understand the origins, contexts, influences and reception histories of biblical writings. I think too of *the Bible's immersion in liturgies and worship* of many types; or in *academic disciplines and forms of study*; or in *practices of preaching, meditation, or ethical and doctrinal deliberation* – and in all these cases the metaphor of immersion can be reversed so that it is they that are immersed in scripture. *This is polymorphous scripture responded to in polymorphous thought.* There can be no overview of it, no systematic integration, only attempts, in the course of learning to take part in the purposes of God in history, to unite our prayers, actions, habits, imaginations, understandings and desires to the glory of God. This I would call *a wisdom interpretation of scripture*, though the justification of that name would require a separate discussion of wisdom as a kind of meta-genre in scripture, which is both scattered through the others in poetic and prose forms and is also vital for the writing, editing, canonizing, reception and ongoing interpretation of each part of the Bible.

Whatever the ways in which his theological appropriation of scripture might be supplemented or revised, however, Jüngel's theology remains a remarkable instance of what I have called wisdom interpretation. The whole of *Gott als Geheimnis der Welt*, indeed, might be seen as *thoughtful theological commentary in a rigorous wisdom mode on two scriptural phrases taken together: 'God is love' and 'the word of the cross'*. It is a 'journey of intensification' (David Tracy) into those phrases, during which a lengthy discourse is generated, within which in turn there are wisdom-like nodes distilled into a further set of phrases, maxims or theses (such as those listed above, pp. 199–200). Perhaps the most constructive response to Jüngel's theology of God is for others to complement it by doing afresh the sort of thing he does rather than saying again what he says. It would be possible to do this using different key scriptural texts from the two I have identified as primary for him – but that would lead into a 'study book' possibly as long as Jüngel's. So in the short space remaining here I will stay with those two – 'God is love' and 'the word of the cross' – and develop what has been said above in the direction of a doctrine of God.

The God of Blessing Who Loves in Wisdom

One conclusion from the discussion so far is the appropriateness of rethinking Jüngel's doctrine of God using wisdom as a leading term. In relation to the Christian tradition this might seem obvious. In Western theology (seen above all in Augustine and Aquinas but continuing into modern German theology through Schleiermacher), as in Eastern theology, wisdom has been a prime attribute of God. I read Jüngel as being in line with Barth's doctrine of the attributes of God in *Church Dogmatics* II/1, where the integrating phrase is: 'The One who loves in freedom'. Throughout *Gott als Geheimnis der Welt* love and freedom also go together. But what if the heading were '*The One who loves in wisdom*'?[25]

This need not be competitive with Barth or Jüngel, and both might agree that each of the attributes of God embraces all the others; but which attributes are especially emphasized does make a considerable difference to the shape and impact of a doctrine of God. Freedom might be seen to be obviously essential to love as conceived by Barth and Jüngel,[26] but both freedom and love benefit (according to both scripture and tradition) from being complemented by an attribute that is more explicitly cognitive. There is in Barth's phrase a bias towards God as will (loving freely) rather than as understanding or intellect (the wisdom that conceives, shapes and directs the willing). But Jüngel's scant attention to wisdom, together with Barth's disappointingly thin (in comparison with his treatment of some of the other attributes) treatment of wisdom as an attribute of God and his structural subordination of wisdom to love and freedom, confirms the suspicion that wisdom is not adequately acknowledged in the 'ecological balance' of either theology. Barth in his introduction to the attributes in *Church Dogmatics* II/1 says a great deal about knowing God, but this makes it all the more striking that in the overarching scheme of his attributes the dimension of God's understanding and wisdom is not so prominent. Likewise Jüngel's massive stress on the importance of theological thinking is not reflected in a corresponding emphasis on whatever analogically corresponds to this in God. In doing theology, Barth's 'knowledge' and Jüngel's 'thought' can be taken up into the more capacious 'wisdom' in a way that is not possible *vice versa*.

In accordance with my own prescription suggested above (pp. 203–5), this conceptualizing of God as the One who loves in wisdom would need

---

[25] Or, given the comments below (though breaking the symmetry with Barth's phrase): 'The One who freely loves in wisdom'.
[26] The pervasiveness of freedom in the strongly biblical theologies of Barth and Jüngel is curious since it is not a very prominent term in the Bible. They have to find it implicitly in lordship, grace, power, joy, or other attributes in order to sustain the biblical support for freedom.

to be tested and developed by multiple 'immersions' – in scripture as an inter-textual canon (*scriptura sui interpres*); in scripture as itself immersed in a complex history of events, contexts and readings; in worship, liturgies and other individual and communal practices; and in ways of learning and studying that seek to correspond to the God of wisdom.[27]

Yet the binary dialectic of love and freedom (explicit in Barth and implicit in Jüngel) or of love and wisdom (as suggested by me) might both be supplemented, and a more adequate dynamic set up, through introducing a third term.[28] Again, it is of course possible to arrive at all the major attributes of God through any one of them, let alone two; but it is still significant which attributes are especially emphasised. In both Barth and Jüngel there is a dimension of God that continually bursts the bounds of what is usually associated with love and freedom. It is seen most clearly in Barth at the culmination of his discussion of the perfections of God: the glory of God articulated in terms of joy and (more cautiously) beauty. What might be a third term most appropriate to love and wisdom?

I would propose: *the God of blessing as the One who loves in wisdom*. What might be some of the advantages of including the notion of blessing here? Jüngel consistently resists the obvious temptation of a 'theology of the crucified' to lose the sense of God *in se*, God in God's self, or the immanent Trinity. For Jüngel, God is interesting for God's sake, and is more than necessary. This priority of 'God for God's sake' is extraordinarily important for the theological health of any doctrine, ethics, politics, or practice of worship. It is perhaps the deepest insight of the biblical wisdom tradition as seen in the Book of Job. I have been convinced that the hermeneutical key to that

---

[27] I have already suggested above how the 'word of the cross' links into the prominent themes of wisdom and love in 1Cor., and how John 1.1–18 is intertextually linked with wisdom literature. Both Paul's Corinthian correspondence and John's Gospel are well suited to the other 'immersions' mentioned above, though space does not permit the demonstration of this here. For my own attempts to distil theological wisdom from the Corinthian correspondence see F. M. Young and D. F. Ford, *Meaning and Truth in Second Corinthians* (SPCK, London, 1987) and D. F. Ford, *Self and Salvation: Being Transformed* (Cambridge University Press, Cambridge, 1999). Together they seek to learn from philological, literary, rhetorical, intertextual, sociological, historical, philosophical and pedagogical approaches and to draw on these for the flourishing of worship, community life and, above all, a habitable contemporary theology. *Self and Salvation* might be seen as a 'journey of intensification' into 2Cor. 3:18 and 4:6, and it both engages in dialogue with Jüngel and attempts a practice of scriptural interpretation partly in line with remarks made above.

[28] Not least because this fits better with the doctrine of the Trinity, even if each of the three is not appropriated simply to one person of the Trinity.

book is in Satan's challenge: 'Does Job fear God for nothing?' (Job 1:9).[29] Job's response to the loss of his property and children is: 'The Lord gave, and the Lord has taken away; blessed be the name of the Lord' (Job 1:21), and after all the complexities of what follows, the message seems clear that Job is vindicated as fearing God for nothing. *The blessing or hallowing of God's name* has been practised by Jews down the centuries, including in many Job-like situations; and for Christians it is the leading – I would say the encompassing – petition of the Lord's prayer. The blessedness of God suggests a certain completeness which is yet full of life and goodness, and free to overflow abundantly. It indicates the abundant God who is the creator of abundant life. Further, it helps to suggest a dynamic, relational divine life – God is the Blessed One, the blessed Trinity (to use a traditional phrase), whose members are a *perichoresis*, or reciprocal coinherence, of mutual blessing.

At the same time, blessing suggests rich and freely responsive 'more than necessary' relations between God and creation. God blesses creation and human beings within it, creation blesses God, human beings bless God and creation and each other. It allows for asymmetry in the relationships (as in radical divine initiative), but also for freedom on both sides, with a sense of non-coercion and non-competitiveness. So the freedom that Barth and Jüngel affirm so strongly is here included in the relational activity of blessing and the relational receptivity of being blessed, with both deeply related to the dynamics of created reality. *Blessing both refers to God in God's self and is immersed in the particularities of nature and history with a view to the eschatological future.* Indeed the fundamental dynamic of creation and history might be understood theologically in terms of blessing: creation, with humanity, being blessed by a generous God, but going wrong; the challenge of receiving and being transformed by blessings that are always more than we can believe possible or want to receive; Jesus Christ as the one who is blessing incarnate, and in his ascension blesses with pierced hands (that might be the key event and image for a Christology of blessing that looks back to his life, death and resurrection under the sign of blessing, and forward to Pentecost and his ultimate recapitulation of all things under the same sign); the Holy Spirit as an anticipation of that eschatological blessing of God; and the need daily to discern in specific ways the blessings of God in creation, in fellow human beings and in our own lives – and at the same time be alert to the many ways in which God's blessings are rejected, distorted, misunderstood, turned into curses.

[29]   Cf. S. Ticciati, 'Job and the Disruption of Identity: Reading Beyond Barth (Continuum/ T&T Clark, London/New York, 2005).

All of this calls for a wisdom of blessing in practice – who to bless, what to bless, and why, when, how, where; this wisdom is itself rooted in the embracing practice of blessing God in thanks and praise; and this is in turn utterly dependent on *being blessed by the God who loves wisely in so many mediated ways, both hidden and revealed.* Finally, nothing could be more fitting than to bless God for the abundant blessings that have been given to so many of us through the life and thought of Eberhard Jüngel.[30]

---

[30] My own debt of gratitude is considerable. It includes generous hospitality as a guest living in Jüngel's home in Tübingen for a whole semester, being welcomed into his group of assistants as a participant in meals and conversations, discussion of my own theological work, gifts of his books, and welcome given to my graduate students.

Chapter Eleven

TRAGEDY AND
ATONEMENT

'Only there is no escape from contingency'. Donald MacKinnon[1]

One of the striking things about Donald MacKinnon's speaking and writing is the way he interprets the Bible. Frequently a passage is focused on, taken up into a discussion, and shown to be fruitful in ways that go beyond the horizons of most scholarly commentaries. Take, for example, his treatment of John, chapter 20 in 'The Problem of the "System of Projection" Appropriate to Christian Theological Statements'.[2] At the culmination of a complex argument involving logical implication, the relation of various types of language to reality and the status of the resurrection of Jesus in Christian faith, John, chapter 20 is introduced as 'one of the classical Christian documents concerning the relation of perceiving (and especially visual, auditory and tactile perception) to faith'.[3] What happens in the interpretation that follows is worth noting.

The main thing going on is what might be called conceptual redescription of the text, like the German *Nachdenken*. The details of the story in all their complex inter-relationships are described in philosophical language, and thought tries to keep closely to the particularities of this text while also exploring its logic. The result is both to sharpen appreciation of the thrust and nuances of the text and to connect its narrative with some perennial philosophical issues. Yet for all the apparent neutrality of the attempt simply to describe, the implications of this approach can be considerable. Treating

---

[1] 'Philosophy and Christology', in *Borderlands of Theology and Other Essays* (Lutterworth Press, London, 1968), p. 81.
[2] *Explorations in Theology, 5* (SCM Press, London, 1979), pp. 70–89.
[3] Ibid., p. 84.

the author of the fourth Gospel seriously, as a thinker whose subtlety can stretch the best of contemporary philosophers, shocks us out of tendencies to paternalism towards him or her. And the consequence of this respectful engagement may be to have our most important conceptions transformed or challenged by the unique nature of what we come to recognize. As MacKinnon concludes:

> One must use these models; yet what one seeks to capture is unique. One's use is part of the way in which one takes hold of the system of projection involved in the Christian faith; the taking hold of a problem from which one continually retreats, preferring the *ersatz* of an allegedly formal orthodoxy, or the security of an absolutely autonomous faith, unbound by the factual, and creative of its own objects, or the greater manageability of more tractable presentations of the fusion of complexity and simplicity characteristic of the evangelists' portrayal of the central figure. Philosophy, whether metaphysics, descriptive or speculative, or logic, is never master in theology, but its indispensable servant, never however giving a service that can be construed after a formula but one that throws light, now in one direction, now in another.[4]

In this chapter I want to see how this sort of approach can be followed through further in exploring one of MacKinnon's main themes, tragedy and atonement. Earlier in the essay quoted above he says that the Christian system of projection is one 'in which one form of expression complements the deficiency of another'.[5] In that essay he demonstrates this in relation to John's narrative and philosophical discourse. In discussing atonement he often adds a third genre, that of tragic drama. My main reference-points will be his writings that combine those three, and I will add three other main partners: Paul's second letter to the Corinthians, Dame Helen Gardner's T. S. Eliot Memorial Lectures of 1968 on 'Religion and Tragedy', and the philosophy of Emmanuel Levinas (joining the discussion in that order).

2 Corinthians and Atonement

The doctrine of atonement has found many of its favourite texts in 2 Corinthians. In particular, chapter 5 has provided them:

---

[4]   Ibid., p. 89.
[5]   Ibid., p. 74.

For the love of Christ controls us, because we are convinced that one has died for all; therefore all have died. And he died for all, so that those who live might no longer live for themselves but for him who for their sake died and was raised. (5:14–15)

Therefore if anyone is in Christ, he is a new creation; the old has passed away, behold, the new has come. All this is from God, who through Christ reconciled us to himself and gave us the ministry of reconciliation; that is, in Christ God was reconciling the world to himself, not counting their trespasses against them, and entrusting to us the message of reconciliation. So we are ambassadors for Christ, God making his appeal through us. We beseech you on behalf of Christ, be reconciled to God. For our sake he made him to be sin who knew no sin, so that in him we might become the righteousness of God. (5:17–21)

Yet the doctrine that has quoted these has often failed to learn from their setting. In MacKinnon's terms, their sense is inseparable from the way they are related to the contingencies of history. The importance of contingency is even clearer in this letter than it is in the Gospels. Paul's gospel is not necessary or general truths but news of a particular person and events. It is itself communicated through involvement in all the contingencies of life, and people have to be appealed to and persuaded to respond to it so that its history is contingent on their responses. The letter itself is part of this, sent into a particular situation as an appeal that tries to change the way the church in Corinth is behaving. It is full of references to the joyful and the painful contingencies of Paul's ministry and his relationship with the Corinthians, seen in the light of the gospel: and this reaches its climax in Paul's account of what he learnt about God's own involvement in contingencies – 'my power is made perfect in weakness' (12:9).

There is a family of metaphors that Paul uses which captures something of this sense of the contingent, the practical and the relational quality of atonement or reconciliation. The doctrine of the atonement is notorious for its inextricability from metaphors – legal, military, medical, social, cultic and financial – and many doctrines seem like the systematization of a central metaphor. Yet the abuse of metaphor is just the other side of its importance, and it has to be thought through. In the passages just quoted from 2 Corinthians a key metaphor is that of exchange. This clearly has cultic resonances in relation to sacrifice, but it also has financial and economic connections, and the rest of 2 Corinthians reinforces this latter line of inquiry. The Holy Spirit is a down-payment or guarantee (1:22, 5:5), the gospel is 'this treasure' (4:7), Paul sees himself as a poor man who makes many rich (6:10) and his activity is characterized as *diakonia*, a basic form of work in the economy of the time. Corinth was a major commercial centre, and Paul himself was a craftsman who manufactured, bought and sold and probably integrated his ministry and his daily work, so it is not surprising that his gospel was expressed partly in economic language about resources, work, money, production, distribution, promises, value and exchange, together with the processes and relationships that these involve.

But it is what he does with this family of metaphors that is most significant. The content of the gospel transforms the concept of economy that is taken up. One obvious feature is its theocentricity. God has set up this economy and has produced a resource comparable to the most fundamental resource, creation (cf. 4:6, 5:17). The nature of this Christ-centred work of God is the key theme of Paul's gospel, and the most astonishing fact about it is that it is simply given by God. God has done something and offered it freely, and this availability of grace, life, the Spirit, glory, reconciliation, freedom, wealth, or however else it is described, determines both Paul's work and the new state of affairs of the world. The distribution of this resource is now the most urgent priority, and Paul calls this 'co-working' with God (6:1; cf. 1Cor. 3:9).

The generative event in this economy is the crucifixion and resurrection of Jesus Christ characterized as an exchange which enables a new economy of exchanges. There is no competition between 'objective' and 'subjective' atonement: intrinsic to the event is its purpose 'that those who live might live no longer for themselves but for him who for their sake died and was raised' (5:15). Believing the gospel means participation in the exchanges of the economy in all the contingencies of life:

> For as we share abundantly in Christ's sufferings, so through Christ we share abundantly in comfort too. If we are afflicted, it is for your comfort and salvation; and if we are comforted, it is for your comfort, which you experience when you patiently endure the same sufferings we suffer. Our hope for you is unshaken; for we know that as you share in our sufferings, you will also share in our comfort. (1:5–7)

One striking feature of that is the repeated note of abundance. It runs through the letter, expressed in thanks, praise, joy, hope and above all glory, summed up in 4:15: 'For everything is for your sake, so that grace abounding through more and more of you may cause thanksgiving to overflow to the glory of God.' The economy of the Roman empire was a 'limited good' economy, with a roughly stable, limited amount of resources. This divine economy was in contrast symbolized by 'grace abounding', 'more and more'. The unit of value was the whole person (Paul says: 'I will gladly spend and be spent on your behalf', 12:15) and the language of the measuring scales in the market is used to reckon cost-effectiveness: 'For this immediate trifle of an affliction produces for us, in extraordinary quantities, an eternal weight of glory' (4:17).

Perhaps the most remarkable thing, however, is what happens in chapters 8–9. There Paul writes about the collection for the Jerusalem Church. He takes the economic language which has already been transformed by the gospel content and he refers it back to literal finances. Financial attitudes and relationships are reconceived, and the literal and divine economies are shown as inextricably interwoven. Paul's terminology is astonishing – Dahl says it is untranslatable.[6] One key 'theological' word after another is applied to the collection. It is called *charis* (grace, gift of grace), *koinonia* (partnership, fellowship, sharing), *eulogia* (blessing, liberality), *leitourgia* (service, voluntary or priestly), *haplotes* (single-minded commitment, generosity) and *perisseuma* (overflow, abundance), among other terms. As Dahl shows, Greek and Jewish economic ideas and ethics are here taken up into something new.

The key theological statement puts a kenotic concept of the atonement in financial terms: 'For you know the grace of our Lord Jesus Christ, that though he was rich, yet for your sake he becomes poor, so that by his poverty you might become rich' (8:9). This is a redefinition of the gospel with very practical implications. The gospel has, in MacKinnon's words, provided 'the terms in which men and women . . . engage with the fundamental problems of their existence'.[7] For Paul the living reality of atonement is represented by the Macedonians:

We want you to know, brethren, about the grace of God which has been shown in the churches of Macedonia, for in a severe test of affliction their abundance of joy and their extreme poverty have overflowed in a wealth of liberality on their part. For they gave according to their means, and, as I can testify, beyond their means, of their own free will, begging us earnestly for the favour of taking part in the relief of the saints – and this, not as we had expected, but first they gave themselves to the Lord and to us by the will of God. (8:1–5)

---

[6] N. A. Dahl, *Studies in Paul* (Augsburg, Minneapolis, 1977), p. 31.
[7] 'The Future of Man', *Explorations, op. cit.*, p. 9.

There is the note of abundance and overflow again, yet without any for-getfulness of the Cross, and it reaches a crescendo in a string of hyperboles: 'in fact, God enables every grace to overflow into you, so that in every way and all the time you have total self-sufficiency to overflow into every act of goodness . . .' (9:8).

Through the economic metaphors, and also in many other ways,[8] this letter attempts to do justice to the crucified and risen Jesus Christ. MacKinnon has written of the letter:

> . . . its background is ontological; what Paul speaks of is not something that he records as 'the contents of his consciousness', but a sense of his mission and its significance that he has won through daring to see it in the light of the Cross. He knows that the ground of his mission, to which it belongs, is all. So there is a deep movement in his language between what is almost autobiographical description, what is theological interpretation, and what is, in effect, the expression of a deepened understanding of the mystery of the Cross through the refraction of that mystery, in the arcana of his own spiritual life and suffering. And yet, because all is under the sign of kenosis, the final note is of a radical self-abandonment.[9]

Yet one question that the letter prompts one to ask MacKinnon is whether he has done justice to the joyful note of abundance. Paul describes himself and others as 'sorrowful, yet always rejoicing' (6:10); can MacKinnon's emphasis on tragedy fully affirm the second half of the paradox? Or, putting another side of the question, is there any sense of tragedy that can go with 2 Corinthians as a whole? This brings us to the next contributor to our discussion.

Tragedy and 2 Corinthians

Dame Helen Gardner agrees with the common view that a characteristic mark of tragedy is the embracing of contraries in tension.[10] There are various ways of formulating the tension: between ultimate sense and non-sense, between two ideals (a conflict in the very ethical nature of reality),

---

[8]   For a fuller treatment of this and other aspects of 2 Corinthians discussed in this essay see Frances M. Young and David F. Ford, *Meaning and Truth in 2 Corinthians* (SPCK, London, 1987).

[9]   'Philosophy and Christology', *Borderlands, op. cit.*, p. 80.

[10]   'Religion and Tragedy', *Religion and Literature* (Oxford University Press, London, 1971), pp. 13–118.

between contradictory aspects of human nature, between the Dionysian and the Apollonian, between protest and acceptance, or between the contingencies of life and their meaningful coherence. From this joining of contraries comes the ambiguity of tragedy, which is notably seen in the vastly varied interpretations that the great tragedies have been able to sustain. Other key marks of tragedy are the stature and dignity of the chief character or characters, the unavoidability of distress and suffering, and the plot, the logic of events which has some sort of resolution.

Paul's gospel, and the drama of which his life, according to 2 Corinthians, is a part, could fit such criteria (one can see contraries in tension, ambiguities, suffering, characters of stature and a plot with resolution), but the pivotal issue is the relation of crucifixion to resurrection. Surely that resolution is untragic? I think not. Indeed, I want to argue that 2 Corinthians shows the tragic being taken into a transformation which sharpens rather than negates it, while yet rendering the category of the tragic inadequate by itself. The genre of tragedy remains a helpful way to illuminate 2 Corinthians and its concept of atonement while yet being unable to do justice to all that is there.

The case is as follows. Paul is as acutely aware as MacKinnon of the dangers of a triumphalist understanding of the resurrection. In 1 Corinthians he had had to reassert the continuing centrality of the cross, and in 2 Corinthians he pursues the theme with a more personal focus. The major issue is his own authority, and he sees the mistake of his opponents being to conceive power and authority in terms that divorce the resurrection from the content of crucifixion. The resurrection is not simply the reversal of death, leaving death behind it. Paul 'carries in the body the death of Jesus' (4:10): the resurrection message has sent him even more deeply into contingency, weakness and suffering. It is an atonement whose power is to allow him to stay close to, even immersed in, the tragic depths of life.

But there is a purpose in this: it is to communicate the gospel. Here is the clue to the new possibility of tragedy. The gospel is the new contingency. It relativizes all the old contingencies of suffering and death. But it does not end contingency; rather, it intensifies it terrifyingly. Paul can hardly bear the tension this means for someone with a responsibility like his: 'For we are the aroma of Christ to God among those who are being saved and among those who are perishing, to one a fragrance from death to death, to the other a fragrance from life to life. Who is sufficient for these things?' (2:15–16). There is the new contingency, the new mystery. Paul even says: 'And even if our gospel is veiled, it is veiled only to those who are perishing. In their case the God of this world has blinded the minds of the unbelievers, to keep them from seeing the light of the gospel of the glory of

Christ, who is the image of God' (4:4. 'The god of this world' is how the Revised Standard Version actually reads, with God in lower case, but I think this is a shying away from the apparently intolerable meaning of the Greek.)

This means that there is no guaranteed happy ending. There is a continuing possibility that can only be called tragic. There is a temptation to resolve this in predestinarian terms (4:4 could be taken like that), but that would make nonsense of the urgency and responsibility of Paul's ministry. Its urgency is only comprehensible if the things he does and says are significant, if tragic disobedience is a possibility, if in some sense the future is open while yet in God's hands. (I will take up this problem in relation to eschatology in the final section.)

Helen Gardner says: 'Tragedy displays causes in calamities and shows design, but in so doing reveals what remains mysterious and inexplicable.'[11] That fits Paul and his gospel. She also argues that what is conceived as calamity changes in emphasis from Greek to Elizabethan tragedy. For the Greek tragedians tragic suffering was connected with the changes and chances of life, the possibility of pollution, and the tensions between arbitrariness and law and between the jealousy and the justice of the gods. For the Elizabethans there was rather the tension between mortality and immortal longings, and between undeserved suffering, guilt and the need for justice. What is calamity for Paul? For him the concerns of both Greeks and Elizabethans are taken up to some extent, but they are relativized by the gospel, and the sense of touching the deepest mystery surrounds the gospel itself. Calamity is rejection of the gospel, or unfaithfulness to it. In this drama ultimately significant events happen, and because contingency, justice, death and suffering are part of them, tragedy continues to illuminate them.

This is intensified by what at first sight may seem to weaken the sense of tragedy in 2 Corinthians: the extraordinary reality of *shared* suffering in the Christian community. Paul draws continual comfort from his joint membership in Christ with others who share both his joy and his suffering. Is it not the case that suffering taken up into this mutual comfort and even rejoicing can hardly be called tragic? And in MacKinnon's treatment of the church, is there again a failure to maintain that combination of 'sorrowful yet always rejoicing' that Paul's grasp of atonement enabled him to affirm?

Helen Gardner's lecture on Shakespearean tragedy concludes with a remarkable comment on *Lear*:

---

[11]   Ibid., p. 104.

King Lear presents an extremity of suffering, physical and mental, falling on man from the hostility of the natural world, the cruelty of others, the visitations of fortune, and the burning shame the thought of his own sins and follies brings. It displays suffering as the universal law of life with all the heightening of common experience that tragedy gives. But without in any way diminishing agony and pain it shows men discovering through their suffering truth, and beyond its demonstration of learning by suffering, the *to pathein mathein* of the Aeschylean tragedy of suffering it displays most movingly the fellowship of suffering, that men are bound to each other in their pain. As the play proceeds the prosperous fall apart; the outcasts draw together, sharing each other's burdens and bearing their griefs.[12]

She sees such mutuality, and the overall ethical temper of Shakespeare's plays, with their valuing of mercy, gentleness and conscience, as signs of their being deeply Christian, usually in a secular way. She also shows how the fellowship of suffering and even the possibility of renewed joy are not incompatible with the greatest tragedy.

The fellowship in *Lear* is hardly comparable with that seen in 2 Corinthians, but yet one can see how the latter does not rule out the tragic either. The focusing of what one might call Paul's concept of the tragic around the gospel means that the community called into being through the gospel is also subject to the threat of tragedy. Indeed, it is almost as if in Paul's dramatic conception of history the spectacle of the people of God, whether Israel or the church, is what chiefly evokes his pity and fear. 'The corruption of the best is the worst', and he is acutely aware of how the place of greatest glory is also the place of greatest responsibility and temptation. MacKinnon, coming after nearly 2,000 years of church history, has even more appalling evidence that the gospel, far from making the category of tragedy less important, both illuminates new ways in which it is relevant and makes possible new forms of communal evil. There is again a heightening or deepening of the tragic even as its ultimate content is transformed by the gospel.

But now we have to ask about that transformation. As MacKinnon says, referring to his philosophical concepts, tragedy has to be used but not allowed to dominate or obscure the uniqueness of what is here. What is this uniqueness?

The Face of Christ

We have already tried to show that any uniqueness is not to be found in such characteristics as taking contingency and evil with ultimate seriousness,

[12]   Ibid., p. 88.

or in leaving behind, in the interests of a happy ending, the tensions between contraries, or in sharing the tragic reality of life in a community that is itself somehow the answer to tragedy. The question symbolized by Paul's phrase 'sorrowful, yet always rejoicing' has also been raised about MacKinnon's way of relating tragedy to the gospel. I have defended him against any simplistic accusation in these terms, such as Paul's opponents in Corinth might have made, but a question remains. How do we identify the inadequacy of tragedy as a genre through which to understand the gospel whose climax is the resurrection joy, but without falling into the traps which MacKinnon has so insistently pointed out?

2 Corinthians suggests a possible answer. Its most powerful and original theology does not come in the passages already quoted in chapter 5 but in the previous two chapters, in the light of which the explicit statements about atonement need to be understood. In chapters 3–4 Paul sets his own ministry in the context of Moses at Sinai and the distinctive content and effects of the gospel. The climactic verse is 4:6: 'For it is the God who said, "Let light shine in darkness," who has shone in our hearts to give the light of the knowledge of the glory of God in the face of Christ.' That verse could inspire a whole systematics, but the phrase I want to explore is 'the glory of God in the face of Christ'.

Could this be one way of beginning to develop the 'radicalized and transformed' notion of the contingent that MacKinnon suggests is required by christology?[13] This face has been through historical contingencies; it is not separable from them yet also not reducible to them. It has also been dead. Yet it is seen as the manifestation of the glory of God, so that in future the glory of God and this death cannot be thought of without each other. It has also been raised from death, and represents the unity beyond paradox of the crucifixion and resurrection. The face of Christ calls for christology as well as soteriology. And for all its definitiveness it also allows one to conceive of continuing involvement in contingency, the sensitivity of a living face to events and people, and a mode of interaction which respects the freedom and randomness of creation while yet continuing to suffer and confront it.

Yet an important thing to note about the phrase 'the face of Christ' is that it is also eschatological (cf. 1 Cor. 13:12 – 'but then face to face'). It can help us to rethink many ideas of eschatology. If the ultimate is recognized in a face, we glimpse a way out of the dilemma of eschatology which so often seems unable to conceive of a definitive consummation of history without also seeing it as predetermined. The face of Christ is definitive, but

[13]   'Philosophy and Christology', *Borderlands, op. cit.*, p. 81.

it does not predetermine. Rather it is the counterpart of a new history of freedom and responsibility, involving a new notion of what glory and freedom are, as the rest of 2 Corinthians makes clear.

What about tragedy? In Helen Gardner's attempt to redefine tragedy with all its apparent paradoxes she eventually chose the analogy of a face:

> I have left to last a formula that for me comes very near expressing the nature of tragedy: the words that Beethoven scrawled, perhaps only in jest, above the opening bars of the last movement of his last quartet: 'Muss es sein?' 'Es muss sein'. He wrote above the whole movement the words 'Der schwer gefasste Entschluss', 'The Difficult Resolution'. The affirmation is in the same words as the question; only a hair's breadth, hardly more than an inflection of the voice separates them. Protest and acceptance are like expressions on the same face. According to their convictions and beliefs men attempt to conceptualize the protest and the affirmation; and according to temperament and even to mood the balance between question and answer quivers. Some find the essence of tragedy in the power with which the question cried out; others in the difficult final resolution.[14]

Perhaps in the light of 2 Corinthians the face could be more than an analogy. The gospel is about someone who has done justice to the tragic. This face, beyond all categories and syntheses, embodies both the powerful question and the difficult final resolution. And it is a resolution that does not fall into triumphalism or cheap joy when it enables the overflow of thanks and Paul's 'always rejoicing'.

At this point MacKinnon's question might be: but what sort of face is this face? In 2 Corinthians it is one of a historical succession of faces, from Moses through to the Corinthians. It is not just an idea or a future ideal but belongs to one who was 'made sin' and crucified. In its affirmation there is an inescapable element of trust in testimony. Yet the shining of this face in the heart is not simply a matter of perception or believing someone else's testimony. The matter is just as complex as in John, chapter 20, and for the same reason: the relationship of faith to sight is extremely difficult to formulate appropriately. What MacKinnon's brilliant redescription of the issue by reference to John 20 does is to leave open the space for such a strange concept as the face of Christ. This face is heard of and anticipated, but not yet seen face to face; it is unsubstitutably identified not by identikit or photofit but by the events of crucifixion and resurrection; it fits no category short of the glory of God; and it is only appropriately recognized in a context such as that in which 2 Cor.4:6 places it – that of the complete

---

[14] 'Religion and Tragedy', *op. cit.*, p. 34.

prevenience of the God who said 'Let light shine in darkness', and of the transformation of selves in community that happens when this face is allowed to shine *kata pneuma* in our hearts. In other words, the trinitarian structure of the verse testifies to the incomparable fact of this face.

This leads into the question of ontology. What sort of metaphysics can do justice to the ultimacy of a face? The philosophy of Emmanuel Levinas attempts to offer one. It hits the same Jewish roots as Paul's writings; and Levinas is also quoted as saying: 'All philosophy is in Shakespeare'. At the heart of his thought is the idea of an irreducible pluralism in being, whose primary form is the 'face to face'. There is no synthesizing of faces, no inclusion of their otherness in an overarching concept of sameness, a general notion of 'being'. The essence of the relationship is that it is ethical: the face of the other represents an appeal, even a command, which lays a primary responsibility on me. Levinas criticizes ontology for often attempting to conceive the unity of being as some sort of totality of which it is possible to have, at least in principle, an overview. The other whom I meet has an exteriority, an alterity, that resists all fusion, all comprehension, all inclusion in sameness.

Levinas connects language and reason as well as ethics with the plural reality of the face to face. The face is an ethical presence, appealing and appealed to, accompanying its presence with speech. Transcendence is to be understood from here, breaking through any idolatry of the face understood as just a visible form:

> If the transcendent cuts across sensibility, if it is openness preeminently, if its vision is the vision of the very openness of being, it cuts across the vision of forms and can be stated neither in terms of contemplation nor in terms of practice. It is the face; its revelation is speech. The relation with the Other alone introduces a dimension of transcendence, and leads to a relation totally different from experience in the sensible sense of the term, relative and egoist.[15]

The theological conclusion of Levinas is: 'Monotheism signifies this human kinship, this idea of a human race that refers back to the approach of the Other in the face, in a dimension of height, in responsibility for oneself and for the Other.'[16] God therefore represents, negatively, a critique of any ontology that unifies being by ignoring the ultimate pluralism of the face to face, and, positively, the priority of ethics over ontology. This allows both the

---

[15]   *Totality and Infinity: An Essay on Exteriority* (Duquesne University Press, Pittsburgh, 1969), p. 193.
[16]   Ibid., p. 214.

question of tragedy (how could a twentieth-century East European Jew fail to be gripped by that question?) and the difficult resolution; and, through and beyond that, the glory of the face.

I suggest that there is here a metaphysics which meets the demand MacKinnon makes, at the end of his chapter on 'The Transcendence of the Tragic' in his Gifford Lectures, for an ontological pluralism which is not atheist and which, by holding to the significance of the tragic, is protected against 'that sort of synthesis which seeks to obliterate by the vision of an all-embracing order the sharper discontinuity of human existence'.[17] But Levinas traces the discontinuity, the pluralism, not only to the sharpness of the tragic but to the face, which can express as well as agony. And in the face of Christ I see a manifestation of the Christian eschatological hope: for a non-tragic outcome of history which yet does full justice to the tragic.

Finally, I want to end with a question. As Kenneth Surin has written, MacKinnon's 'preference is for an interrogative, as opposed to an affirmative, mode of theological discourse'.[18] The question is from John Donne's sermon on the verse 'Jesus wept'. In it the themes of this essay converge – tragedy, atonement, eschatology, the face and the possibility of being 'sorrowful, yet always rejoicing'. And this genuinely open question comes from the sorrowful side, in deepest gratitude to Donald MacKinnon whose thought and, dare I say it, whose face have shown the intensity and yet sensitivity of the interrogation that the tragic must be allowed to conduct in theology and philosophy:

> When God shall come to the last Act in the glorifying of Man, when he promises, *to wipe all teares from his eyes*, what shall God have to doe with that eye that never wept?[19]

---

[17] *The Problem of Metaphysics* (Cambridge University Press, Cambridge, 1974), p. 135.
[18] 'Christology, Tragedy and Ideology', *Theology*, 89 (July 1986), p. 285.
[19] Quoted in 'Religion and Tragedy', *op cit.*, p. 78.

Chapter Twelve

APOPHASIS AND THE SHOAH: WHERE WAS JESUS CHRIST AT AUSCHWITZ?

George Steiner in his autobiography recalls his friendship with Donald MacKinnon and says:

> There could, for Donald, be no justifiable future for Christianity so long as Christian theology and practice had not faced up to, had not internalized lucidly, its seminal role in the millennial torments of Judaism and in the Holocaust. Primarily, this signified coming to terms with the horror of Golgotha, a horror unredeemed – this was Donald's compulsive instinct – by the putative wonder of resurrection or by any promise of celestial reparation.[1]

Steiner also writes of MacKinnon 'trying to "think" Auschwitz and Golgotha as implicated in some interrelated finality'.[2]

Golgotha and Auschwitz are also connected by Rabbi Dr Nicholas de Lange in his 1997 Cardinal Bea Memorial Lecture, in which he presses the question which I have included in my title, 'Where was Jesus Christ at Auschwitz?',[3] and de Lange is himself drawing on what his own teacher, Ignaz Maybaum, said on this theme.[4]

Both Jesus Christ and the Holocaust (or Shoah, as I will refer to it) invite thought about 'silence and the word', and I will explore the theme with special reference to one text by Anne Michaels related to the Shoah, and another on Christology by Dietrich Bonhoeffer.

[1] George Steiner, *Errata, An Examined Life* (Yale University Press, New Haven, CT and London, 1997), p. 152.
[2] Ibid.
[3] Nicholas de Lange, 'Jesus and Auschwitz' in *New Blackfriars*, vol. 78, no. 917/918, pp. 308-16.
[4] See Ignaz Maybaum, *The Face of God After Auschwitz* (Polek and Van Gennep, Amsterdam, 1965).

Silence and the Word in *Fugitive Pieces*

Anne Michaels is a poet–novelist who steeped herself in the history and eyewitness testimony of the Shoah during the writing of her novel, *Fugitive Pieces*.[5] What emerges is a somewhat fragmented yet often profound work on the Shoah. It has something of the impact of Solzhenitsyn's novels about the Gulag Archipelago. Anne Michaels does not combine her fictional skill with Solzhenitsyn's personal testimony, and her main authorial standpoint is that of the generation after the survivors; but this helps her into a more penetrating and self-aware appreciation of the levels and complexities of the language and silence of testimony, of the significance of time for memory, and of the subtle interrelations of evil, beauty, goodness and truth. In both of them the complementarity of history and fiction is instructive: neither the Gulag nor the Shoah can be done adequate justice to in 'straight' history. There is also a fascinating question about the optimum time for mature testimony to 'epoch-making events'.[6] There is a period at some distance from the events − when the first shock, surprise and even speechlessness has been come through, and when there has been time for meaning to have been distilled into a combination of testimony with wisdom − yet before the last eyewitnesses have died: that is the period, soon to end, in which we live now. It may therefore be the best time for producing classic testimonies to the Shoah in various genres and media.

Fugitive Pieces is largely about Jakob Beer, who when he was seven was in hiding behind the wall of the room where his parents were murdered during a Nazi action, and his older sister Bella disappeared. He was rescued by Athos, a Greek geologist and archaeologist, who hides him in his own home on a Greek island during the war and later emigrates with Jakob to Canada. Jakob becomes a poet who writes about the Shoah, and he also edits Athos's posthumous work, *Bearing False Witness*, about the Nazi falsification of archaeological evidence. The second part of the book concerns Ben, an admirer of Jakob's poetry who discovers his lost journals in Greece. There is a complex interweaving of testimonies by and to Jakob and to the Shoah, covering three generations, and this allows for fascinating interrelationships of time, memory, language and truth to be explored. And again and again there is the theme of silence.

---

[5] Anne Michaels, *Fugitive Pieces* (Bloomsbury, London, 1998). She underlines this by acknowledging her principal sources at the end of the hook.
[6] Cf. Paul Ricoeur, *Time and Narrative*, vol. 3 (University of Chicago Press, Chicago 1988), chapter 8, 'The Interweaving of Fiction and History', especially on 'epoch-making events'.

The book is like a phenomenology of silence in various forms.[7] It describes the silence of the room after the traumatic event of the action, of a parent's apartment after his death; more metaphorical silences after a marriage fails ('And then the world fell silent' – p. 139) and after the Shoah itself; and the 'ghastly silence' (p. 285) when the sound of the waves stops in Hawaii before an earthquake. There are silences of absence, of overwhelming grief, of a past that has been erased, of lack of news, of response to emptiness and to plenitude, of sleep, of lack of forgiveness because the one who could forgive has gone, and of long intervals between notes as a child tries to play a piano piece without making mistakes.

In Ben's family, where the parents survived the camps but the father could not talk of it,

> [t]he code of silence became more complex as I grew older. There were more and more things to keep from my father. The secrets between my mother and me were a conspiracy. What was our greatest insurrection? My mother was determined to impress upon me the absolute, inviolate necessity of pleasure . . . Loss is an edge; it swelled everything for my mother, and drained everything from my father. Because of this, I thought my mother was stronger. But now I see it was a clue: what my father had experienced was that much less bearable. (p. 223)

The father has a special relationship with his daughter–in–law, who respects his silence, broaching the rich theme of reserve:

> What I had mistaken for confidentiality from my father was simply the relief of a man who realizes he won't have to give up his silence. It's the ease Naomi's grace encourages in everyone. She will honour privacy to the end. (p. 249)

Ben only discovers after his parents' death that he had had a brother and sister who died in the Shoah:

> I'll never know whether the two names on back of my father's photograph, if they had ever been spoken, would have filled the silence of my parents' apartment. (p. 280)

---

[7] I am grateful to Rachel Muers for her work on silence from which I have learnt much, not least her survey of the phenomenological literature. See Rachel Muers, *Keeping God's Silence* (Blackwell, Oxford, 2004).

Perhaps at the heart of the novel's sensitivity to 'silence and the word' is its treatment of testimony to the Shoah. The awesome task of giving testimony is traced from many angles:

> I began to understand how here, alone, in the red and yellow of poppies and broom, you had felt safe enough to begin *Groundwork* [Beer's first volume of poetry on the Shoah]. How you descended into horror slowly, as divers descend, with will and method. How, as you dropped deeper, the silence pounded. (p. 266)

> Truth grows gradually in us, like a musician who plays a piece again and again until suddenly he hears it for the first time. (p. 251)

> Grief requires time. If a chip of stone radiates its self [the previous page was about radiocarbons and rock magnetism], its breath, so long, how stubborn might be the soul. If sound waves carry on to infinity, where are their screams now? I imagine them somewhere in the galaxy, moving forever towards the psalms. (p. 54)

> I listened to these dark shapes as if they were black spaces in music, a musician learning the silences of a piece. I felt this was my truth. That my life could not be stored in any language but only in silence; the moment I looked into the room [where his parents lay murdered] and took in only what was visible, not vanished. The moment I failed to see Bella had disappeared. But I did not know how to seek by way of silence. So I lived a breath apart, a touch-typist who holds his hands above the keys slightly in the wrong place, the words coming out meaningless, garbled. Bella and I only inches apart, the wall between us. I thought of writing poems this way, in code, every letter askew, so that loss would wreck the language, become the language.

> If one could isolate that space, that damaged chromosome in words, in an image, then perhaps one could restore order by naming. Otherwise history is only a tangle of wires . . .

> English was a sonar, a microscope, through which I listened and observed, waiting to capture elusive meanings buried in facts. I wanted a line in a poem to be the hollow ney of the dervish orchestra whose plaintive wail is a call to God. But all I achieved was awkward shrieking. Not even the pure shriek of a reed in the rain. (pp. 112–13)

The content of the testimony has an utter realism which again and again rings true as it evokes well-known elements of the Shoah: sheer terror;

children killed wantonly, playfully; starvation; humiliation; the brutality of an action beginning with beating on doors; torture; forced marches; prisoners exhuming thousands of rotting corpses; 'those who breathed deep and suffocated' (p. 139); the scholars of Lublin sobbing as they 'watched their holy and beloved books thrown out of the second-storey window of the Talmudic Academy and burned' as a military band played and soldiers sang (p. 138); and the devastation of so much ordinary life:

> That they were torn from mistakes they had no chance to fix; everything unfinished. All the sins of love without detail, detail without love. The regret of having spoken, of having run out of time to speak. Of hoarding oneself. Of turning one's back too often in favour of sleep.
>
> I tried to imagine their physical needs, the indignity of human needs grown so extreme they equal your longing for wife, child, sister, parent, friend. But truthfully I couldn't even begin to imagine the trauma of their hearts, of being taken in the middle of their lives. Those with young children. Or those newly in love, wrenched from that state of grace. Or those who had lived invisibly, who were never known. (p. 147)

For all the vividness, it is a realism which conveys not just the inexpressibility of the Shoah but its pressure to find new forms of inexpressibility, more adequate forms of silence. Beer's life is dedicated to witnessing to the Shoah in poetry, but we are only given (p. 268) a two-line fragment of his poetry – and that is not directly about the Shoah. So the novel surrounds with words the crucial testimony which is never made explicit – and which, of course, only exists in a fictional oeuvre. It evokes chasms of silence of many sorts in survivors, families, victims, perpetrators, nations, genres. It also describes a life dedicated to a discipline of words inextricable from a discipline of silence. There is a simultaneity of word and silence embodied in Jakob Beer's life and work, testified to by himself and others, and all related to (though not by any means reducible to) the Shoah.

Resonances with Anne Michaels: Silence and the Word in Bonhoeffer's *Christology*

At this point the startling opening of Bonhoeffer's *Christology* is apposite:

> Teaching about Christ begins in silence. 'Be silent, for that is the absolute' (Kierkegaard). This has nothing to do with mystical silence which, in its

absence of words, is, nevertheless, the soul secretly chattering away to itself.
The church's silence is silence before the Word. In proclaiming the Word, the
church must fall silent before the inexpressible: Let what cannot be spoken
be worshipped in silence (Cyril of Alexandria). The spoken Word is the
inexpressible: that which cannot be spoken is the Word. It must be spoken,
it is the great battle cry of the church (Luther). The church utters it in the
world, yet it still remains the inexpressible. To speak of Christ means to keep
silent; to be silent about Christ means to speak. The proclamation of Christ
is the church speaking from a proper silence.

We are concerned here with the meaning of this proclamation. Its content
is revealed only in the proclamation itself. To speak of Christ, then, will be
to speak within the context of the silence of the church. We must study
christology in the humble silence of the worshipping community. Prayer is
to be silent and to cry out at the same time, before God in the presence of
his Word. We have come together as a community to study Christ, God's
Word. We have not met in church, but in the lecture room. We have academic
work to do.[8]

The simultaneity of silence and crying out, understood in the context
of prayer 'before God in the presence of his Word' leads into Bonhoeffer's
basic Christological principle: the priority of the 'Who?' question.
Thought about Christ is continually in danger of being captured by
'How?' questions, trying to understand how Jesus Christ fits into our frameworks, disciplines and classifications, how he can be understood in causal
terms or in coherence with other ideas, how incarnation might be possible,
how the history of Jesus might be proved, and so on. At the heart of Christology is the perception that the appropriate framing question is the one
addressed to Jesus Christ in prayer: 'Who are you?'[9] The answer (in brief −
Bonhoeffer spends most of the lectures expanding on it) is: the historical
(geschichtliche), crucified and risen Jesus Christ who is God and human for
us. There is an asymmetrical simultaneity of life, death and resurrection in
this person who is hiddenly present, mediated through word, sacrament and
community.

Intrinsic to this interrogative encounter is silence:

'Who are you?' asks Pilate. Jesus is silent. Man cannot wait for the dangerous
answer. The Logos cannot endure the Anti-Logos. It knows that one of them
must die. So it kills the person of whom it is asked.[10]

[8]   Dietrich Bonhoeffer, *Christology* (Collins, London and New York, 1971), p. 27.
[9]   Ibid., pp. 28ff.
[10]   Ibid., pp. 33–4.

The silence of the Word who is killed is the key to Christian silence, and the risen Christ is always *simul* (simultaneously) the crucified one. It is the silence of this particular person, who both speaks and is silent as incarnate, crucified and risen. The simultaneity of silence and word is here defined through the simultaneity of the life, death and resurrection of Jesus Christ.

And there is a further *simul:* the question we address to Christ, 'Who are you?', is reversed as we are addressed by him: 'Who are *you?*' – 'The Christological question "Who?" is finally formulated only where this reversed question is also heard.'[11]

The resonances between the simultaneities of Michaels and Bonhoeffer should be clear. Bonhoeffer, as is appropriate for his lecture genre, conceptualizes the key issue of the priority of the 'Who?' question, while Michaels' novel conveys it through narrative. By the end of *Fugitive Pieces* she has portrayed silence as constitutive in the identities of her key characters. The 'How' questions have not been ignored – how to 'seek by way of silence', how to cope with the silence of absence and death, how to describe and interpret the forms and codes of silence, how language relates to silence, how silence is part of the 'descent into horror'. Indeed, Michaels gives these a significance which might invite us to open up Bonhoeffer's theology to such questions more than he does. Especially on questions to do with language he has little to say. But Michaels does implicitly follow Bonhoeffer's priority of the 'Who?' while doing so polyphonically through a range of characters.[12]

But does Michaels have anything resembling the *simul* of Bonhoeffer's incarnation, crucifixion and resurrection? I have already described her realism about the horror of the Shoah, analogous to that of the crucifixion. The novel is also pervaded by what might be read as an incarnational realism, savouring ordinariness, physicality, the life of the senses, the natural world, pleasure, human relationships, without any hint of dualism or dichotomy as regards what is 'spiritual'.

But there is also a clear indication that the horror of the Shoah does not have the last word. This third dimension of her realism is signalled by the occurrence, without any loss of the other two dimensions, and in close (often inextricable) relationship with them, of words such as truth, goodness, beauty, dignity, gratitude, grace, revelation, faith, trust, hope, singing, poetry and, above all, love.

[11]   Ibid., p. 34.
[12]   For polyphony as a hermeneutical key to Bonhoeffer's theology see David F. Ford, *Self and Salvation: Being Transformed* (Cambridge University Press, Cambridge, 1999), chapter 10.

In the Golleschau quarry, stone-carriers were forced to haul huge blocks of limestone endlessly, from one mound to another and back again. During the torture, they carried their lives in their hands. The insane task was not futile only in the sense that faith is not futile. (p. 53)

A camp inmate looked up at the stars and suddenly remembered that they'd once seemed beautiful to him. This memory of beauty was accompanied by a bizarre stab of gratitude. When I first read this I couldn't imagine it. But later I felt I understood. Sometimes the body experiences a revelation because it has abandoned every other possibility. (p. 53)

Irony as scissors, a divining rod, always pointing in two directions. If the evil act can't be erased, then neither can the good. It's as accurate a measure as any of a society: what is the smallest act of kindness that is considered heroic? In those days, to be moral required no more than the slightest flicker of movement — a micrometre — of eyes looking away or blinking, while a running man crossed a field. And those who gave water or bread! They entered a realm higher than the angels' simply by remaining in the human mire. (p. 162)

Yet it is also clear that the simultaneity of these realisms is not symmetry. They are not in balance. There is far more than survival in the aftermath of the Shoah; nor is it a matter of reaffirming natural and social life as if there had been no cataclysm.

Since his death, I've come to respect my father's caches of food around the house as evidence of his ingenuity, his self-perception. *It's not a person's depth you must discover, but their ascent. Find their path from depth to ascent.* (pp. 249–50)

To remain with the dead is to abandon them.
   All the years I felt Bella entreating me, filled with her loneliness, I was mistaken. I have misunderstood her signals. Like other ghosts, she whispers; not for me to join her, but so that, when I'm close enough, she can push me back into the world. (p. 170)

The hope is not only personal; there are hints of it even on the metanarrative level of history:

Athos's backward glance gave me a backward hope. Redemption through cataclysm; what had once been transformed might be transformed again. (p. 101)

But the primary level of this realism of hope and redemption is the face to face. Perhaps the climactic moment in the novel is Jakob Beer's discovery of the joy of love with his second wife Michaela. The key image for it is taken from a story of a Polish painter born 10 years before the war who said at the party where Jakob met Michaela: 'All my life . . . I've asked myself one question: How can you hate all you have come from and not hate yourself?' (p. 184) He had bought himself tubes of bright yellow paint but could not bring himself to use them.

> The first morning I woke to Michaela – my head on the small of her back, her heels like two islands under the blanket – I knew that this was my first experience of the colour yellow. (p. 184)

> Your poems from those few years with Michaela, poems of a man who feels, for the first time, a future. Your words and your life no longer separate, after *decades of hiding in your skin* . . .

> *Is there a woman who will slowly undress*
> *my spirit, bring my body to belief* (pp. 267–8)

There are obviously immense differences between the testimony of Bonhoeffer to Jesus Christ and that of Anne Michaels to the Shoah and the fictional Jakob Beer, but their structures of simultaneous, asymmetrical, multiple realisms, to which silence and speech are intrinsic, and which are embodied in particular persons, are sufficiently analogous to be mutually illuminating and interrogating.

Perhaps the most penetrating question suggested by Michaels about Bonhoeffer's concept of silence is whether he allows silence a full simultaneity with speech beyond the crucifixion. For Michaels, the horror of the Shoah does not have the last word, but nor does it have the last silence: there is a further rich phenomenology of silence beyond it – analogies of 'the colour yellow' at the heart of the silences of love. Silence for Bonhoeffer retains the sense of a limit-concept, and its pivotal event is the crucifixion. It is never developed as a habitable medium which is as important to communication and to joy in God as are words. His dismissal of mystical silence as 'the soul secretly chattering away to itself' no doubt has relevance to some practices; but the silence of many mystics could also be heard as an other-oriented adoration which takes seriously Bonhoeffer's own principle of the simultaneity of word and silence, and which allows for the ultimacy of silence as well as word.

Beyond Resonances: Where was Jesus Christ at Auschwitz?

Resonances such as those between Bonhoeffer and Michaels are not sufficient answer to the hard questions posed earlier by MacKinnon and de
Lange. Those questions call for theology which grapples both with what
MacKinnon calls 'the millennial torments of Judaism' during the past two
thousand years, and with de Lange's challenge to Christians about the presence of Jesus Christ in Auschwitz. They are vast topics, and I will offer just
one theological approach to each question.[13]

The Gentile sub-plot: a non-supersessionist Christian theology

The first approach will be dealt with very briefly, because, while I see it as
a minimal essential requirement for Christian theology which takes
MacKinnon's point seriously, yet for my purposes here it is the framework
for answering my title question rather than the central issue, and I have also
discussed it elsewhere.[14] This is the issue of supersessionism.

Supersessionism sees the church as superseding the Jews as the people of
God. This can be accompanied by active hatred and attacks on Jews for their
role in killing Christ and rejecting the Christian message, or it can encourage attempts to convert them, or it can be neutral or even benignly tolerant
towards them; but the key point is that the theology of supersessionism
opens the way for writing the Jews out of any positive role in the 'divine
economy' of history. A contemporary way of putting it might be that
Judaism is an anachronism in the Christian metanarrative: Jews have no
good future unless they become Christians. Supersessionism is an answer to
'How?' questions such as: how are Christians to account for the continuing
existence of Judaism, and how are they to legitimate themselves theologically? It theologically silences contemporary Jews; or they are regarded as
'noise' over against the Christian Word. Auschwitz can be seen as a secular-
ized attempt to fulfil the supersessionist meta-narrative, the logic of which
is that there is no place for Judaism. There are, of course, many complicating
factors (such as the fact that the Nazi racial anti-semitism eliminated converted Jews too), and I would not want to overstress the religious genesis
of Nazism. Being an exceptional event does not mean that it must have had
one exceptional cause. But even if many other indictments are issued —

---

[13]   What follows is complementary with my article, 'A Messiah for the Third Millennium'
in *Modern Theology*, vol. 16, no. 1, January, 2000, pp. 75–90, and there is some overlap.
[14]   See 'A Messiah for the Third Millennium'.

against, for example, racism, militarism, nationalism, bureaucracy and 'scientism' – the terrible truth for Christians is that the logic of their theology had fatal affinities with Nazi ideology.

One common way of approaching this has been through Romans 9–11, that agonized wrestling by Paul about the salvation of his people. One key element in a non-supersessionist theology is clear there: Gentile Christians are 'grafted in' to a heritage which remains that of the Jews – there is no second covenant, no cancelling. This is of the utmost importance, since it is precisely this that the church, when it became largely Gentile, often denied, whether explicitly or implicitly. The unsurpassable horizon of history remains that of God and the Jews. The main plot of the metanarrative is to do with God and the people of God. The grafting in of Gentiles, while embracing far greater numbers, is in fact a sub-plot. Eugene Rogers, following on from George Lindbeck's contention that both the church and Israel should be regarded as types, not of Christ, but of 'the people of God in fellowship with God at the end of time',[15] makes a convincing case for the contribution of an 'anagogical' interpretation of scripture, reading it in the light of the eschatological community as Paul does in Romans 9–11. He reads the plot as a Jewish one oriented towards consummation, with Gentile redemption a sub-plot. God's faithfulness to the covenant with Israel is permanent. There 'are not two stories, much less two covenants, but two ways the Spirit excites gratitude for the blessings of Abraham in the readers of the bible, who in this too can become sources of mutual blessing'.[16]

That can be supported and developed in many ways,[17] but for now the important point is that if, in common Jewish and Christian terminology, the hope is for the coming of the Kingdom of God, yet there are likely to be enormous differences between the two (and, of course, within each) about the 'Who?' questions regarding God, the Messiah, and Jesus Christ as inaugurator of the Kingdom of God. The newness seen by Christians in Jesus Christ can fill their horizon and supersede the previous plot. Paul in Romans chapters 9–11 is resisting just this temptation. Is it possible to sustain a non-supersessionist account of the person of Jesus Christ? De Lange's question about Jesus Christ at Auschwitz, which can be seen as a horrendous consummation of Christian supersessionism, goes to the heart of the matter.

[15]   Eugene F. Rogers, Jr, 'Supplementing Barth on Jews and Gender: Identifying God by Anagogy and the Spirit', in *Modern Theology*, vol.14, no. 1, January 1998, p. 63.
[16]   Ibid. p. 64. It is worth remembering that many Gentiles are not Christians. There are major implications, beyond the scope of this article, of non-supersessionist Christian theology for Christian theology in relation to others besides Jews.
[17]   For my own way, see 'A Messiah for the Third Millennium'.

Where was Jesus Christ at Auschwitz?

In agreement with Ignaz Maybaum, Nicholas de Lange sees the Shoah as the third *Churban* (destruction) – the others being the Babylonian exile and the Roman destruction of the Temple in 70 AD.[18] He calls it a twentieth-century Calvary and reads the Gospels as post-Holocaust literature, with the cross being a symbol or allegory of the Shoah. He speaks of Jewish wrestling with the question: 'Where was God at Auschwitz?' and throws out a challenge:

> We have reached the point now, I believe, where we cannot engage in mean-ingful dialogue with any Christian who has not similarly confronted the question: 'Where was Jesus Christ at Auschwitz?'[19]

He sharpens this by a series of disturbing quotations from Dietrich Bon-hoeffer, Martin Niemöller and Jürgen Moltmann,[20] and a vivid evocation of the crucified Jesus as the persecutor of his own people:

> It is painful to contemplate the thought of those pierced hands dripping with the spilt blood of so many innocent victims.[21]

A Christian response to that cannot treat the crucifixion of Jesus as nothing but symbol or allegory; but nor can it treat Auschwitz as illustrating or symbolizing the crucifixion. MacKinnon saw them as implicated in some 'interrelated finality', and it is one which does not permit overviews or integrations. How can we think them together in Christian theology?

Bonhoeffer's approach to the 'Where?' question is as follows:

> If we look for the place of Christ, we are looking for the structure of the 'Where?' within that of the 'Who?'[22]

His further specification of the 'Where' within the 'Who' is:

> 'Where does he stand?' He stands *pro me*. He stands in my place, where I should stand and cannot.[23]

---

[18] Nicholas de Lange, 'Jesus Christ and Auschwitz'.
[19] Ibid., p. 309.
[20] In conversation with me (April 1999) Professor Moltmann has rejected Dr de Lange's interpretation of his position.
[21] Ibid., p. 311.
[22] Ibid., p. 61.
[23] Ibid.

What if 'my place' is facing Auschwitz? How might Jesus Christ face Auschwitz? – in compassion; in judgement; in anguish; in silence; in death? Facing Auschwitz leads deeper into all the simultaneities discussed earlier: life, death and resurrection; speech and silence in many modes; radical questioning which is at the same time reversed onto ourselves. Above all, the Shoah stretches the conceivability of the *simul* of death and resurrection to breaking-point – a horror, in Steiner's phrase about MacKinnon, 'unredeemed . . . by the putative wonder of resurrection or by any promise of celestial reparation'. Is it possible to think the resurrection without in some sense leaving the horror of the death behind?

But note: these are 'How?' questions. At the heart of an answer to de Lange in line with Bonhoeffer is the basic testimony: however he might be there, or conceived to be there, the hidden, incomprehensible reality which is trusted in is that this person *is* there, facing Auschwitz. That is where a Christian response starts, with this 'Who'. There are then two massive questions: how does the response go on after starting like this? And is this not the ultimate in triumphalist supersessionism, a Christian subsumption and takeover of the Shoah?

A theology of Jesus Christ facing Auschwitz

There are already hints above at the lines of development of a theology of Jesus Christ facing Auschwitz. It is a theology of interrogative faith before the face of one who was a baby, ate, drank, taught, proclaimed the Kingdom of God, was transfigured, prayed in Gethsemane, was kissed by Judas, was arrested, tried, flogged, crucified, rose from the dead and ascended; and is looked to in hope for the world. It is simultaneously interrogative faith before the faces of the victims, of the perpetrators, of the silent and speaking witnesses, and of others. What it means to face Auschwitz in this sense can be entered into through testimonies, fiction such as *Fugitive Pieces*, and many other media and genres. Interrogative faith is stretched in study, imagination and feeling to do justice to the Shoah and to God in relation to it. But above all faith is exercised in practical response before one who is believed both to take radical responsibility for the world, to the point of death, and also to call others into comparable responsibility. It is the content of that responsibility that is most urgent for the church and its theology after Auschwitz.

To be before this face that has witnessed Auschwitz is to be summoned to face Auschwitz in his spirit and to accept responsibility for such things not happening again. It is also, however, to accompany such Auschwitz-centred responsibilities (as MacKinnon, de Lange and Bonhoeffer all do) with interrogative faith in the full flourishing of creation in the Kingdom of God. The asymmetrical simultaneity of life, death and resurrection which, in the light of faith in the resurrection, allows trust that Auschwitz is not the last word (or the last silence) about human flourishing, works asymmetrically (and simultaneously) in the other direction too, seeing crucifixion and resurrection in the service of the message and realization of the Kingdom of God. The desire for the Kingdom of God above all else is, perhaps, the point of deepest convergence between Jews and Christians — and there are analogous though perhaps lesser convergences in relation to many other faiths and worldviews.

Yet that still leaves the second question about whether the priority of the 'Who?' question addressed to Jesus Christ is a form of Christian supersessionism.

The face of the Messiah

How might this theology of the face of Christ avoid being dominating, triumphalist, exclusivist, supersessionist and other bad things? Christian theology has often been rightly subject to such accusations and suspicions. Yet the face and facing of Jesus Christ also holds the possibility of an alternative which helps Christian theology to be both radically self-critical in facing its own past and present and also dialogical with others. What follows is just a set of headlines for what this might be like.[24]

The very idea of facing can be seen as resistant to totalizing overviews and syntheses. This particular face can be seen as challenging Christian (and other) ideologies of domination and coercive practices. It is the face of one who is silent, who listens to cries, who is self-effacing, suffers violence, and dies. Its reality can represent a continual critique of power in the interests of the weak and suffering, an ethic of gentleness and being for others, and forms of communication that have the crucifixion as their central criterion and dialogue as their central practice. To face Jesus Christ means learning to be responsible before him, learning to be judged by him, to look on others as he looks on them, to have 'the mind of Christ', to be vigilant, and to speak and be silent in his Spirit.

It is also to be open to radical surprise. Christians have no overview of how Jesus Christ relates to other Christians or even themselves, let alone

---

[24] For a fuller theology of the face of Christ, see David F. Ford, *Self and Salvation* (Cambridge University Press, Cambridge, 1999).

to Jews, Muslims, Hindus, agnostics, atheists, and so on. We trust that he relates in ways that are good beyond anything we or they can imagine. But what about Jews who reject him as Messiah and await the true Messiah? Neither Jews nor Christians can claim a total overview. Both affirm in radical ways that the category of 'surprise' is inseparable from eschatology. If anything is clear from Jesus's own teaching about God's future it is that those who are most confident that they have it worked out are likely to be most surprised. This above all is the place for reserve, for an agnostic yet expectant silence which is open to the unexpected. It is a silence to be filled with the prayer, vigilance and service which are the practical forms of anticipating the good surprise of welcome by the Messiah who is now met with incognito in responding to others.

Learning New Speech and Silence

In his 'Thoughts on the Day of the Baptism of Dietrich Wilhelm Rüdiger Bethge' written in May 1944 in Tegel Prison, Dietrich Bonhoeffer concludes on a prophetic note about language and silence. He says:

> Reconciliation and redemption, regeneration and the Holy Spirit, love of our enemies, cross and resurrection, life in Christ and Christian discipleship – all these things are so difficult and so remote that we hardly venture any more to speak of them. In the traditional words and acts we suspect that there may be something quite new and revolutionary, though we cannot as yet grasp or express it. That is our own fault. Our church, which has been fighting in these years only for its self-preservation, as though that were an end in itself, is incapable of taking the word of reconciliation and redemption to mankind and the world. Our earlier words are therefore bound to lose their force and cease, and our being Christians today will be limited to two things: prayer and righteous action among men. All Christian thinking, speaking, and organizing must be born anew out of this prayer and action . . . It will be a new language, perhaps quite non-religious, but liberating and redeeming – as was Jesus' language; it will shock people and yet overcome them by its power; it will be the language of a new righteousness and truth, proclaiming God's peace with men and the coming of his kingdom . . . Till then the Christian cause will be a silent and hidden affair, but there will be those who pray and do right and wait for God's own time . . .[25]

[25] Dietrich Bonhoeffer, *Letters and Papers from Prison*, ed. Eberhard Bethge (SCM, London, 1971), pp. 299f.

There is something in that of Anne Michaels' 'seeking by way of silence' in the aftermath of trauma which has left a 'damaged chromosome in words'. It is analogous to her attempt to 'find [a] path from depth to ascent'.

How might such seeking proceed? Again, Bonhoeffer seems to seek new words rather than new silences, whereas Michaels seeks new silences too. Bonhoeffer's concept of silence is rooted in the crucifixion and a constraining reserve which is to be overcome by the gift of new words. Together they suggest the need for a new ascesis of language and silence, disciplined by facing the Shoah and, in Bonhoeffer's case, by a new appraisal both of modernity and of the self-discrediting of Christianity during this period. They are united in the crucial importance of 'righteous action' in the ascesis, and in finding speech and silence inextricable from the rest of our ethics. There are only hints of worship in Michaels:

> If sound waves carry on to infinity, where are their screams now? I imagine them somewhere in the galaxy, moving forever towards the psalms. (p. 4; cf. p. 195)

Bonhoeffer makes prayer central, and it is linked to the 'discipline of the secret' (*disciplina arcani*) of early Christian eucharistic practice. I understand him to mean by this secret the hidden reality of the crucified and risen Jesus Christ.[26] Eberhard Bethge has written that in the *arcanum* Christ takes everyone who really encounters him and turns them around to face other people and the world.[27] Prayer is the place where the priority of the 'Who?' question is sustained above all, and also the *simul* of speech and silence. In the growing number of Jewish and Christian liturgies focused on the Shoah, one striking feature is that same inter weaving of words and silence.[28] To hear testimonies of victims and survivors and to be silent before them and before God as Jews and as Christians (with some liturgies created for joint Jewish–Christian worship): that is to learn, or at least to seek and desire, new speech and new silence. And Michaels invokes Muslim worship in an image of desire and failure which somehow draws us deeper into the mystery:

---

[26] David F. Ford, *Self and Salvation*, p. 263.
[27] Eberhard Bethge, *Dietrich Bonhoeffer: Theologian, Christian, Contemporary* (Collins, London and New York, 1977), p. 787.
[28] See Marcia Sachs Littell (ed.), *Liturgies on the Holocaust. An Interfaith Anthology* (Edwin Mellen, Lewiston NY and Queenston, ONT, 1986).

English was a sonar, a microscope, through which I listened and observed, waiting to capture elusive meanings buried in facts. I wanted a line in a poem to be the hollow ney of the dervish orchestra whose plaintive wail is a call to God. But all I achieved was awkward shrieking. Not even the pure shriek of a reed in the rain. (pp. 112–13)

CONCLUSION: TWELVE THESES FOR TWENTY-FIRST CENTURY CHRISTIAN THEOLOGY

These 12 theses articulate the main elements of what I hope twenty-first-century Christian theology might be about:[1]

1 God is the One who blesses and loves in wisdom.
2 Theology is done for God's sake and for the sake of the Kingdom of God.
3 Prayer is the beginning, accompaniment and end of theology: Come, Holy Spirit! Hallelujah! and Maranatha!
4 Study of scripture is at the heart of theology.
5 Describing reality in the light of God is a basic theological discipline.
6 Theology hopes in and seeks God's purposes while immersed in the contingencies, complexities and ambiguities of creation and history.
7 Theological wisdom seeks to do justice to many contexts, levels, voices, moods, genres, systems and responsibilities.
8 Theology is practised collegially, in conversation and, best of all, in friendship; and, through the communion of saints, it is simultaneously premodern, modern and postmodern.
9 Theology is a broker of the arts, humanities, sciences and common sense for the sake of a wisdom that affirms, critiques and transforms each of them.

[1] David F. Ford, 'Epilogue: Twelve Theses for Christian Theology in the Twenty-first Century', in *The Modern Theologians: An Introduction to Christian Theology Since 1918*, ed. David F. Ford with Rachel Muers, 3rd edn (Blackwell, Oxford, 2005), p. 761.

10   Our religious and secular world needs theology with religious studies in its schools and universities.

11   Conversation around scriptures is at the heart of interfaith relations.

12   Theology is for all who desire to think about God and about reality in relation to God.

SUBJECT INDEX

INDEX OF
BIBLICAL REFERENCES